Indian Artifacts of the Midwest

by
Lar Hothem

COLLECTOR BOOKS
A Division of Schroeder Publishing Co., Inc.

The current values in this book should be used only as a guide. They are not intended to set prices, which vary from one section of the country to another. Auction prices as well as dealer prices vary greatly and are affected by condition as well as demand. Neither the Author nor the Publisher assumes responsibility for any losses that might be incurred as a result of consulting this guide.

Searching For A Publisher?

We are always looking for knowledgeable people considered to be experts within their field. If you feel that there is a real need for a book on your collectible subject and have a large comprehensive collection, contact Collector Books.

Printed by IMAGE GRAPHICS, INC., Paducah, Kentucky

Table of Contents

Acknowledgments 4

Author's Note 5

Chapter One – The North American Midwest..................................7

Chapter Two – The First Hunters 9

Chapter Three – The Hunters And Gatherers..................................25

Chapter Four – The Mound Builders 113

Chapter Five – The Farmers 155

Chapter Six – Important Midwestern Collections 179

Chapter Seven – Midwestern Prehistoric Facts 185

Value Guide 197

Acknowledgments

Even a cursory glance through this book will indicate the importance of the many photographs in presenting an accurate picture of the material culture of the prehistoric Midwest. The below contributors aided very greatly by sending photographs for this project, and all are gratefully acknowledged and thanked for their help. Without their fine assistance this book would not have been possible.

ALABAMA
Cliff Markley

COLORADO
Marguerite & Stewart Kernaghan

ILLINOIS
Dale Richter
Don Simmons
Duane Treest
Eldon Launer
Ellis J. Neiburger, DDS
Gregory L. Perdun
Russell & Rhonda Bedwell
The Guy Brothers
Tim & Patty Wiemers
Tom Razmus
William Gehlken

INDIANA
Kenneth Spiker

IOWA
Bruce Filbrandt
Dale & Betty Roberts
Dwight Stineman
Floyd & Judi Goddard
Gary D. Klebe
Jim Roberson
Lane Freyermuth
Paul Witt
Richard Holliday
Verlin Hepker

KENTUCKY
Mike Darland
Private Collection
Steven R. Dowell

MICHIGAN
John Baldwin

MISSOURI
Aaron Rampani
L.A. Noblett
Mike George
Robert M. Rampani
Victor A. Pierce

NORTH CAROLINA
Rodney M. Peck

OHIO
Charles West
Del Hetrick, Sr.
Donald E. Shuck
Edward Tyson
Glenn Spray
Paul Rankin
Private Collection
Richard E. Jones
Steve Puttera, Jr.

PENNSYLVANIA
Gary Fogelman
Lee Fisher
Lee Hallman

TENNESSEE
Blake Gahagan

Author's Note

A brief explanation is in order for the four large prehistoric periods as covered in the book. Many artifacts existed only in one prehistoric time-frame, and so are included in only one section of this book. An example would be the fluted-base points of the Paleo period, or the twin-lobed or bifurcated based points or blades that are unique to the Early Archaic period in the Midwest. These examples were made in the same or closely related period throughout the Midwest and are only in that particular photo-section.

However, some point types such as the Agate Basin began very nearly in the Late Paleo and continued into the Early Archaic. They are pictured in the Paleo section because this was their first temporal appearance, and it is not known precisely how long they were used. Birdstones are in both the Archaic and Woodland section, because they were made in both, though in different forms (elongated and other forms first, bust-types later).

The reader will note that the Archaic section of this book is quite large. The main reason for this is that this time-frame is by far the largest known to the Midwest, running some seven thousand years. Thus, during this long time there were astronomical numbers of artifacts made, in a wide range of types and styles and sizes.

In conformity with various state and federal legislations, and with awareness of the sensitivity of Native American groups to the issue, no photographs of known burial-related items or of any grave-associated artifacts are included in this book.

While values are listed for most items, these do not constitute offers to buy or sell. They are included as a general guide to those who are beginning to collect. They are to be considered as one factual aspect of prehistoric artistic appeal to today's collector. In fact, exact comparisons to items a reader-collector might have are difficult to make, as each item is distinct and unique. Hopefully, the one thing such values will help do is to make the reader aware of why such a figure or range is applied of that particular artifact. And this may encourage questions such as why, relating to the object, the figure might be high, or low, or average. This is one – and not the only – way of looking at an artifact and trying to understand and appreciate its appeal.

Finally, the age of the artifacts is important in several ways. The reader can catch glimpses of what life was like long ago in the Midwest by studying the artifacts and imagining how they were used. With points, game was brought down. With axes, wood was cut up. With bannerstones...well, no one knows for sure how those artifacts were really used.

This is the time-period generally accepted as accurate for the North American Midwest:

Paleo	13,000(?)	-	8000 BC
Archaic	8000 BC	-	1000 BC
Woodland	1000 BC	-	AD 800
Mississippian	AD 800	-	AD 1650

Chapter I

The North American Midwest

Looking at a map of North America, any collector of prehistoric Amerind artifacts sooner or later begins to focus attention on a certain region. Often that area is the Midwest of the United States, sometimes considered different regions by different persons but here treated as a six-state area. These are the states of Iowa, Illinois, Indiana, Kentucky, Missouri and Ohio.

Indian-related images begin with the present words for the states themselves. Iowa was named for an Indian tribe that lived in Iowa, Minnesota and Missouri. Illinois was named for a confederacy of tribes that lived in Illinois, Iowa, Missouri and Wisconsin. Indiana was named for Indian groups of that region in general, with a geographic suffix.

Kentucky was named for the hunting grounds of the canebrakes and bluegrass, the original meaning something like "prairie lands." Missouri was named for a Siouan tribe that lived in the northern part of the state. And Ohio was named for an Iroquois word meaning "grand river" or "beautiful river," of course the Ohio River.

But the story of human life in these states, this six-state region, goes back to and beyond historic times (before about AD 1650) that gave us state names. As collectors know, the Midwest is exceptionally rich in prehistoric artifacts. Certainly no other block of adjoining states has a similar quantity and quality and variety of prehistoric artifacts. Most collectors will agree that, per square mile, there are more high-quality prehistoric artifacts in this region than in any other comparable region of North America.

There are solid reasons for this. The region was preferred by early inhabitants because, simply, it met their basic needs. It was a good place to live. The topography in general was moderate, a land of rolling terrain and open meadows and forested slopes. Much of this pleasing landscape was due to the flattening action of past glaciers which turned large hills into small ones, terraced the valleys, and smoothed wrinkles from the face of the earth.

The climate also had much to do with regional attractiveness. It was much like that today, though somewhat colder in the earliest centuries of human occupation. Winters were not too cold and summers were not too hot. This moderate climate was well within the scope of management, even with relatively primitive technology.

The evidence suggests that people who came into the Midwest tended to stay on, generation after generation.

Enhancing the overall hospitable environment were other factors of supreme importance. These included the basics of food, clothing and shelter. Food, according to remains found in early kitchen middens, included just about every form of living thing that was in abundance. Early explorers in historic times often recorded, sometimes with near-disbelief, how incredibly much wild game was about.

Deer were so thick at some saline springs or salt-licks that, upon shooting one, the others might nearly destroy the fallen game in their stampede. Wild turkeys were so common that it was easy to tire of the taste, and they were so tame they could be killed with stones or ramrods. Squirrels were so thick that early pioneers held killing drives to protect the corn crop. "Wild cattle" or forest bison existed in some Midwestern states, along with elk. Passenger pigeons flew into overnight roosts in flocks that darkened the sun, and their weight broke branches, even trees.

Clothing was often a by-product of food-getting. Leathers were made from the pelts of deer, bison or elk, and furs came from a large variety of animals, from weasels to bears. Plant fibers and the inner bark of trees were woven into sandals and carrying bags and body-coverings of many kinds. Further, animals provided the bone to make tools and weapons and ornaments.

Shelter ranged from the totally natural (shallow caves or rock-shelters) to lightweight tent-like dwellings, to large and elaborate and long-term housing. Saplings and grapevines and bark and grasses could be made into marvelous shapes, housing for an individual or for many families.

Water was the major key, the essential ingredient, to life at all. In this, the entire Midwestern region was exceptionally well-endowed. Here, freshwater existed in lakes large and small, swamps and marshes, mighty rivers and small creeks, artesian wells and springs. All this provided water for drinking, cooking and washing, as well as transportation. As has often been noted, major prehistoric sites are never far from some source of year-round water.

The basics for an adequate lifeway were present, and so were the extras that allowed a good, even excellent, lifeway. If the average person is asked why there were so many prehistoric peoples in the ancient Midwest, no answer or a general answer might be forthcoming. Ask a collector of Amerind artifacts, and the reply (perhaps after some serious thought) would likely deal with the raw materials available for making tools and weapons, the artifacts.

In the six-state region that this book concerns, there would be at least one hundred different sources, major and minor, of chert and flint. These, depending on the specific material and quarry or distribution area, were in the form of loose pebbles, loose or imbedded nodules, and outcroppings or workable veins or beds.

Not only were there many kinds of chert (non-glossy, with some impurities) and flint (glossy, few impurities), but these were often of very high grades, good quality. In prehistoric times the better the material the easier it was to chip the material into the desired form, and the more attractive that form was. While this of course was a matter of utmost importance long ago, it also means that today's collectors and students of Amerind artifacts can acquire some very high-grade artifacts.

Some of this flint—such as Ohio's Flintridge and Kentucky's Carter County and the Independence of Illinois and Indiana—can be highly translucent or colorful or both. Many grades are actually of gem or near-gem quality, and are sold in rock shops by the pound for working into jewelry. This attraction was noticed by ancient artisans and some Amerind groups purposely selected only certain cherts or flints for most of their artifacts. Some groups, such as the Hopewell of Middle Woodland times, often brought materials from very distant quarries for their finest pieces.

As much as anything, the fine materials for tools and weapons brought Amerinds into the prehistoric Midwest, and kept them there. Adding to the permanent and long-existing deposits, the succession of glaciers brought additional high-grade materials. These included colorful, durable hardstones for axes and celts and some ornaments.

In the upper Midwestern tier, hematite and copper and silver could be found in the glacial drift. For ornaments and decorative objects, glacial slate in dozens of hues and color combinations was used, including black, blue, brown, green and red. These could be solid-colored, or mixed, or banded, with the latter usually being given preference. With a widespread and varied supply of raw materials, prehistoric artisans of the Midwest created a dazzling array of beautiful artifacts and artworks. Many types (birdstones, lizard effigies) were not made outside the Midwest or an adjoining state, though some were exported elsewhere.

The American Midwest has another distinction. The rich, well-watered and well-drained land was ideal for agricultural purposes. Countless million acres have been under tillage, some areas since the early to mid-1800's. This farming activity gradually uncovered the ancient camp and village sites, and the artifacts that were in them.

The Midwest, just as in prehistoric times, has a relatively heavy population. This meant that more collectors of Amerind objects were in the region, and their surface-hunting recovered millions of fine artifacts. Farmers also picked up specimens encountered during agricultural operations, and there was a time when almost every farm had a collection of field-found artifacts. Some of the greatest old-time collections of Amerind artifacts were put together in the Midwest, and there is a book chapter on that.

One indication of the status of Midwestern artifacts is that often out-of-area collectors come to surface-hunt. And large auctions of Midwestern artifacts invariably attract buyers from across the country. All this is not to say that other states and other regions do not have top-quality artifacts. They do. But in terms of almost any combination of quantity and quality one cares to arrange, the Midwest does very well in comparison. Very well indeed.

Chapter II

The First Hunters

Paleo Period (10,000 BC – 8000 BC)

The first humans in the Midwest were the Paleo-Indians, who arrived at least 12,000 years ago, perhaps earlier. Of medium height and sturdily built, they are distinctive for several reasons. Their tools and weapons are for the most part different, for they brought the designs with them. And Paleo points and blades were never afterward precisely duplicated. In this very early time, chert and flint were the major raw materials for tools and weapons, and almost all Paleo artifacts were chipped into the desired form.

The Paleo people probably moved into the Midwest from the south, for all the land to the north was blocked by the final surges of the Wisconsin glacier. The ice-walls had slowly begun to melt and retreat back into Canada, and the land recovered only gradually from the great frigid invasion. Only slowly did the native plants and animals return, and with them came the Paleo hunters. This may all have been a very gradual process, covering dozens or scores or even hundreds of years.

It is almost impossible to correctly imagine the land back then, what it was like when the first hunters arrived. Evidence suggests that the climate was colder and wetter, at least for a time, and vegetation was a mix of northern and midwestern land and plant species. In the regions that were in fact glaciated, the entire surface of the land was devastated and rolled-out and gentled.

A legacy of the last glacier was a great change in water-courses. This was not caused so much by the ice itself, but by the enormous amounts of earth and rock that were pushed ahead and carried along. These masses were large enough to actually change and shift entire watershed regions. Rivers were dammed to create lakes, which eventually broke the unnatural boundaries and created new streambeds. Scooped-out areas became lakes and ponds, swamps, marshes and bogs. Sand and gravel formed high hills and in some cases raised the valley floors and formed high valley terraces.

In unglaciated areas of the Midwest, and in areas freed from ice and snow as the glacier retreated, a bewildering array of animals could be hunted. At least a dozen kinds of very large animals were present, and some—mammoth, mastodon, short-faced bear, elk-moose, giant beaver and ground sloth—became extinct about 9000 BC. Whether hunting people hastened their ends is a matter of scholarly debate, but what is known is that shortly after the first hunters came, many of the larger animals died out.

Still, many other animals survived and there is evidence that the early hunters made heavy use of caribou, deer and elk. The former could be ambushed along seasonal migration routes, and deer could be felled using many different tactics and techniques. Elk or wapiti, and caribou, now live far to the north of the Midwest. Smaller game was taken whenever needed, for both food and furs.

The Paleo peoples, it appears, mainly followed major river valleys like the Mississippi, Missouri and Ohio. From these main waterways, they took tributaries and then minor streams, covering finally most of the interior of the Midwest. Their sites, wherever located, were generally close to a year-round source of water. Different kinds of sites have been noted. Some were workshops near quarries, while others appear to be campsites, the temporary villages of that early time. A few kill-sites have been found. These include the Adams Site in Kentucky, and the Kimmswick Site in Missouri, where Paleo tools have been found with the bones of extinct large mammals.

The Paleolithic or Paleo time-period is divided into two sections, and two somewhat distinct lifeways apparently were involved. The Early Paleo period was ca. 10,000(?) - 9000 BC, while the Late Paleo was ca. 9000 - 8000 BC. This 2000-plus year period was relatively short for North American prehistory, so no Middle Paleo period has been delineated. Of course such dates are flexible and fluid; no one really knows exactly when the first Paleo hunters walked into today's Midwest or when the early hunting lifeway really ended.

Collectors know Early Paleo because of a special weapon-tip and tool called the Clovis point. Clovis points (named for the original type site near Clovis, New Mexico) are found all across North America, with many picked up in the Midwest. Made of high-grade cherts and flints, the points are distinctive in general shape, being long and slender, with a concave or incurvate baseline. They are not notched or stemmed, and instead are unique in being fluted. That is, a long, narrow flake was driven off near the base bottom on one or both faces, extending toward the tip. Sometimes several long, thin flakes or flutes were removed in this manner.

9

This special configuration permitted the attachment of a thin and narrow shaft or foreshaft. It allowed the point to penetrate very deeply into the game animal. Further, after striking, the projecting ears kept the point in place. Many different radio-carbon (C-14) dates have been obtained at Clovis sites, and almost all are in the 9500 - 9000 BC range, or, 11,500 to 11,000 years ago. So these beautifully designed and superbly made points were used for a relatively short time-period. Other, usually smaller, fluted points of a number of slightly different designs continued to be used even into the Late Paleo period.

Late Paleo people, or the concept of new point types, came into the Midwest from the west and northwest. Their major hunting tool was quite different. These were the lanceolate-makers, and their points were long and narrow and unfluted. Many different lanceolate or lance-like points developed, from rectangular bases and tapered bases to stemmed and shouldered varieties. Dozens of different lanceolate combinations were possible, and some examples (probably knives) were large and beautifully chipped.

While the design of points and weapon-tips tends to separate the two early periods, such is not usually the case for the chipped tools. (A major characteristic of Paleo times is that the process of chipping made almost all of the surviving material culture.) A whole range of tool forms is associated with the Paleo period, and like the points, many of them are large and sturdy and made of high-grade materials.

The Paleo tool-kit — and these artifacts are amazingly alike in all the Midwest, and in North America, for that matter — includes many uniface blades. The word simply means that most of the chipping was done on one side or face of a large and usually long flake. Edge treatment determined the artifact purpose and use, and this might be for knives or scrapers. Small projecting tips were apparently used as gravers to mark or cut bone or antler or ivory.

Drills were made, some of them so long and finely crafted they may have actually been hairpins. Scrapers were made in a huge number of shapes and sizes. A Paleo characteristic is the graver spur located on one or both corners of an end-scraper. Planes and wedges and shaft-scrapers and perforators and chisel-tips (burins) are just a few of the diagnostic Paleo tools that have been found in the Midwest.

Another Paleo diagnostic artifact is the combination tool. This combined two or more functions in a single artifact, such as a scraper at one end and a reamer at the other, sometimes with a knife-edge between the two. Combination tools with four or five different working areas have been seen. Likely, such designs preserved valuable material and made handy, lightweight tools that could easily be transported from place to place.

While there are many Early and/or Late Paleo sites in the Midwest, the primary collector items — fluted points and lanceolates — are not easy to find. Most are isolated and rare field pickups, and even then they are likely to have use-damage or have suffered detraction from farming equipment strikes. Most surface hunters would consider themselves lucky to spot one fine and complete example in a lifetime.

PLATE 1: *Clovis Fluted Point,* Early Paleo period and ca. 9500-9000 BC. It is made of Kentucky nodular flint and was found in western Kentucky. Size is 1¾6" x 1½". This is a very well-made and attractive point, rare wherever found. Courtesy Donald E. Shuck collection, Ohio.

PLATE 2: *Clovis Point,* shown obverse and reverse. This large point is 3½" long, made of a white chert, and is in undamaged condition. It was found near the Iowa River in Johnson County, Iowa, by the late Bill Jones in 1974. Mr. Jones taught the owner how to surface-hunt for artifacts. This Clovis is a very good type example, well-fluted. Courtesy Verlin Hepker collection, Iowa.

PLATE 3: *Agate Basin Point,* Late Paleo, from Ohio. It is made of black flint and measures 3" long. This is a nice early piece. Private collection; photograph by Del Hetrick.

PLATE 4: *Clovis Fluted Point,* Early Paleo period, from Adams County, Illinois. This is a fine artifact, fluted both lower sides, and made from dark Knife River flint. It measures 1¼" x 3⁹⁄₁₆". This is a superior and rare early piece. Courtesy Donald E. Shuck collection, Ohio.

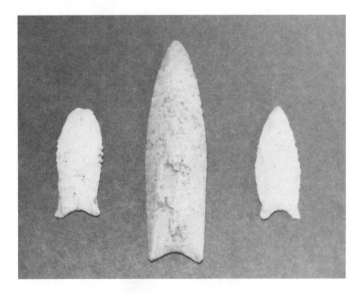

PLATE 5: *Paleo Points,* Early in center, left and right Late. All are from either Jersey or Madison Counties, Illinois. Left and right, Quad points with the typical flared bases. Center, large Clovis fluted point, mottled flint. Courtesy Gregory L. Perdun collection, Illinois.

PLATE 6: *Ross County type Clovis point,* Early Paleo, made of coal-black Zaleski flint from southcentral Ohio. This artifact has typical Ross County features, including the large, flat flake scars across both faces. It is 1⁵⁄₁₆" x 4⅜" long. This is a fine early piece, larger and better-made than average. From Mercer County, Ohio. Courtesy Charles West collection, Ohio.

PLATE 7: *Clovis Fluted Point,* Early Paleo, made of dark high-grade flint. It is 1⅛" x 4¹⁄₁₆" long, and from Indiana. Clovis points of this size and fine condition are rarely found, adding to rarity. Courtesy Charles West collection, Ohio.

PLATE 8: *Clovis point,* Early Paleo and ca. 9500-9000 BC. Made of a good grade of dark flint, this artifact is 1" x 3¼", and is from Indiana. Clovis points from anywhere in the Midwest are scarce. Courtesy Charles West collection, Ohio.

PLATE 9: *Lanceolate,* Late Paleo period, made of high-grade glossy flint. It measures 1⅛" x 5¼" long, and is from Clermont County, Ohio. Most fine lances of this size from the Late Paleo are badly damaged or broken due to length combined with relative width, making them fragile. Courtesy Charles West collection, Ohio.

PLATE 10: *Fluted Clovis,* Early Paleo, a 1990 field-find by twelve-year-old Neil Holman. It is fluted one side for ⅔ of length, and ¾" x 1⁹⁄₁₆". Material is sugar quartzite; it came from Sandusky County, Ohio. Courtesy Tyson-Holman collection, Ohio; Del Hetrick, photographer.

PLATE 11: *Lanceolate,* Late Paleo, ⅝" at the base, 1¼" maximum width, and 3¼" long. This artifact is from Wyandot County, Ohio, and is a good example of an early piece. Courtesy Private Collection; Del Hetrick, photographer.

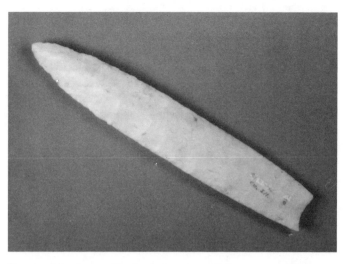

PLATE 12: *Agate Basin lanceolate,* Late Paleo, made of a quality mottled flint. It is 1⁹⁄₁₆" x 4" long and is from Brown County, Illinois. Agate Basins are usually, as here, very well made and with extensive grinding on lower side edges and the base bottom. Courtesy Charles West collection, Ohio.

PLATE 13: *Agate Basin point,* Late Paleo, a very fine piece made of a light-colored glossy flint. It measures 1" x 5½" and is from Brown County, Illinois. This is an exceptional lanceolate. Courtesy Charles West collection, Ohio.

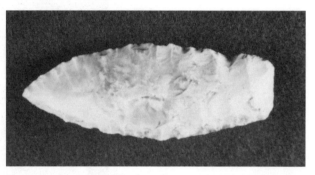

PLATE 14: *Agate Basin point,* from Dupage County, Illinois. It is Late Paleo, 2⅞" long, and made of an unusual material. This is sugar quartzite or Hixton silicified sandstone which is quite difficult to work well. Personal find by owner on April 19, 1989. Courtesy Duane Treest collection, Illinois.

PLATE 15: *Agate Basin point,* Late Paleo, 2¾" long and made of local chert. It was found in Kane County, Illinois, by the owner on July 15, 1990. Courtesy Duane Treest collection, Illinois.

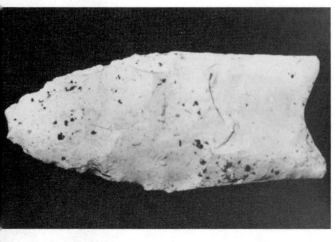

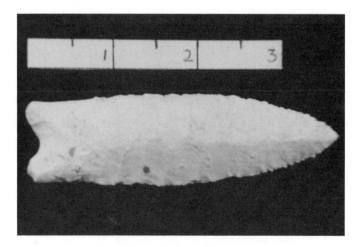

PLATE 16: *Clovis point,* Kane County, Illinois. Early Paleo, it is 2½" long and fluted both lower faces. Fluting is ½" and ¾" long, respectively. Material is a local chert. This point was found by the owner on Nov. 14, 1982. Courtesy Duane Treest collection, Illinois.

PLATE 17: *Dalton point,* Late Paleo/Early Archaic, ca. 7500 BC. Made of white Crescent chert, it was found by Steve Rampani on June 27, 1979 in Bridgeton, St. Louis County, Missouri. It is 1⅛" x 3⅜", and a finely made piece in excellent condition. Courtesy of Bob Rampani collection, Bridgeton, St. Louis County, Missouri.

PLATE 18: *Late Paleo stemmed lanceolates,* both very thin for size, and both Ohio. Left, black Coshocton flint, 2" x 5⅝", ex-collection of Belden, Akron, fine large blade. Right, Delaware chert, 1½" x 6", from Champaign County. It is ex-collections of Earl Townsend, Robert Meyers and Dave Farrow. The difference in blade edges suggests knife use. Courtesy Steve Puttera Jr. collection, Ohio.

PLATE 19: *Late Paleo points or blades,* all Upper Mercer flints, all Ohio. Left, found by George Muessar in 1974, Cuyahoga County; 2nd from left, Lorain County, ex-collection of DeMuth; 2nd from right, Medina County, ex-collection of Mayne; right, found by Dan Rosette in Cuyahoga County, Ohio, in the early 1970's. Courtesy Steve Puttera Jr. collection, Ohio.

PLATE 20: *Folsom point,* Late Paleo, made of pink and grey material. It is 1⅞" long, fluted full-face on obverse and ⅓" length on reverse. This was found in Holt County, Missouri. Courtesy Mike George collection, Missouri.

PLATE 21: *Late Paleo blades or points,* typical lanceolate forms, all from a cache found in Henry County, Ohio. Longest specimen is 5". These are all beautifully made early pieces, of an unidentified flint. Cache specimens of this nature are best kept together, the cache intact, for study purposes. Courtesy Steve Puttera Jr. collection, Ohio.

PLATE 22: *Agate Basin point,* Late Paleo, 4½" long, made of brown material with heavy patination. This fine early piece is in perfect condition, and a rare find. Courtesy Mike George collection, Missouri.

PLATE 23: *Ross County fluted point,* Early Paleo period, made of dark-colored flint. It is from Boone County, Kentucky, and a rare very early artifact. Courtesy Cliff Markley collection, Alabama.

PLATE 24: *Knife,* probably Paleo, from Perry County, Missouri. The size, general configuration, dissimilar edge treatment and irregular base suggest early placement. Material is a light and dark striated flint. Courtesy Cliff Markley collection, Alabama.

PLATE 25: *Clovis point,* Early Paleo, found in a sand-pit in Scott County, Illinois. This is a fine very old artifact, in mottled cream flint, 3" long. Courtesy private collection, Scott County, Illinois; photograph by Eldon Launer.

PLATE 26: *Tang knife,* Late Paleo (probably), an extrememly rare form that was originally much wider before resharpening. In use one edge may become beveled. The original form is an ovoid blade, and they are so-called by Perino in *Selected Preforms, Points And Blades...,* 1985, p. 114. This was in the J.W. Tweed collection in 1876; from Brown County, Ohio. Courtesy Charles West collection, Ohio.

PLATE 27: *Lanceolate point or blade,* Late Paleo, light-colored flint or chert. It is a well-formed piece, from Adams County, Illinois. Courtesy Cliff Markley collection, Alabama.

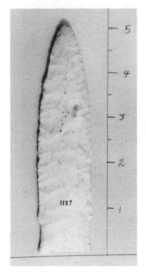

PLATE 28: *Scottsbluff,* a fine and large specimen, Late Paleo. This general form is fairly common throughout the Midwest. This example is from Perry County, Missouri. Courtesy Cliff Markley collection, Alabama.

15

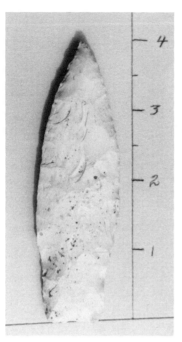

PLATE 29: *Lanceolate point*, Late Paleo, made of speckled light-colored chert. This is an excellent early piece, from Jackson County, Missouri. It has slight stemming. Courtesy Cliff Markley collection, Alabama.

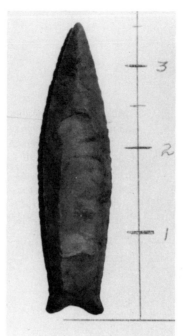

PLATE 30: *Cumberland fluted point*, Late Paleo era, beautifully made specimen in a dark high-quality flint. This rare piece is from Taylor County, Kentucky. Even broken Cumberland examples are quite collectible. Courtesy Cliff Markley collection, Alabama.

PLATE 31: *Paleo knife*, with material Flintridge (OH) or Carter County (KY) mottled amber. From Butler County, Ohio, it is 1" x 3⅛" and somewhat uniface on the reverse. Ex-collections of Johnston and Saunders. An interesting early piece. Courtesy Richard E. Jones collection, Ohio.

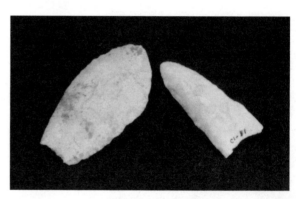

PLATE 32: *Paleo points or blades*, both probably early in the period. Left, 2" x 4½", mottled flint, Butler County, Ohio. Right, 1½" x 4", tan and greyish flint, fluted one side, from Clay County, Indiana. Courtesy Lee Fisher collection, Pennsylvania; Anthony Lang, photographer.

PLATE 33: *Paleo points and blades*, from Iowa and Missouri, grey, cream and tan varieties of chert. The top center example is 3⅞" long. There is a good type-range of early pieces here. Courtesy Verlin Hepker collection, Iowa.

PLATE 34: *Late Paleo points and blades*, with a few Early Archaic pieces. All are from Iowa, Illinois and Missouri sites. A wide variety of grey, tan and cream cherts is represented. The longest artifact here is 3⅞". Courtesy Verlin Hepker collection, Iowa.

PLATE 35: *Lanceolate points*, Late Paleo. Left, 1" x 2½", ~ink and tan flint, found April 4, 1988 in Crawford County, ~llinois. Right, ¹⁵⁄₁₆" x 2½", dark grey flint, found July 24, ~988, Crawford County, Illinois. Neither point has lower side ~r base grinding. They are excellent examples of fairly scarce ~aleo points. Personal finds, courtesy of collection of Don ~immons, Robinson, Illinois.

PLATE 36: *Late Paleo lanceolates*, various Ohio counties, two-inch scale indicating sizes. This is a fine array of point sizes, types and materials, typical of the variety made in Late Paleo times. This is an excellent collection of single-period chipped points and blades. Courtesy Fogelman collection, Pennsylvania.

PLATE 37: *Knife,* from Champaign County, Illinois. This is an unusually long specimen at 11", and it is in perfect condition. The overall design of the artifact appears to be Late Paleo. A very fine Midwestern piece. Courtesy Dale Richter collection, Illinois.

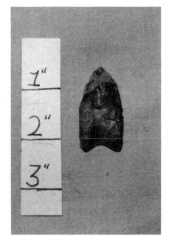

PLATE 38: *Clovis point,* Early Paleo period, 1⅝" long. It is made of a cream and green material known as Indiana Green. This piece is fluted on both lower sides and was found in Benton County, Indiana. Courtesy private collection of Kenneth Spiker.

PLATE 40: *Agate Basin points*, Late Paleo lanceolates, both from Illinois. Left, blue and grey Avon chert, Fulton County, 3¼" long. Right, dark white chert with grey spotting, 4" long, from Fulton County. Courtesy collection of Russell & Rhonda Bedwell, Illinois.

PLATE 39: *Paleo points or blades,* from the Eagle's Point ~ite, Ohio County, Kentucky. The examples shown are not ~arge, but are very well made. Courtesy Steven R. Dowell col-~ection, Kentucky.

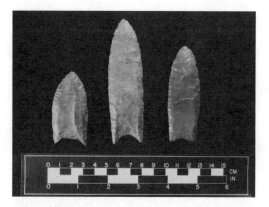

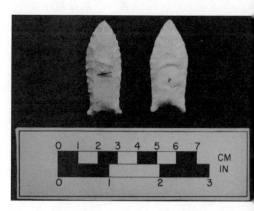

PLATE 41: *Clovis Points*, Early Paleo, all from Barren County, Kentucky. Left, 60mm long, grey Onondaga flint. Center, 102mm, blue-grey Onondaga flint. Right, 78mm, grey Onondaga flint. Courtesy Rodney M. Peck collection, Harrisburg, North Carolina.

PLATE 42: *Fluted Paleo points*, both from St. Charles County, Missouri, and both 45 mm long. Left example is fluted about midway. Right, white flint; this example is fluted Cumberland-style to the tip on both faces. Courtesy Rodney M. Peck collection, Harrisburg, North Carolina.

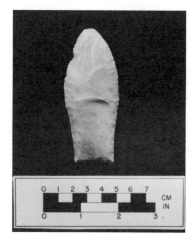

PLATE 43: *Ross County fluted point*, Paleo period, from Oakland Farm, Delaware County, Ohio. It is 9 x 36 x 89mm, and material is a brown flint. This point was illustrated under the type name (reverse side drawn) in *Ohio Flint Types*. Courtesy Rodney M. Peck collection, Harrisburg, North Carolina.

PLATE 44: *Clovis point*, Early Paleo, base missing. Judging from the break location, this 3¼" specimen would originally have been just over 4". It was found in Wapello County, Iowa, by the owner. The material is a light-colored chert. Such pieces are often restored by collectors since the general form is known. Courtesy Verlin Hepker collection, Iowa.

PLATE 45: *Agate Basin*, Late Paleo period, from Lee County, Iowa. Ex-collection of DeRosear, it is made of high-grade cream chert. Size is ¼" x 1⁵⁄₁₆" x 4⅛" long. The basal one-third of point length has grinding on the edges and base bottom. This is a fine and large piece. Courtesy Jim Roberson collection, Muscatine, Iowa.

PLATE 46: *Agate Basin point*, Late Paleo, this found in two pieces during 1984 in Louisa County, Iowa. It is made of Burlington chert in white and tan with crystal inclusions; lower side edges have grinding. Size is ⁵⁄₁₆" x 1¹⁄₁₆" x 5¼" long. This artifact was a personal find by the owner. Courtesy Jim Roberson collection, Muscatine, Iowa.

PLATE 47: *Clovis points*, Early Paleo, and both classic long points. Left, tan (probably Burlington) chert, 1" x 3", fluted both lower faces, Pike County, Missouri. Right, white chert, 1" x 3³⁄₁₆", fluted both lower faces; found in Ralls County, Missouri, 1979. Courtesy collection of Bob Rampani, Bridgeton, St. Louis County, Missouri.

PLATE 48: *Large blade or point*, probably Late Paleo, in a material with shades of brown, grey and white. Found in Muscatine County, Iowa, it is ex-collection of Paul. Size is ⁷⁄₁₆" x 1⁹⁄₁₆" x 5⅞". This is a colorful point or blade. Courtesy Jim Roberson collection, Muscatine, Iowa.

PLATE 49: *Agate Basin*, Late Paleo, found in Hancock County, Illinois. Material is mixed pink, white and brown. Size is ⅜" x 1³⁄₁₆" x 4¹³⁄₁₆" long. There is only slight basal grinding; ex-collections of Spangler and DeRosear. Courtesy Jim Roberson collection, Muscatine, Iowa.

PLATE 51: *Lanceolate point*, probably Late Paleo, found in Benton County, Iowa. It is made of grey, tan and pink material, and is ¼" x 1¹⁄₁₆" x 2¹³⁄₁₆" long. Ex-collection of Kline. Courtesy Jim Roberson collection, Muscatine, Iowa.

PLATE 50: *Agate Basin*, Late Paleo period, found in Knox County, Illinois. Ex-collection of Grotte, it is made of Avon chert in white with chocolate-colored inclusions. The bottom one-third has basal grinding on the sides; size, ¼" x 1⅜" x 4⁵⁄₁₆". Courtesy Jim Roberson collection, Muscatine, Iowa.

PLATE 52: *Clovis point*, Early Paleo period, in white Crescent chert. It is fluted both sides and is 1⅛" x 2⅝"" overall. This excellent very early piece was a personal find by the owner in St. Charles County, Missouri, on August 27, 1987. Courtesy Aaron Rampani collection, St. Ann, St. Louis County, Missouri.

PLATE 53: *Clovis point*, Early Paleo period, made of flint with "bullseye" of white against grey. One-third of the lower length has edge-grinding. Size is ³⁄₁₆" x 1⅛" x 2⅞" long. Ex-collection of Hirl, this very old artifact is from Muscatine County, Iowa. Only a small portion of the tip is missing. Courtesy Jim Roberson collection, Muscatine, Iowa.

PLATE 54: *Paleo point,* Clovis family, unfluted example. The basal area and sides up for about ¾" are heavily ground. This point is 3⅝" long and from Rock Island County, Illinois. Courtesy Lane Freyermuth collection, Iowa.

PLATE 56: *Agate Basin,* Late Paleo, found in Muscatine County, Iowa. It is made of off-white chert and has heavy basal grinding and excellent chipping overall. Ex-collection of Hirl. Size, ¼" x 1³⁄₁₆" x 4". Extra-good specimen for type. Courtesy Jim Roberson Collection, Muscatine, Iowa.

PLATE 55: *Clovis point,* Early Paleo and ca. 9500-9000 BC, from Mercer County, Illinois. It is 3" long, made of near-white chert, and has heavily ground lower edges. Note the small rust-like spotting on the obverse, such natural deposits sometimes seen on lighter-colored flint and chert. Nice piece. Courtesy Lane Freyermuth collection, Iowa.

PLATE 57: *Lanceolate points or blades,* Late Paleo period. Left, dark material with streaking, 2⅞". From Rock Island County, Illinois, it is very well made with basal grinding. Middle, and right, both from Mercer County, Illinois, both with basal grinding. Courtesy Lane Freyermuth collection, Iowa.

PLATE 58: *Stemmed lanceolate,* Late Paleo, made of creamy white chert. It is 3⅞" long, and from Mercer County, Illinois. This is an unusual specimen, with very narrowed stem. Courtesy Lane Freyermuth collection, Iowa.

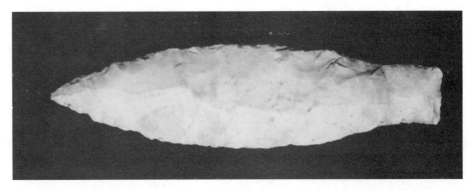

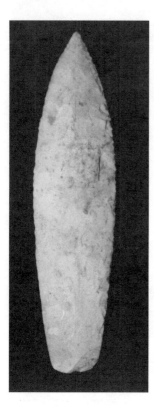

PLATE 59: *Agate Basin point*, Late Paleo, creamy white flint. It is from Lee County, Iowa, and a large and well-formed artifact. Size is ⁵⁄₁₆" x 1⅛" x 4½". Nice piece. Courtesy William Gehlken collection, Illinois; Lane Freyermuth, photographer.

PLATE 60: *Agate Basin point*, Late Paleo, 4½" long. This classic example is from Rock Island County, Illinois, and is very thin and well-designed. Chipping is fine and sides are gently excurvate; it has basal grinding for about one-third the lower sides. A top specimen in every way. Courtesy Gary Klebe collection, Muscatine, Iowa.

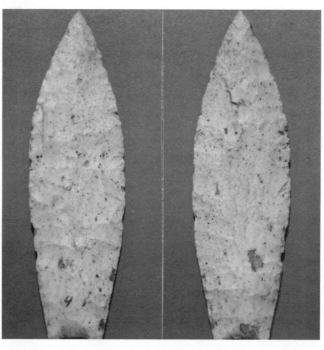

PLATE 61: *Agate Basin*, Late Paleo, obverse and reverse views. It was found in Henry County, Iowa, and is ex-collection of White. Material is a tan chert and it measures ¼" x 1⅜" x 4⅝" long. Courtesy Jim Roberson collection, Muscatine, Iowa.

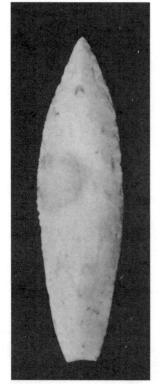

PLATE 62: *Agate Basin point*, Late Paleo, made of white flint with a yellow inclusion, unusual. It is from Rock Island County, Illinois, and ⅜" x 1" x 4" long. The lower sides are ground, as is common for the type. A fine specimen. Courtesy William Gehlken collection, Illinois; Lane Freyermuth, photographer.

PLATE 63: *Sloan Dalton*, Late Paleo/Early Archaic, from Fulton County, Illinois. One of the numerous Dalton forms, this is a very well-made piece with parallel flaking. Made of white and tan flint, it is ¼" x 1⅛" x 3" long. A fine type example. Courtesy William Gehlken collection, Illinois; Lane Freyermuth, photographer.

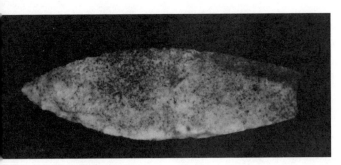

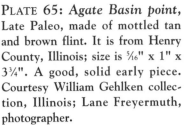

PLATE 65: *Agate Basin point*, Late Paleo, made of mottled tan and brown flint. It is from Henry County, Illinois; size is ⁵⁄₁₆" x 1" x 3¾". A good, solid early piece. Courtesy William Gehlken collection, Illinois; Lane Freyermuth, photographer.

PLATE 64: *Agate Basin point*, Late Paleo, with base and lower sides ground for about 1 inch. As example, Agate Basins are almost always very well made. It is from Rock Island County, Illinois, and measures 3¾" long. Courtesy Lane Freyermuth collection, Iowa.

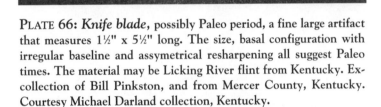

PLATE 66: *Knife blade*, possibly Paleo period, a fine large artifact that measures 1½" x 5½" long. The size, basal configuration with irregular baseline and assymetrical resharpening all suggest Paleo times. The material may be Licking River flint from Kentucky. Ex-collection of Bill Pinkston, and from Mercer County, Kentucky. Courtesy Michael Darland collection, Kentucky.

PLATE 67: *Agate Basin point*, Late Paleo, found in 1970 by the owner in Mercer County, Kentucky, near the Salt River. MD: "This field had footprints all around this area but they started in another direction. When I went the other way this is the point I found." This high-grade and rare artifact is 4¹³⁄₁₆" long. Courtesy Michael Darland collection, Kentucky.

PLATE 68: *Agate Basin point*, Late Paleo, an unusually fine specimen that is well-chipped and with basal grinding. Material is a white flint, and it is from Tama County, Iowa. Size is ⁵⁄₁₆" x 1" x 4" long. Superb specimen. Courtesy William Gehlken collection, Illinois; Lane Freyermuth, photographer.

PLATE 69: *Paleo point*, Clovis family but unfluted. The upper portions of this piece have been resharpened, suggesting knife use. Creamy-tan material, length 3¾", provenance Rock Island County, Illinois. Courtesy Lane Freyermuth collection, Iowa.

PLATE 70: *Paleo points and artifacts*, all from southern Illinois. Early Paleo specimens are top right and second from right, bottom row. Most of the others are Late Paleo. Different colors of flint and chert make up the materials, and size range is 2¾" to 5¼". The three pieces at lower left are from the same site. Fine early artifacts. Courtesy the Guy Brothers collection, Pinckneyville, Illinois.

Chapter III

The Hunters and Gatherers

Archaic Period (8000 BC – 1000 BC)

It required some seventy centuries, but the Midwestern Archaic peoples gradually took full control of a non-specialized lifeway. They were no longer only hunters and they were not yet farmers. The Archaic peoples took their food from the forests and prairies, lakes and marshes, and they probably doubled in population every few generations.

While most prehistoric groups were highly conservative, keeping to old, established, and tried and proven ways, the Archaic had time for many inventions and new ways of doing things. The first small villages developed, a few houses grouped in a sheltered valley, a few families banded together for mutual support and protection. Early in the Archaic, if not before, dogs were domesticated and became a great help. They were sentinels by day or night, were companions, tracked game and brought it to bay, and helped keep camps and villages clean.

The main change however was a broad dependence on nearly everything the natural world offered. This was both practical and profitable, and no doubt provided a better-balanced diet and a more even supply of food. Small game of all kinds was hunted and trapped, plus larger game like deer and bear was brought down. Fish were caught using a variety of methods, and tiny bones in kitchen middens suggest that minnow-sized fish were scooped from backwaters with woven baskets, these also made in the Archaic.

The presence of mortars or grinding stones means that plant seeds of various kinds were utilized, plus probably roots and berries as well. Nuts or tree-seeds (as the remains of the hulls and shells prove) were in big demand, for they were easy to gather, simple to store, and fast to prepare, compact and nutritious. While we can know little about such things, probably new ways of preparing and seasoning and cooking and preserving foods developed.

Birds of many kinds were hunted or captured, and a new device may have been used. Bolas-like entangling cords or weighted throwing nets may have been employed, and their probable weights are known to collectors today as plummets. Even frogs and turtles contributed their calories to the cooking fires.

Technology took several great strides forward in the Midwestern Archaic. While knapping or shaping chert and flint by chipping had long been known, many new point and knife designs arose. While the overall Archaic lifeway in the Midwest was similar, different regions developed different tool and weapons forms. Compared with Paleo times, there were dozens of additional styles and forms. Likely, smaller regions developed satisfactory designs and largely kept to them; since they worked, there was no real need to change. The relatively few designs of the earlier Paleo may have been the result of both a highly specialized hunting economy and a semi-nomadic lifeway that did not allow much settling-down and the development of unique regional forms.

One interesting thing about the Archaic in the Midwest is that when a person today goes out and finds an "arrowhead," it probably really is not. Instead, the odds are that it is an Archaic lance-tip or knife-blade. There are at least a hundred different chipped point and blade types, plus innumerable sub-types and blending forms. Chert and flint artifacts, because they are still relatively common, are the single largest collecting category today. And besides the known and named point or blade types there are many that have not yet been named; due to scarcity or small numbers or lack of study in this particular field they may never be properly identified.

Sometime early in the Archaic, the idea arose that tools could be made by a different method, called pecking and grinding. This was a simple enough process or series of steps, but it had never before been done in North America on a large scale. Some prehistoric genius discovered that even if hardstone and glacial slate could not be chipped into finished forms, like blades and points could be, the stone and slate could still be shaped. The new method was almost a form of sculpting.

First, repeated blows from a hammerstone took away most of the unwanted material. This was actually a careful and delicate process, so as not to damage or destroy the object being fashioned. This was the longest major step and some artifacts undoubtedly took many days of this tedious work before the preform was completed. The same process was used to make tools like axes or adzes, and ornamental objects like bannerstones, birdstones and pendants.

After the artifact was generally shaped by pecking, the next step was to grind the preform. Large areas (axe-blades, pendant or gorget faces) were flattened and smoothed by rubbing the artifacts against a large sandstone slab or even into bedrock grooves. At times, the artifact was held and a smaller abrading stone was used freehand to work smaller areas. All this helped wear away the pitted surface left by pecking and prepare the surface for the last step, polishing. Actually, no one knows precisely how polishing was done, but it probably involved leather, animal fat and fine grit or sand. For ornamental objects, especially with colorful hardstones or banded slates, the fat not only aided the polishing process but helped bring out the colors.

While this wearing-away method doesn't seem too important, it prepared the way for making very durable tools and highly sophisticated ornaments. As just one example, sturdy adz-heads could now be made. These in turn were secondary wood-working tools that helped shape dugout watercraft, handles for Atl-atls or lance-throwing sticks, wooden bowls, hollow-log mortars, and the like. So the new Archaic technology of pecking and grinding had long-term benefits in food preparation, hunting and transportation.

The artifacts from Midwestern Archaic times are much-admired today. This area was the heartland for bannerstones, those strange and beautiful objects that may once have served as counter-balance weights for Atl-atls, or they may have been symbols of rank or importance. Hardstone was used mainly for the more compact forms of banners, and beautiful material like rose quartzite was sometimes imported for the purpose.

Glacial slate was used for most bannerstone forms, and almost all of the very large types — notched ovates, knobbed lunates — were made of this material. A few forms like curved-pick banners were made of rare materials like green or yellow chlorite. While the word slate does not itself sound attractive, glacial slate was a different matter. Whether monochrome in greys, browns, blacks, blues or even reds, or beautifully banded in almost any color arrangement or pattern, slate was a favored material for Archaic (and later) times.

Hardstone was also used to make a few gorgets (flat, usually drilled with holes equidistant from ends) and pendants (flat, usually one hole near one end). Both of these artifacts were usually of slate material. An interesting thing is that when hardstone was used for ornamental artifacts usually made of slate, the forms tend to be both very well made and more highly developed forms. So, many hardstone artifacts may have been made in later

Archaic times.

Two unusual and valuable artifacts are unique to the Midwest and a few states adjoining the Midwest. They are different in form but are probably related. The "lizard" or effigy stone is 4 to 6-plus inches long, flat on the underside and with (supposedly) a head, wider body, and long, tapering tail. Most have a somewhat streamlined configuration. Most are not drilled but may have notches or grooves as if for attachment to something. Almost all examples are made of glacial slate and timewise they are probably Middle Archaic. The lack of hardstone effigies suggest they are not particularly late in the Archaic.

Birdstones are probably the descendants of effigy stones and many of these forms do look like setting birds or birds at rest. Strangely, legs and wings are rarely depicted in any way, but there is a raised head with beak, a lower body, and a raised and sometimes flared tail. There are many different forms, from chunky animal-type to turtle-like to the classic Glacial Kame or Gravel Knoll forms with elongated body and flowing lines. Often, for whatever reasons, eyes are present in some fashion and this area is emphasized.

Birdstones have a flattish, rectangular base beneath the body section, which is usually drilled at each end with small connecting or "L"-shaped holes. Other birdstone varieties, such as the short pop-eyes, may have a front and rear bottom ridge, with holes drilled through the ridge center. Pop-eyes are more rounded forms and hardstone examples may be made from porphyry, a dark very compact material with irregular inclusions that may be milky-white, cream, yellow or orange. Birdstones were made in the Late Archaic period, and several types continued into the Woodland period.

Both effigies and birdstones were probably associated with Atl-atls, though many guesses are made as to where they were fastened on the lance-throwing stick. There are some indications that they were decorative handles or hand-guides, but this is only the best speculation so far. As to meaning or what the forms signify, effigies may represent snakes that have captured and swallowed prey, and thus may have been hunting charms. Birdstones may represent the lance itself in flight, and an early magical effort to make a guided missile. But only when a birdstone is found that is still secured to whatever it was will the questions really be answered.

PLATE 71: *Lizard effigy*, probably Middle Archaic period, made of dark hardstone or very dense slate. This example has a finely tapered body and distinct head region. It is 4⅝" long, from Delaware County, Ohio. It is ex-collection of Dr. Gordon Meuser, sale lot number 2698. Fine piece. Courtesy Charles West collection, Ohio.

PLATE 73: *Hematite bell pestles*, Archaic, from the Eagle's Point Site in Ohio County, Kentucky. Left, 4" x 7¾"; the grainy texture indicates it has never been used. Right, 4¼" high, in contrast has been used until the surface was polished to glass-like smoothness. Courtesy Steven R. Dowell collection, Kentucky.

PLATE 74: *Archaic axes*, probably Middle to Late. Left, full groove from Montgomery County, Kentucky. It is 7⅛" long and has an unusually small bit for size. Right, ¾ groove from Adams County, Ohio. It is 6¾" long and made of speckled granite. Courtesy Steven R. Dowell collection, Kentucky.

PLATE 72: *Archaic axes*, various materials. Top left, Ohio, ¾ groove, 5¼" long, well polished. Bottom center, angle-edged full groove, unusual type, sketched in *Indian Axes And Related Stone Artifacts*. Top right, Daviess County, Kentucky, ¾ groove, 5" long. Courtesy Steven R. Dowell collection, Kentucky.

PLATE 75: ¾ *groove axe*, from Madison County, Illinois, and made of spotted granite material. It is Archaic period and 4½" x 7½". This is a better-than-average field find for anywhere in the Midwest. Tim & Patty Wiemers collection, Edwardsville, Illinois.

PLATE 76: *Archaic points or blades,* all from the Eagle's Point Site in Ohio County, Kentucky. A wide range of Kentucky flints and cherts is represented here. Courtesy Steven R. Dowell collection, Kentucky.

PLATE 77: *¾ groove axe,* Archaic, from Pike County, Illinois. It is 2⅜" x 3¾" x 6½" long; shown are two views of this fine piece, made of high-quality porphyry material. Courtesy of Rodney M. Peck collection, Harrisburg, North Carolina.

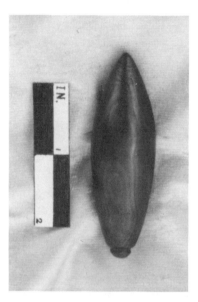

PLATE 78: *Gilcrease grooved plummet,* Terminal Archaic, ca. 920 BC (ref. *Early Woodland Archeology,* 1986, pp 340, 342 figure 16.5, rows 2 & 3). Material is silver-grey hematite and size is 1" x 3". This beautiful artifact was found on February 3, 1988, along the Wabash River in Sullivan County, Indiana. Despite many theories, exact plummet use is unknown. Personal find, from the collection of Don Simmons, Robinson, Illinois.

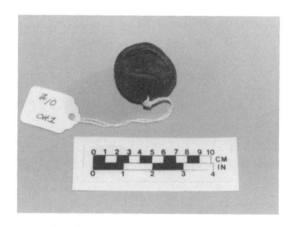

PLATE 79: *Bowl-type pipe,* Archaic period. It is from the Eagle's Point Site in Ohio County, Kentucky. This artifact is unusual in that it has a drilled hole in one side, possibly for suspension. A one-of-a-kind find, the pipe is 1½" in diameter. Courtesy Steven R. Dowell collection, Kentucky.

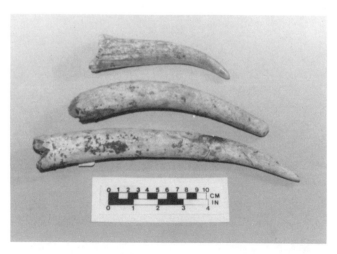

PLATE 80: *Antler flakers,* flint-working tools from Early to Middle Archaic. These came from the Eagle's Point Site in Ohio County, Kentucky. Size, 4½" to 7½" long. Courtesy Steven R. Dowell collection, Kentucky.

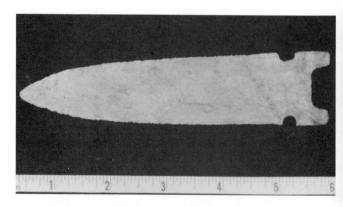

PLATE 81: *Graham Cave variant,* Early Archaic, from Illinois. It is made of pink and white chert and is 1¼" x 5⅜". This piece has an unusual "U"-shaped base rather than the more typical deeply concave baseline. Ca. 8000-6000 BC. The type is named after Graham Cave, Missouri. Courtesy Tom Razmus collection, Georgetown, Illinois.

PLATE 82: ¼ *groove axes*, Archaic, from either Tama County or Marshall County, Iowa. The small axe at the center is 3¼" long. All pieces have outstanding workmanship, color and material, plus condition, especially for smaller axes. Collection of Floyd and Judi Goddard, Wilton, Iowa.

PLATE 83: ¼ *groove axe*, found in Tama County, Iowa, by Don Rank. It is made of black, green and white hardstone and measures 3⅛" x 6¼". This is a rare and unusual axe, having large groove ridges and deeply fluted both top and bottom. It is also well polished. Collection of Floyd and Judi Goddard, Wilton, Iowa.

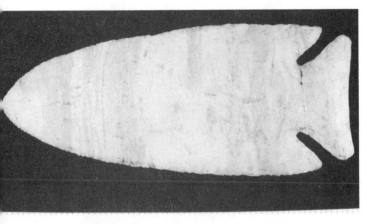

PLATE 84: *Early Archaic blade*, diagonal-notch type, from Illinois. Material is typical for the region and is a good grade of white chert; there is some striping, especially near the tip. Size is 1⅞" x 4¼". This is a well-made early knife form. Courtesy Tom Razmus collection, Georgetown, Illinois.

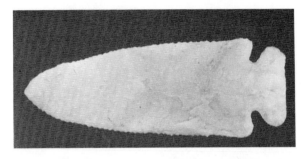

PLATE 85: *Thebes blade*, Early Archaic, made of white chert. It is from St. Louis County, Missouri, and size is 1½" x 4¼". This is a large and well-made artifact, in top condition. Note the fine edge-serrations found on some of the type. Ca. 7500 BC. Courtesy Tom Razmus collection, Georgetown, Illinois.

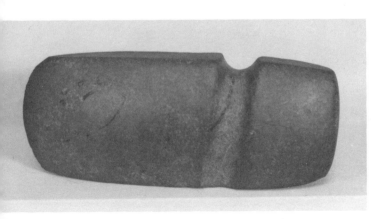

PLATE 86: ¼ *groove axe*, Archaic period, found in a gravel pit near the Boyer River, Crawford County, Iowa. This is simply a very beautiful axe, made of grey-green quality hardstone. It is very highly polished and 8¼" long. The axe has good size, clean lines, and top workstyle. Collection of Floyd and Judi Goddard, Wilton, Iowa.

PLATE 87: ¼ *groove axe*, Archaic period, found in Marshall County, Iowa. Material is a black and grey hardstone, and it is 7" long. This is an outstanding axe in every way, with artistic design, top workstyle, crisp lines and superb condition. This is a museum-grade artifact, highly polished. Collection of Floyd and Judi Goddard, Wilton, Iowa.

PLATE 88: *Bannerstone*, Archaic period, banded glacial slate, found in Vermillion County, Indiana. This is a blending banner form, Reel and Double-bitted axe form. (See Knoblock, *Bannerstones Of The North American Indian*, 1939, pp 310-313.) Picked up when a water line was dug, this superb specimen is 1⅛" x 6½". Courtesy Tom Razmus collection, Georgetown, Illinois.

PLATE 89: *Flared-bit axes*, ¾ grooved, Archaic. These are excellent axes with very pronounced raised groove ridges. Left, Tama County, Iowa, made of greenish and white hardstone with black and porphyry spots. Right, Scott County, Iowa, black, brown and white hardstone. Collection of Floyd and Judi Goddard, Wilton, Iowa.

PLATE 90: *Bannerstone*, angular Geniculate type, Archaic period. This has the hole typical of the class, which is oval instead of being round. This piece was found in Vermillion County, Indiana, and is 2⅛" x 2⅜". Material is a high grade of banded slate. Fine piece. Courtesy Tom Razmus collection, Georgetown, Illinois.

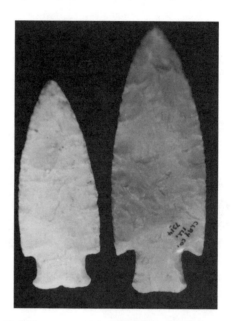

PLATE 91: *Hardin points or blades*, Early Archaic, both from Illinois. Left, off-white material, Fulton County, 3½" long, found in 1946. Excellent specimen. Right, glossy grey and brown material, Clay County, 4½" long, fine piece. Collection of Russell & Rhonda Bedwell, Illinois.

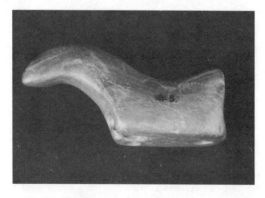

PLATE 92: *Birdstone*, Late Archaic, found near Danville, Vermillion County, Illinois. It is made of green slate and measures 1" x 2⅞". This is a well-shaped small birdstone, with tally-marks on the base. Courtesy Tom Razmus collection, Georgetown, Illinois.

PLATE 93: *¾ groove axe*, found in St. Louis County, Missouri. It is 6½" long, made of dark green hardstone with small light green inclusions throughout, attractive material. This is a top-grade axe, good design and lines, with high polish. Superb piece, and ex-collection of Dennis DeRosear. Collection of Floyd and Judi Goddard, Wilton, Iowa.

PLATE 94: ¼ *groove axe*, from Ver County, Illinois. Made of dark granite-like hardstone, it is 6" at greatest dimension. This is a good, sturdy utilitarian Archaic axe. Courtesy Dale Richter collection, Illinois.

PLATE 95: *Plummets*, made of hematite, all personal field-finds by Stanley Razmus over a period of 25 years. These came from Vermillion County, Indiana, and range in size from 2½" to 3". Stanley Razmus, now 82 years old, contributed all his personal finds to his son, Tom. These are very fine Late Archaic specimens. Courtesy Tom Razmus collection, Georgetown, Illinois.

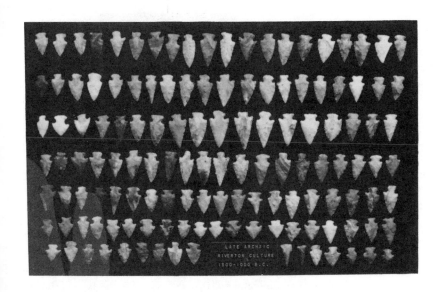

PLATE 96: *Riverton points*, Late Archaic period and ca. 1000 BC. All points were personal field-finds made by Tom and Stanley Razmus in Vermillion County, Indiana. These examples are made of river pebble cherts, and many seem to be of heat-treated materials. Size range, ½" to 1½". Courtesy Tom Razmus collection, Georgetown, Illinois.

PLATE 97: *Plummets*, Late Archaic, all personal field-finds by Stanley Razmus over a 25-year period. These were all given to his son, Tom. Stanley Razmus found a total of nine plummets over the quarter-century, giving an idea of rarity. The size range here is 1¾" to 2⅞". All are from Vermillion County, Indiana. Courtesy Tom Razmus collection, Georgetown, Illinois.

PLATE 98: ¼ *groove axe*, Archaic period, from Ver County, Illinois. Made of a medium-color hardstone, the surface is well-polished; piece is 5½" long. Courtesy Dale Richter collection, Illinois.

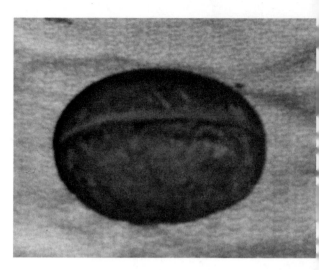

PLATE 99: *Pendant*, probably Archaic, from Ver County, Illinois. Made of slate, it is 3" at greatest dimension. Some of the pendants can be quite early in the period. Courtesy Arnold Richter collection, Illinois.

PLATE 100: *Loafstone*, made of medium-dark slate, 2" long. It has the typical thin incised groove running length-wise. An interesting Archaic piece, from Champaign County, Illinois. Courtesy Arnold Richter collection, Illinois.

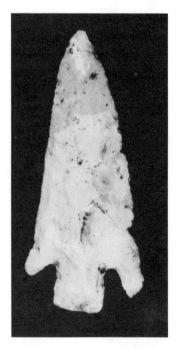

PLATE 101: *Etley or Mehlville point or blade*, made of Ozark chert, white and heavily patinated. Archaic, this knife has obviously dissimilar edge treatment typical of knife use. Size, 1¾" x 4⅛". This was a personal find by the owner in Warren County, Missouri, on February 3, 1990. Courtesy Aaron Rampani collection, St. Ann, St. Louis County, Missouri.

PLATE 102: *Kings corner-notch point or blade*, of off-white Crescent heat-treated chert. A well-made artifact from the Archaic, it has a needle-point tip and serrations. At 1⅛" x 1¾", this was a personal find by the owner in St. Louis County, Missouri, on October 10, 1988. Use for the type is thought to have continued into Woodland times. Courtesy Aaron Rampani collection, St. Ann, St. Louis County, Missouri.

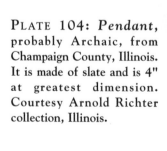

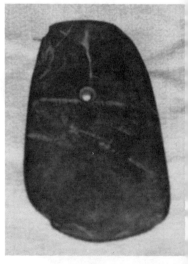

PLATE 103: *Bannerstone*, Archaic, early simple winged form. It is made of banded slate with the material worked into the final artifact form, encircling the central drill-hole. This piece is from Champaign County, Illinois, and is 5" wide. Nice piece. Courtesy Arnold Richter collection, Illinois.

PLATE 104: *Pendant*, probably Archaic, from Champaign County, Illinois. It is made of slate and is 4" at greatest dimension. Courtesy Arnold Richter collection, Illinois.

PLATE 105: *Tapered-tube pipe*, made of steatite, probably Late Archaic. This is the so-called "cloud-blower" type, and size is 2⅜" x 3½" long. This is not at all a common pipe form; from Meigs County, Ohio. Courtesy Charles West collection, Ohio.

PLATE 106: *Archaic corner-notch points or blades*, all Ohio. Left, 1⅛" x 2⅝", blue Upper Mercer with crystal inclusion, Knox County. Center, blue Upper Mercer with lightning lines, serrated edges, ¹³⁄₁₆" x 2⅜", ex-collection of DH#529. Right, 1³⁄₁₆" x 3⅛", mottled blue Upper Mercer, probably late in the period and a Meadowood type. Hothem collection, Ohio.

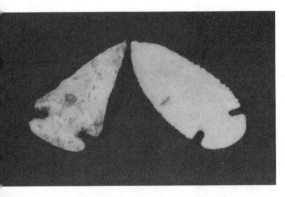

PLATE 107: *Blades or knives*, Early Archaic. Left, Thebes, 2¼", from Franklin County, Indiana. Right, Dovetail, 2¹¹⁄₁₆", from Henderson County, Kentucky. Courtesy Lee Fisher collection, Pennsylvania; Anthony Lang, photographer.

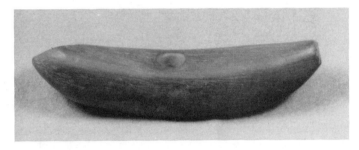

PLATE 108: *Pick bannerstone*, brown slate, from Pike County, Illinois. This has a well-drilled center hole, and overall measures 1 x 5¼". Courtesy Lee Fisher collection, Pennsylvania; Anthony Lang, photographer.

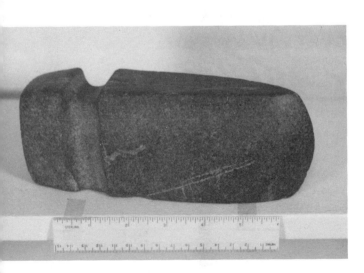

PLATE 109: *Iowa Straight-side ¾ groove axe*, found in 1988 by Gene Barry in Jasper County, Iowa. It is a classic form, and quite honestly one of the best axes ever found in Iowa. It is made of a pepper-grey-green fine-grained hardstone, and is 8" long. A few plow-scars do not detract from this top-of-the-line piece. Collection of Floyd and Judi Goddard, Wilton, Iowa.

PLATE 110: *Atl-atl weight*, Archaic, grooved and humped variety. This is a fine example of an unusual weight type, with groove around both sides and top. Size is ¾" wide, ¹³⁄₁₆" high and 2¾" long. Material is green granite. This piece was found February 17, 1989 along the Embarras River, Jasper County, Illinois. Personal find, from the collection of Don Simmons, Robinson, Illinois.

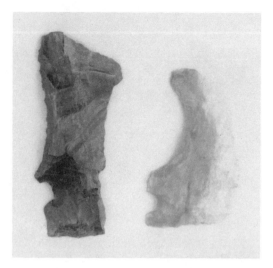

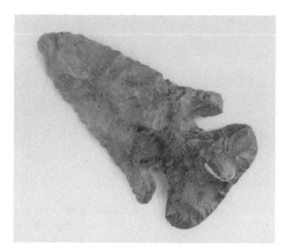

PLATE 111: *Hafted shaft-scrapers*, uncommon artifacts from the Early Archaic in the Midwest. Left, blue-black striated flint, 1" x 2½", ex-collection of R. Cox, Hocking County, Ohio. Right, grey and cream unknown material, 1³⁄₁₆" x 1⅞", ex-collection of B. Champion, from Perry County, Ohio. These artifacts are usually isolated surface finds, and scarce wherever picked up. Hothem collection, Ohio.

PLATE 112: *Archaic deep-notch blade*, probably one of the Thebes cluster members, Early Archaic. Material is a mottled Upper Mercer (eastern Ohio) in light blue, from Coshocton County. Size, 1⅝" x 3", intact wing-tips or shoulders despite resharpening. This piece is both serrated and beveled, good size and fine condition. Hothem collection, Ohio.

PLATE 113: *Archaic knives*, all made of Indiana Green material, and all from Benton County, Indiana. The largest piece at center measures 1¾" x 4⅜". (Some examples may be Paleo, but most are Archaic). Courtesy private collection of Kenneth Spiker.

PLATE 114: *Archaic blades*, both Ohio. Left, possibly a Palmer corner-notch, 1¼" x 2¹⁄₁₆", black Upper Mercer, county unknown. Right, stemmed Early Archaic blade, 1" x 3¼", mottled blue Upper Mercer, Coshocton County. Hothem collection, Ohio.

PLATE 115: *Heavy-duty blade*, Archaic period, from Hocking County, Ohio. Material is a mottled high-grade Upper Mercer, so common in Archaic artifacts for the region. Size, 1¼" x 3⅛" and ex-collection of B. Champion. Hothem collection, Ohio.

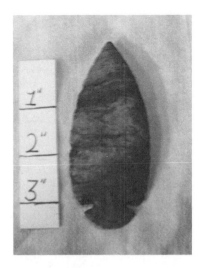

PLATE 116: *Hardin points or blades*, both found in Benton County, Indiana. Left, 1⅜" x 3¼". Right, 1¼" x 3⅞". Courtesy private collection of Kenneth Spiker.

PLATE 117: *St. Charles or Dovetail blade*, found in Tippecanoe County, Indiana. This fine knife is made of Indiana Green flint and is 1½" x 3⅞" long. It is Early Archaic and an excellent example of early flintworking. An exceptional piece. Courtesy private collection of Kenneth Spiker.

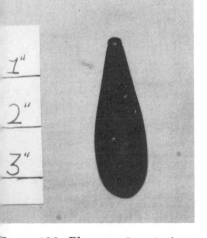

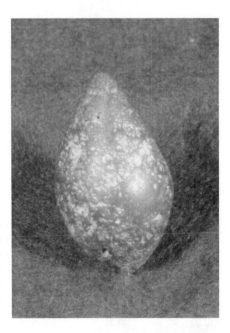

PLATE 118: *Drills*, possibly Archaic, 2½" and 3" long, respectively. Left example is from Lincoln County, Missouri, and right example is from Adams County, Illinois. These are well-made specimens. Courtesy Lee Fisher collection, Pennsylvania; Anthony Lang, photographer.

PLATE 119: *Plummet*, Late Archaic, 1¼" x 2". This well-made example is hematite and the smaller (top) end is grooved. It is from Brown County, Ohio. Courtesy Lee Fisher collection, Pennsylvania; Anthony Lang, photographer.

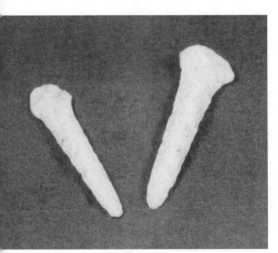

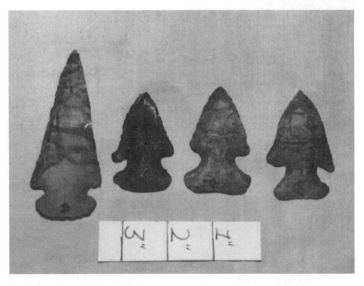

PLATE 120: *Plummet*, Late Archaic, found in Newton County, Indiana. It is grooved near the top and overall size is 1" x 3". Made of quality hematite or natural iron ore, this is a better-than-average specimen of an uncommon artifact. Courtesy private collection of Kenneth Spiker.

PLATE 121: *Thebes cluster points or blades*, Early Archaic period, all from Benton County, Indiana. Material is Indiana Green and the largest specimen is 1½" x 3⅝". Courtesy private collection of Kenneth Spiker.

PLATE 122: *Bell-type pestle*, Ohio, 2½" across the base and 4¼" high. It is made of quartzite and in this size might well be considered a miniature form. It is ex-collections of Dunn, Tyson and Hetrick. Private collection; Del Hetrick, photographer.

PLATE 123: *Hafted end-scraper*, Thebes family cluster, Early Archaic. It is 1½" wide and 1½" long. Made of black flint, it is from Ohio and ex-collection of Norm Dunn. Private collection; Del Hetrick, photographer.

PLATE 124: *Sedalia*, a Late Archaic point, from Pike County, Illinois. This is an excellent large specimen in whitish chert, and measures 1¾" x 5". Lee Fisher collection, Pennsylvania; Anthony Lang, photographer.

PLATE 125: ¾ *groove axe*, Archaic period, made of fine blue and green speckled granite. This high-grade piece is 2¼" x 5¼". Note the clean, crisp, artistic lines and high polish of this top specimen. Courtesy Dale & Betty Roberts collection, Iowa.

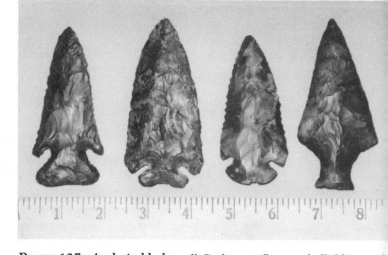

PLATE 126: *Winged bannerstone*, Archaic, from Mercer County, Ohio. The material is an attractive green banded slate; size is 2" x 3½". Fine piece. Courtesy Lee Fisher collection, Pennsylvania; Anthony Lang, photographer.

PLATE 127: *Archaic blades*, all Coshocton flints and all Ohio; scale indicates sizes. All left to right: Ohio-notch Thebes, found in 1987 near Atwood Lake. Thebes, Union County, ex-collections of Baker, Tackett, Ebosh and Sadofsky. Notched-base, Holmes County, ex-collections of Scott, Cox, Davis; reddish flint. Ashtabula, ex-collection of Pholey. Courtesy Steve Puttera Jr. collection, Ohio.

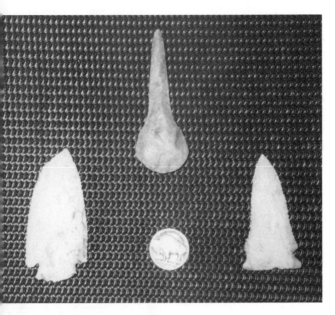

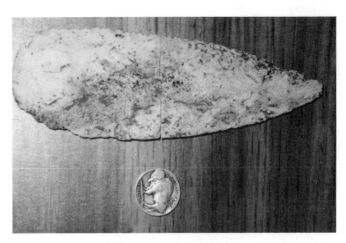

PLATE 128: *Midwestern chipped artifacts*, from Hancock County, Illinois. These were all found the same day on the same Archaic site by Mr. Launer. The fine drill is 3" long and is made of Brown County chert. Courtesy Eldon Launer collection, Illinois.

PLATE 129: *Archaic knife*, probably a Stanfield from the early centuries, from Scott County, Illinois. This is a reassembled artifact, having been found in two pieces; the fitting line is about mid-length. Size, 5½" long. Courtesy Eldon Launer collection, Illinois.

PLATE 130: *Sedalia point*, Late Archaic, a well-known type from Illinois and Iowa. This example, about 3¼" long, is made of light-colored chert and is from Wapello County, Iowa. It was found by a friend of the owner. Courtesy Verlin Hepker collection, Iowa.

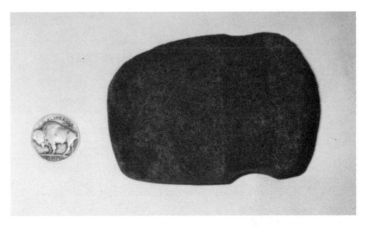

PLATE 131: *Archaic knife*, made of a milky chert, from Scott County, Illinois. It is 4" long, and a solid, sturdy piece. Courtesy Eldon Launer collection, Illinois.

PLATE 132: ¾ *groove axe*, from Scott County, Illinois, picked up along the river bottoms. It is 3¾" long, and a well-made smaller example. This was a personal find by Mr. Launer. Courtesy Eldon Launer collection, Illinois.

PLATE 134: *Large knife blade*, probably Archaic period, from Rock Island County, Illinois. It is made of bluish fossiliferous chert and is ⁵⁄₁₆" x 1⅝" x 5³⁄₁₆" long. This is a fine blade. Courtesy Jim Roberson collection, Muscatine, Iowa.

PLATE 133: *Slant-grooved ¾ axe*, Archaic, from Marion County, Iowa. Size is 1⅜" x 2" x 4⅜". Material is a beautiful speckled hardstone in black and white, and the surface has overall very high polish. Courtesy Jim Roberson collection, Muscatine, Iowa.

PLATE 135: *¾ groove axe*, Archaic, made of a speckled tan hardstone. From Marion County, Iowa, it is ex-collections of Williams, DeRosear, and Goddard. This is a well-designed and very well finished axe, 1¾" x 2⁹⁄₁₆" x 5⅜" long. Courtesy Jim Roberson collection, Muscatine, Iowa.

PLATE 136: *Slant-grooved ¾ axe*, Archaic period, from Marion County, Iowa. It is 1⅞" x 2½" x 5⅛" long. This axe is very unusual in that the groove, poll and bit areas are highly polished (dark portions) while the faces were repecked for unknown reasons. This is the only axe in this condition the owner has seen. Courtesy Jim Roberson collection, Muscatine, Iowa.

PLATE 137: *Knife blade*, probably Archaic, a personal find during 1988 by the owner, in Louisa County, Iowa. Made of white flint, this artifact is ¼" x 1⅝" x 5½" long. This is a fine piece, in top condition. Courtesy Jim Roberson collection, Muscatine, Iowa.

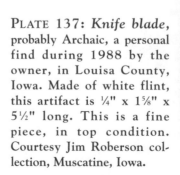

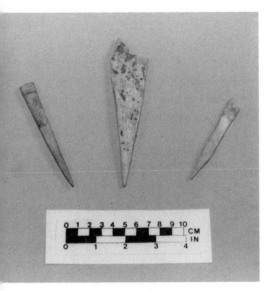

PLATE 138: *Bone needles,* Early to Middle Archaic, from the Eagle's Point Site, Ohio County, Kentucky. Two have holes at the wide end, while example on left was perhaps salvaged from an awl and is grooved. Lengths, 1¾" to 3". Courtesy Steven R. Dowell collection, Kentucky.

PLATE 139: *Hematite plummet,* probably Late Archaic, from Muscatine County, Iowa. This fine specimen is drilled through the small end, and overall plummet length is 3⅜". Examples this large and fine are quite rare. Courtesy Richard Holliday collection, Muscatine, Iowa.

PLATE 140: *Bannerstone,* Archaic period, reel group or type, made of mottled dark diorite. This is a well-made form in very fine condition, and from Greene County, Illinois. Good specimen. Courtesy Gregory L. Perdun collection, Illinois.

PLATE 141: ¾ *groove axe,* Archaic, well-defined groove, speckled hardstone. This well-made axe is from Jersey County, Illinois. Courtesy Gregory L. Perdun collection, Illinois.

PLATE 142: *Early Archaic points and blades,* all from Jersey County, Illinois. Various side and corner notched examples are represented, as well as St. Charles (Dovetails) and Hardins. This is a fine representative selection of very old artifacts. Courtesy Gregory L. Perdun collection, Illinois.

PLATE 143: *Dalton points or blades,* Early Archaic, from the Illinois River Valley of Illinois. These examples were found in Jersey and Greene Counties. The resharpening (reduction of length and/or width) is evident on some specimens. Note the wide type range. Courtesy Gregory L. Perdun collection, Illinois.

PLATE 144: *Sloan Dalton*, an early knife form in the Dalton family of the Early Archaic. Fine work-style and basal thinning are typical, though the straight-base sub-variety is unusual. Size is 5¾" and material is a fine white chert. It was found during a house-site excavation in Holt County, Missouri. Courtesy Mike George collection, Missouri.

PLATE 145: ¼ *groove axe*, from Ohio, Archaic period, made of a good grade of hardstone. This piece, 3⅞" high, is highly polished overall. Ex-collection of Norm Dunn. Private collection; photograph by Del Hetrick.

PLATE 146: *Hardin*, Early Archaic, beveled and extensively resharpened. From Ohio, this 2⅞" specimen is made of grey, lavender and maroon flint. Ohio Hardins are very uncommon. Private collection; photograph by Del Hetrick.

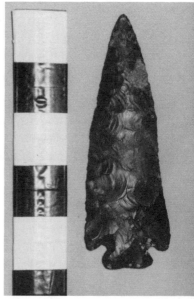

PLATE 147: *Corner-notched point or blade*, 1¾" x 5". Material is black Coshocton (Upper Mercer) flint with light blue inclusions. It was collected by a Mr. Belden of Akron prior to 1930. Slightly pentagonal in upper blade outline, this could be Glacial Kame or Intrusive Mound, as no basal grinding is present. The author suggests Late Archaic, possibly Glacial Kame. An excellent Ohio flint. Courtesy Steve Puttera Jr. collection, Ohio.

PLATE 148: *St. Charles or Dovetail blade*, Early Archaic, made of white and brown flint. This is a classic piece, from Holt County, Missouri. It was a surface find after a 5½" rain. The blade is 5¼" long. Courtesy Mike George collection, Missouri.

PLATE 149: ¼ *groove axe*, made of light-colored speckled granite, from the Midwest. It is 3¾" x 4⅞", and is ex-collection of Paul Rankin. Private collection; photograph by Del Hetrick.

40

PLATE 151: ¾ groove axe, this piece found by Mr. Dullard on the Des Moines River in Wapello County, Iowa. This small axe has much color, being a grey-green with cream inclusions. Size is 2⅝" x 4¾", and it is well patinated. Courtesy Bruce Filbrandt collection, Iowa.

PLATE 150: *Dalton point or blade*, Early Archaic, 2¾" long, made of white chert. This was found in Holt County, Missouri. These pieces retain some features of Late Paleo points or blades. Courtesy Mike George collection, Missouri.

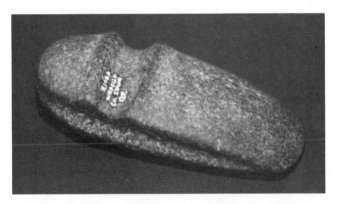

PLATE 153: *Illinois River type axe*, found in the 1930's in Wapello County, Iowa, near the Des Moines River. It is made of a quality hardstone, has well-defined features, and has the edge or side flutes completely around the axe, sides and poll. Size, 2¾" x 6¾", with weight of about two pounds. Courtesy Bruce Filbrandt collection, Iowa.

PLATE 152: *Sedalia point or blade*, 4¼", with material a tan and brown flint. It has basal grinding and is from Holt County, Missouri. Archaic era. Courtesy Mike George collection, Missouri.

PLATE 154: *Stone mortar*, possibly Archaic, from northern Ohio. Collected by Mr. Belden, it is 5 high and 10" long; weight is 15¼ pounds. Note the projecting carrying or handling lugs at each end. This is a very unusual artifact. Courtesy Steve Puttera Jr. collection, Ohio.

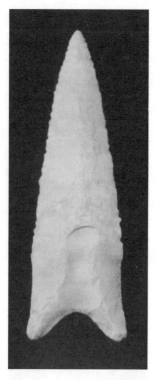

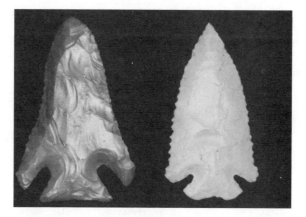

PLATE 156: *Archaic blades*, both Kentucky. Left, Lost Lake with steep bevel in KY nodular flint. Found by Rev. Roy Francis, Todd County. Ex-collections of Jeff Sadofsky and Harry Cline. Right, Dovetail that is very finely edge-serrated, also found by Rev. Francis in Todd County. Ex-collections of Sadofsky and Cline. Perfect condition, top workstyle. Courtesy Steve Puttera Jr. collection, Ohio.

PLATE 157: *Graham Cave blade*, an Archaic knife form, made of brown flint. It is 2⅜" long, probably considerably shorter than the original length due to resharpening or rechipping. Found in Holt County, Missouri. Courtesy Mike George collection, Missouri.

PLATE 155: *Dalton point or blade*, Early Archaic, 3¾" long, from Missouri. Like a few Daltons, it has fluting, here about 1" long. This is a fine and highly collectible early piece made of high-grade white chert. Courtesy Collection of Russell & Rhonda Bedwell, Illinois.

PLATE 158: *Missouri points or blades*, l. to r.: Nebo Hill, pink flint or chert, 6" long, found by Bill Bodine in Cooper County. Good sturdy piece in nice color. Sedalia, 5¼", found by Bill Bodine in Saline County. Side-notched blade, 5½" long, found southwest of Nelson, Saline County. Courtesy Steve Puttera Jr. collection, Ohio.

PLATE 159: *Illinois points or blades*, l. to r.: Super-quality Thebes, 2½" x 4¾", glossy pink flint, Rock Island County, ex-collections of Norm Dunn and Jack Hooks. This is Early Archaic, others also. Lost Lake, southern Illinois, heavily resharpened, exquisite workstyle. Holland, southcentral Illinois, 4¼" long, very finely chipped, serrated. Hardin barbed, Adams County, near-jewel flint, 1½" x 3⅛". Top piece and near-museum quality. Courtesy Steve Puttera Jr. collection, Ohio.

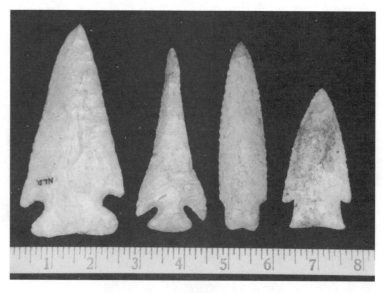

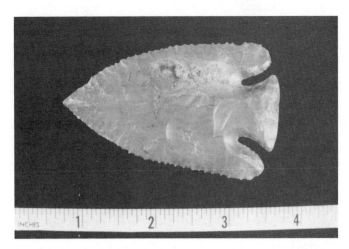

PLATE 160: *Large stone hammers or mauls,* possibly Archaic, both full-grooved and both Ohio. Left, ex-collection of C.T. Crocker, from Geauga County, weight 5 pounds. Right, northcentral part of state, ex-collection of Gene Liebchin, weight 7 pounds. Excellent specimens. Courtesy Steve Puttera Jr. collection, Ohio.

PLATE 161: *Lost Lake,* Early Archaic, ca. 8000 BC. This piece is made of grey Indiana hornstone and is from Parke County, Indiana. This is a very well-made blade and the excurvate sides indicate it was not heavily resharpened. Serrations are typical of knife use. It is about 3" long. Courtesy Tom Razmus collection, Georgetown, Illinois.

PLATE 162: *Adzes,* both possibly Archaic, both from Ohio. Left, grooved elongated form in green granite, 1½" x 6¼", from Crawford County. Right, high-quality granite adz in perfect condition from Lorain County. Size, 2⅛" x 5¼". Courtesy Steve Puttera Jr. collection, Ohio.

PLATE 163: *St. Charles or Dovetail point or blade,* Early Archaic and ca. 7500-6000 BC. It is made of red chert, darker toward the tip, with top workstyle, size, color and condition. Superb specimen. It is 1½" x 5³⁄₁₆", and is from St. Clair County, Illinois. Courtesy collection of Bob Rampani, Bridgeton, St. Louis County, Missouri.

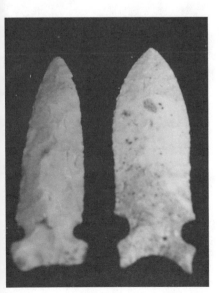

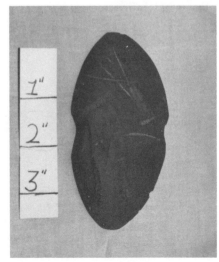

PLATE 164: *Archaic blades,* both from Illinois. Left, Osceola, off-white, Fulton County, 3¼" long, with much age patination. Found in the 1940's. Right, Graham Cave, white and purple chert, 3½", from Adams County. Courtesy collection of Russell & Rhonda Bedwell, Illinois.

PLATE 165: *Winged bannerstone,* Archaic period, from Benton County, Indiana. Made of banded glacial slate, it is 2¼" x 4¼". The lines or marks on one wing are probably from plow or disc strikes, not unusual on field-found artifacts. Nice piece. Private collection of Kenneth Spiker.

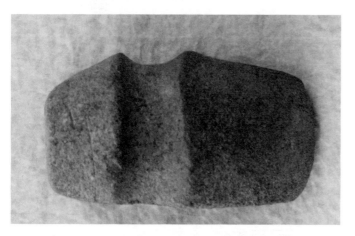

PLATE 166: ¼ *groove axe*, from Logan County, Illinois, and 2½" x 4⅝". It is a Missouri straight-back type, with raised groove borders. Material is a high grade of brown granite that took a solid polish. Courtesy collection of Bob Rampani, Bridgeton, St. Louis County, Missouri.

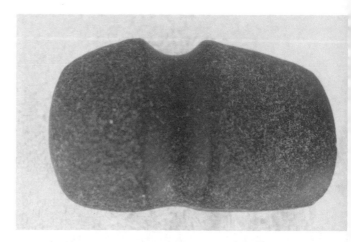

PLATE 167: ¼ *groove axe*, found in Bridgeton, St. Louis County, Missouri. It was picked up March 26, 1987 by a friend of the owner, and is 3½" x 5¾". Material is a black speckled granite with good overall polish. A superior piece. Courtesy collection of Bob Rampani, Bridgeton, St. Louis County, Missouri.

PLATE 168: *Saddle-face bannerstone,* found in Williamson County, Illinois, in October of 1974. It came from near the Big Muddy River and the finder said it was lying with the smooth side up, clean and shining in the ground. Material is granite-like green and white speckled hardstone. Size is 2⅜" wide and 2½" long. A superior and rare specimen. Courtesy Tom Razmus collection, Georgetown, Illinois.

PLATE 169: *Saddle-face bannerstone,* Archaic period, side view. See accompanying photograph caption for additional information.

PLATE 170: ¼ *groove axe,* Archaic, near-miniature in size. This fine specimen is made of high-grade speckled hardstone and is well-shaped and nicely polished. Size is 2" x 4¼"; it is from Hamilton County, Ohio. Courtesy Charles West collection, Ohio.

PLATE 171: *Gouge,* Archaic period, made of very high grade dark hardstone that took a beautiful polish. This rare artifact (more common to Northeastern U.S.) is not frequently found in the state of origin. It is from Miami County, Ohio, and is 1⅞" x 6⅞". Ex-collections of G.C. Kiefer and C. Theler. Courtesy Charles West collection, Ohio.

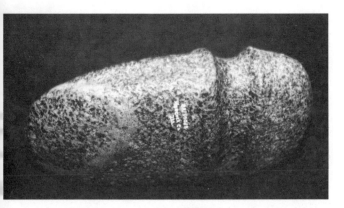

PLATE 172: ¼ *groove axe*, from Hancock County, Illinois. It was found on a farm just east of Dallas City. Material is grey and black hardstone, with a white inclusion, possibly of porphyry, near the bit. This axe has fluting on both sides below the groove. Size, 5¼" x 10". Courtesy Bruce Filbrandt collection, Iowa.

PLATE 173: *Half-groove axe*, from Lee County, Iowa. It was found many years ago and was in the Copeland collection, and purchased at the Max Shipley auction. This is a very fine axe, 2½" x 4½" x 9¼". Weight is 8 to 9 pounds. Material is a dense black hardstone, and both sides have slight fluting. Courtesy Bruce Filbrandt collection, Iowa.

PLATE 174: ¼ *groove axe*, found in Muscatine County, Iowa, many years ago. It came from the bluff area overlooking the bay region south of Muscatine. It is made of black hardstone and is well-detailed and highly polished. Size is 3½" x 6⅜" and weight is 2½ pounds. Courtesy Bruce Filbrandt collection, Iowa.

PLATE 175: ¼ *groove axe*, from East Moline, Illinois, and found many years ago. This is strange material, being grey quartzite with flint-like inclusions on the poll area and handle side. This is a highly developed form and is heavily polished. This axe is 3⅝" x 6¼" and weighs about 3½ pounds. Courtesy Bruce Filbrandt collection, Iowa.

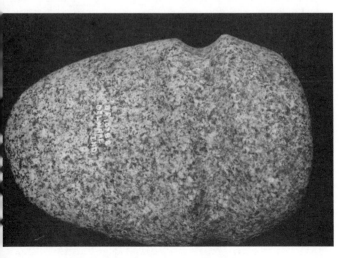

PLATE 176: *Full-groove axe*, from Delaware County, Indiana. It is made of light-colored granite with speckled inclusions, nice material. Ex-collection of Wood, it is 6½" x 8½" and weight is 5-6 pounds. Courtesy Bruce Filbrandt collection, Iowa.

PLATE 177: ¼ *groove axe*, found by the owner in the spring of 1971 in Crow Creek, Scott County, Iowa. It is made of black hardstone and is well-polished in the groove and lower blade regions. This axe is 5½" x 10½"; Mr. Filbrandt is holding this axe in *Who's Who In Indian Relics No. 5*, page 56. A fine axe and a remarkable personal find. Courtesy Bruce Filbrandt collection, Iowa.

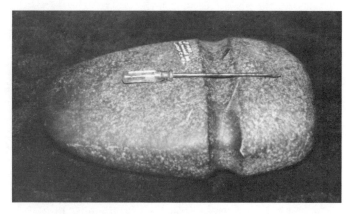

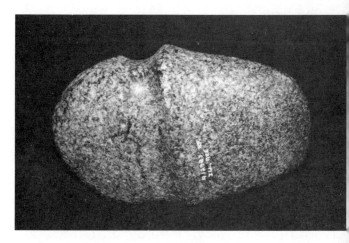

PLATE 178: ¼ *groove axe*, known as the Monroe Axe, found in Old Monroe, Missouri by a Mr. Piper. This is a very large axe, 2¾" x 6½" x 10¾". It is well-shaped, expertly worked and heavily polished. Material is a greenish granite or hardstone, and lower blade region is heavily polished. Courtesy Bruce Filbrandt collection, Iowa.

PLATE 179: ¼ *groove axe*, from Illinois. It is made of black to tan granite or hardstone and has high overall polish. This axe was deacquisitioned from a Tennessee museum 23 years ago. It is 4½" x 8½" and a high-grade piece. Courtesy Bruce Filbrandt collection, Iowa.

PLATE 180: *Full-groove axe*, greenish porphyry with yellow-white inclusions. This axe was a 1971 personal find by the owner, and it came from Scott County, Iowa. It is 5½" x 7". Weight is about five pounds. Courtesy Bruce Filbrandt collection, Iowa.

PLATE 181: ¼ *groove axe*, Archaic, from central Illinois. Material is dark grey, possibly porphyry, with straw-like white streaking. This axe was obtained at the George Whitney collection auction in May of 1989. A fine axe, it is 3½" x 5¾", and weight is about two pounds. Courtesy Bruce Filbrandt collection, Iowa.

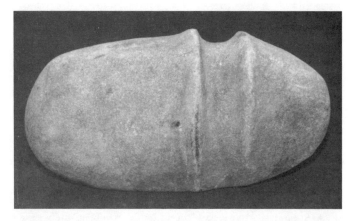

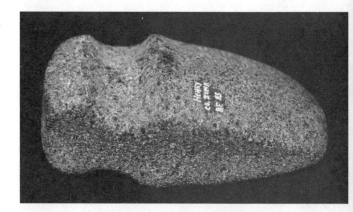

PLATE 182: ¼ *groove axe*, very large size, from Rock Island County, Illinois. It was found in 1946 by Sherman Powell, who was digging a corner posthole. This fine axe is made of brownish hardstone and is 6" wide, 11¼" long. Weight is over 12 pounds. The axe is exceptional both in size and artwork. Courtesy Bruce Filbrandt collection, Iowa.

PLATE 183: *Half-groove axe*, speckled greenish hardstone. This piece was purchased by Floyd Goddard at a Mt. Pleasant, Iowa, auction and was obtained from him by the present owner. This is a fine axe, 3½" x 6½", with weight of 3-3½ pounds. Courtesy Bruce Filbrandt collection, Iowa.

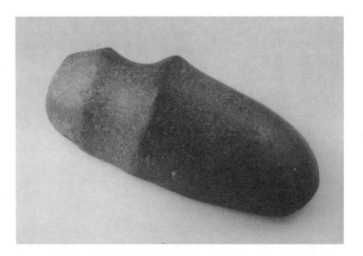

PLATE 184: ¼ *groove axe*, Archaic period, an extremely fine example from St. Charles County, Missouri. This axe has good styling, high-grade mottled hardstone material and excellent lines. It is 5¼" x 7¼". Fine axe. Courtesy Charles West collection, Ohio.

PLATE 185: *Miami Valley axe*, a rare Ohio axe form in full or ¼ groove. It is made from medium-dark dense hardstone and has the typical comparatively wide poll and groove region, ridged groove, and the smaller blade and bit region. Size is 4¼" x 5¾" and the axe is from Hamilton County, Ohio. Courtesy Charles West collection, Ohio.

PLATE 186: ¼ *groove axe*, made of very dark hardstone, Archaic period. This is a top artifact in terms of design and workstyle, despite the fairly small size. It is 1½" x 4⅜", and from Hamilton County, Ohio. This axe is also highly polished. Courtesy Charles West collection, Ohio.

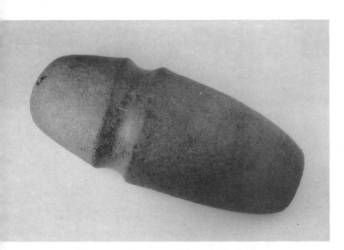

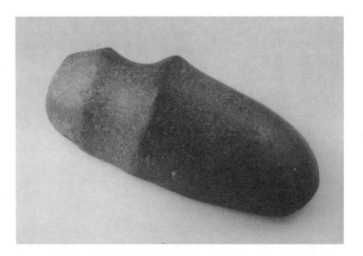

PLATE 187: *Hump-backed adz*, Archaic period, thick and very nicely grooved. This is a large and solid piece, very well shaped and worked, made of a medium-dark hardstone with good polish. Size is 3" x 7⅝"; it is from Adams County, Illinois. Courtesy Charles West collection, Ohio.

PLATE 188: *Hump-backed adz*, grooved and very boldly ridged, Archaic period. This is a rare artifact type for the state, and a highly artistic example in dark hardstone, well-polished. It is from Franklin County, Ohio, and measures 2⅜" x 5½". Courtesy Charles West collection, Ohio.

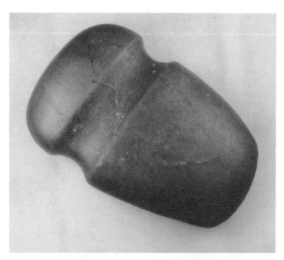

PLATE 189: *Full groove (¼) axe,* one of the better examples of the type. It is made of dark quartzite, is well-shaped and highly polished. Measurements, 3¾" x 6"; it is from Posey County, Indiana. Quartzite is not a common axe material. Courtesy Charles West collection, Ohio.

PLATE 190: ¼ *groove axe,* a fine small Archaic arti fact made of white quartzite. It was a personal find b the owner on Easter Sunday, 1974, near Penny Sloug in Henry County, Illinois. It is 2½" x 3½" and weight i about one pound. Courtesy Bruce Filbrandt collection Iowa.

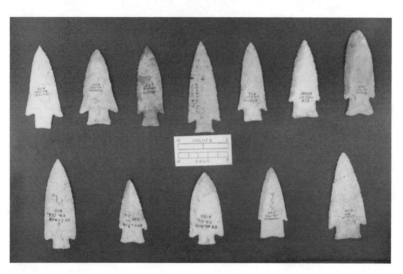

PLATE 191: *Hardin barbed points or blades,* from various counties in Illinois and Missouri. Most are made of local Burlington and Crescent cherts. These are Early Archaic, and ca. 7500-6500 BC. This is a fine selection of type and variety, nicely showing intergrades. Courtesy Collection of Bob Rampani, Bridgeton, St. Louis County, Missouri.

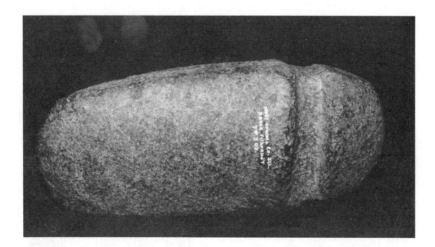

PLATE 192: *Half-groove axe,* Keokuk type, shown with slight groove or fluting on the upper side. This axe was found in Hancock County, Illinois by Henry Siegfrid. It is a large axe at 4⅛" x 10⅜", and 10½" around at the groove. This is a fine axe in dark, mottled hardstone. Courtesy Bruce Filbrandt collection, Iowa.

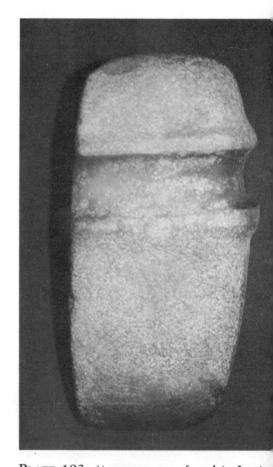

PLATE 193: ¼ *groove axe,* found in Louisa County, Iowa. It is made of grey quartzite and i one of the largest quartzite axes ever found ir Iowa. Recovered August 23, 1990, it is 3" x 6' x 12" and weight is nearly 12 pounds. There i deep polish in the groove and on the lower blade portion. An exceptional axe in every way. Courtesy Bruce Filbrandt collection, Iowa.

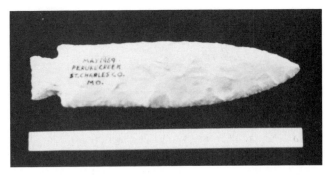

PLATE 194: *Wadlow blade*, a preform for the Etley point or blade. It was found in Scott County, Missouri, and is 1⅝" x 6⅞". This piece, of Burlington chert, is Late Archaic/Early Woodland and ca. 1500-1000 BC. A well-made artifact in exceptional size. Courtesy Collection of Bob Rampani, Bridgeton, St. Louis County, Missouri.

PLATE 195: *Etley point or blade*, found in St. Charles County, Missouri, a personal find of Steve Rampani in May of 1969. It is 1⅞6" x 6¼", Late Archaic/Early Woodland period. It is made of white Crescent chert, a top specimen with above-average length. Courtesy collection of Bob Rampani, Bridgeton, St. Louis County, Missouri.

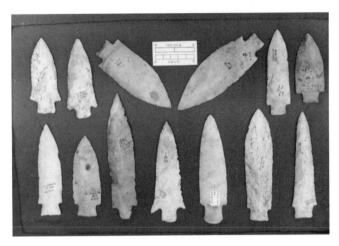

PLATE 196: *Sedalia points or blades*, from various counties in Illinois and Missouri. These are Late Archaic and ca. 2500-1500 BC in time. Materials are mainly Burlington and Ozark cherts. Note the stylistic range from specimen to specimen and size differences. An excellent grouping. Courtesy collection of Bob Rampani, Bridgeton, St. Louis County, Missouri.

PLATE 197: *Etley points or blades*, a representative grouping from various counties in Illinois and Missouri. The Etley is Late Archaic/Early Woodland and is sometimes found associated with pottery. This is a nice display of type examples and varieties. Materials are Burlington and Crescent cherts. Courtesy collection of Bob Rampani, Bridgeton, St. Louis County, Missouri.

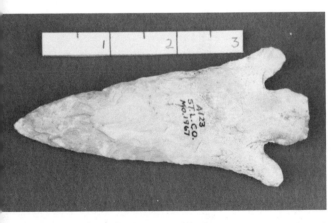

PLATE 198: *Mehlville point or blade* (see Perino, *Selected Preforms . . .* p 250) From Archaic times, this has the typical form and is made of tan chert. It is 2" x 4⅜"; this is a sturdy and solid piece. The Mehlville was found by Bob Rampani in St. Louis County, Missouri, in 1967. Courtesy collection of Bob Rampani, Bridgeton, St. Louis County, Missouri.

PLATE 199: *Hardin point or blade*, Early Archaic period, this piece is made of heavily patinated off-white chert and has fine edge-serrations. It is 1⅞6" x 3½". This was a personal find by Bob Rampani in St. Louis County, Missouri, in 1988. Courtesy collection of Bob Rampani, Bridgeton, St. Louis County, Missouri.

PLATE 200: *Graham Cave point or blade*, made of white Crescent chert. It is Early Archaic, ca. 7000-5500 BC, and 1¼" x 4¾". This is a finely made and well-serrated classic specimen, found by Bob Rampani in 1950 in St. Louis County, Missouri. Courtesy collection of Bob Rampani, Bridgeton, St. Louis County, Missouri.

PLATE 201: *Sedalia point or blade*, Late Archaic, 1½" x 5⅞". It is made of Ozark chert, nicely multi-colored. It is a good type example, with good length. This piece was found in Cooper County, Missouri. Courtesy collection of Bob Rampani, Bridgeton, St. Louis County, Missouri.

PLATE 202: *Stanfield knife*, this blade ca. 7000 BC and from the Early Archaic. Material is tan Burlington chert. This piece has good workstyle and length; 1¼" x 5⅞", and from St. Louis County, Missouri. Courtesy collection of Bob Rampani, Bridgeton, St. Louis County, Missouri.

PLATE 203: *Pebble pendant*, 3⅛" long, Archaic period. The suspension hole is drilled from both sides and the lower edges are tally-marked. This was found in Kane County, Illinois, by the owner in spring of 1974. Courtesy Duane Treest collection, Illinois.

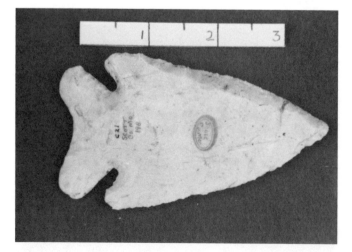

PLATE 204: *Thebes point or blade*, Early Archaic period. The Thebes is the main member of a large family of similar and/or related early blades. This piece is white Crescent chert, 2¼" x 4", and very well made. It has the beveled-edge resharpening. Found in Scott County, Missouri, and ex-collection of Beuell. Courtesy collection of Bob Rampani, Bridgeton, St. Louis County, Missouri.

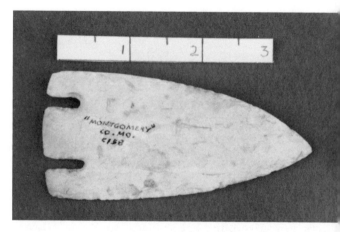

PLATE 205: *Smith point or blade*, Late Archaic period. This is a true-to-form Smith, and a superbly made specimen. It is 1¾" x 3¾", made of tan chert, and from Montgomery County, Missouri. Excellent. Courtesy collection of Bob Rampani, Bridgeton, St. Louis County, Missouri.

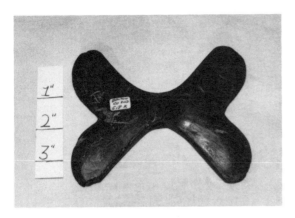

PLATE 206: *Double crescent bannerstone*, Archaic, an extremely rare banner form from Benton County, Indiana. Made of glacial slate, it is 4¼" x 5½" and has had some restoration done. Private collection of Kenneth Spiker.

PLATE 207: *Fox Valley points or blades*, also known as Clipped Wing or Truncated Barb points. All were found in Kane County, Illinois, by the owner. This type has bifurcated and non-bifurcated sub-divisions. Courtesy Duane Treest collection, Illinois.

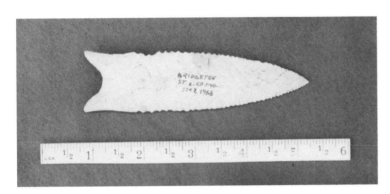

PLATE 208: *Dalton point or blade*, Early Archaic, ca. 7500 BC. It is made of white Crescent chert and is 1⅛" x 4½". This is a classic specimen, with parallel flaking, good serrations on edges and short basal flutes. It is very well made, and in a fine material. This Dalton was found by Bob Rampani in 1966 in St. Louis County, Missouri. Courtesy collection of Bob Rampani, Bridgeton, St. Louis County, Missouri.

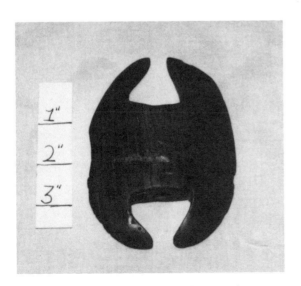

PLATE 209: *Double-notched ovate bannerstone*, banded slate, from Benton County, Indiana. Size, 3½" x 4⅝". Bannerstones themselves are not common and this particular form is quite rare. Private collection of Kenneth Spiker.

PLATE 210: *Fox Valley points or blades*, all found in Benton County, Indiana, by the owner. This is an Early Archaic type, sometimes called a Frederick. Fox Valley examples are small, averaging about 1½" in length. Private collection of Kenneth Spiker.

PLATE 211: ¼ *groove axe*, Benton County, Indiana, Archaic period. This is a solid, utilitarian axe in very good condition. Size, 3⅜" x 6", and material is a dark hardstone. Courtesy private collection of Kenneth Spiker.

PLATE 212: ¼ *groove axe*, Benton County, Indiana. Size is 3½" x 5⅛". This Archaic piece is a utilitarian tool, nicely formed. Courtesy private collection of Kenneth Spiker.

PLATE 213: *Pick bannerstone*, Archaic, from Benton County, Indiana. Made of banded glacial slate, it measures 2¼" x 8" long. This is a fine, large specimen, and a rare form in this size. Courtesy private collection of Kenneth Spiker.

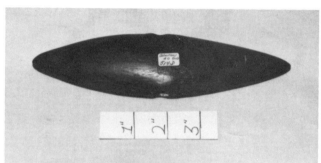

PLATE 214: *Full groove or ¼ axe*, from Benton County, Indiana. At 5¼" x 7⅝", this is the first axe ever found by the owner. Courtesy private collection of Kenneth Spiker.

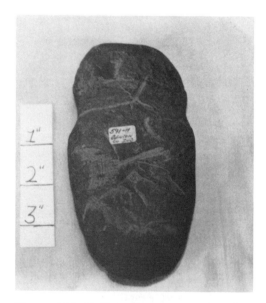

PLATE 215: *Full-groove or ¼ axe*, found in Benton County, Indiana. Size is 3⅛" x 5¾"; good example of a typical utilitarian axe. Courtesy private collection of Kenneth Spiker.

PLATE 216: *Osceola point or blade*, Middle Archaic and ca. 3000 BC. It is made of light-colored chert and is 3½" long. It was found in Kane County, Illinois, by the owner on May 4, 1984. Courtesy Duane Treest collection, Illinois.

PLATE 217: *Table Rock or Bottleneck point or blade*, found by the owner in fall of 1989. From Kane County, Illinois, it is Late Archaic and ca. 2500 BC. The material is an agatized flint in brown, white and grey, unusual for the area. Length is 2¾". Courtesy Duane Treest collection, Illinois.

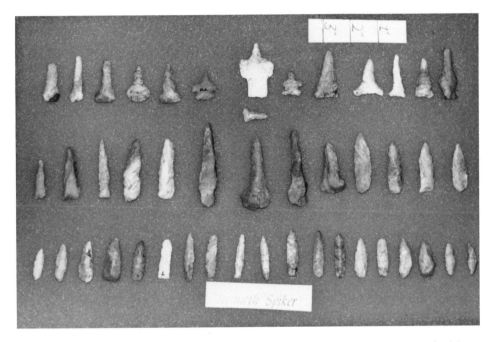

PLATE 218: *Drills and perforators*, all Indiana, and made of various materials. Many are no doubt Archaic, though several Woodland examples are to left and right of the top center piece. Courtesy private collection of Kenneth Spiker.

PLATE 219: *Stanfield knife*, Early Archaic, 5⅛" long. The material has crinoid fossil inclusions in the lighter-colored chert. This was found in Kane County, Illinois, by the owner in spring of 1974. Courtesy Duane Treest collection, Illinois.

PLATE 220: *Godar point or blade*, 2¾" long, from Kane County, Illinois. It was found by the owner on February 2, 1975. This is a good Archaic piece in light-colored chert. Courtesy Duane Treest collection, Illinois.

PLATE 221: *Thebes*, Early Archaic, very steeply beveled due to frequent resharpening. It is made of black flint, is from Ohio, and is 3³⁄₁₆" long. This is a solid early knife blade. Private collection; photograph by Del Hetrick.

PLATE 222: *Thebes*, Early Archaic, Coshocton dark mottled flint, from Ohio. It is 2⅝" long and like most of the type indicates resharpening by the beveled edge. Private collection; photograph by Del Hetrick.

PLATE 223: ¾ *groove axe*, Ohio, county unknown. It is 9¼" long and is made of dark granite. The groove area is lightly ridged; a superior specimen. Courtesy Rodney M. Peck collection, Harrisburg, North Carolina.

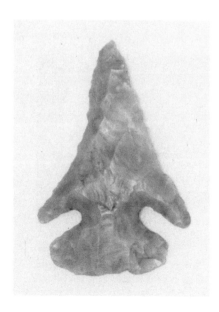

PLATE 224: *Thebes*, an Early Archaic blade, from Ohio. Material is grey translucent flint and length is 2½". The indented sides and beveling indicate that the blade sides were heavily resharpened, typical for the type. Private collection; photograph by Del Hetrick.

PLATE 225: *Thebes*, Early Archaic, with deep and upswept Ohio-type notching. From Shelby County, Ohio, it is 2¼" long. At one time, before extensive resharpening, the blade was considerably longer. Private collection; photograph by Del Hetrick.

PLATE 226: ¼ *groove axe*, Archaic, from Delaware County, Ohio. It is 9¼" long, and very highly polished. This is a superb early stone artifact. Courtesy Rodney M. Peck collection, Harrisburg, North Carolina.

PLATE 227: ¼ *groove axe*, Archaic, slightly raised ridges around the groove; it is from Coles County, Illinois. This piece is 2½" x 4½" x 10¼" long, and the material is high-grade hardstone, brown porphyry. Ex-collection of Ben Thompson; see CSAJ Vol. 37 No. 1, 1990, pp 30-31. Beautiful axe. Courtesy Rodney M. Peck collection, Harrisburg, North Carolina.

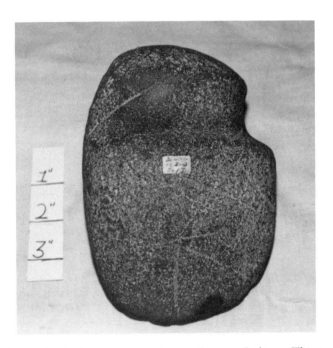

PLATE 229: ¼ *groove axe*, Benton County, Indiana. This is an unusual form, with the lower portion below the groove projecting beyond the poll. A well-designed axe, 4¾" x 6¾". Private collection of Kenneth Spiker.

PLATE 228: ¼ *groove axe*, Middle-Late Archaic, 4⅝" x 6¼". Material is a dark hardstone; this is a good utilitarian axe and was obtained from an old-time collector in Kane County, Illinois. Not many axes are found in the area anymore. Courtesy Duane Treest collection, Illinois.

PLATE 230: ¼ *groove axe*, Archaic period, from Brown County, Ohio. It is made of a high quality mottled granite-like material and measures 4" x 7¾". This specimen is interesting in that the blade bit region is the widest axe portion. Courtesy Charles West collection, Ohio.

PLATE 231: ¼ *groove axe*, Archaic, from Benton County, Indiana. This is a fine angular axe with well-shaped and deep grooving, and high overall polish. Size is 3½" x 6¾". This is a beautiful example of Archaic stoneworking. Courtesy Charles West collection, Ohio.

PLATE 232: ¼ *groove axe*, Archaic, made of dark, speckled granite-like stone. This specimen measures 4¾" x 6¼" and is from Knox County, Indiana. Ex-collection of Dr. Hoover, this axe is well-shaped and highly polished. Courtesy Charles West collection, Ohio.

PLATE 233: ¼ *groove axe*, Archaic period, from Clermont County, Ohio. It is made of high-grade granite-like hardstone and is well-ridged, accurately grooved and highly polished overall. This piece was found on the Ohio River bank after the 1937 flood. Found near Moscow, Ohio, it is 3½" x 8¾". This is one of the finest axes ever found in the state. Courtesy Charles West collection, Ohio.

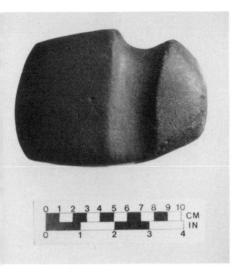

PLATE 234: *Slant-groove ¾ axe*, Archaic, from Jefferson County, Kentucky. It is 5⅝" long and the material is dark quartzite. This is a nicely shaped piece. Courtesy Rodney M. Peck collection, Harrisburg, North Carolina.

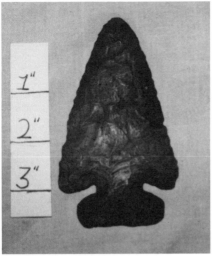

PLATE 235: *Thebes point or blade*, Early Archaic, made of Indiana Green flint or chert. From Indiana, this fine and large specimen is 2⅜" x 4⅛" and appears to be in nearly unresharpened condition due to extreme width. Unusual in this size. Courtesy Private collection of Kenneth Spiker.

PLATE 236: *Pestle or monolithic maul*, Archaic period, 3½" x 6" high. It is made of a dark, close-grained hardstone that took a high polish. This piece is from Hamilton County, Ohio. Courtesy Charles West collection, Ohio.

PLATE 237: *Pestle or double-ended maul*, close-grained granite-like hardstone, 3½" x 5". This is a scarce type, and very well crafted; from Spencer County, Indiana. Courtesy Charles West collection, Ohio.

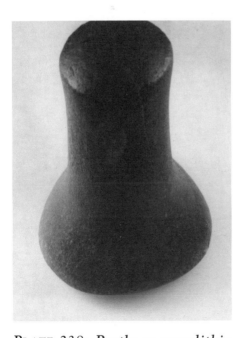

PLATE 238: *Pestle or monolithic maul*, dark close-grained granite-like hardstone, from Ohio. This is a well-shaped and highly polished specimen, size 3½" x 4½". Archaic. Courtesy Charles West collection, Ohio.

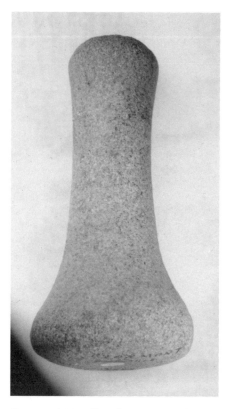

PLATE 239: *Pestle or monolithic maul,* fine-grained light-colored granite material, from near Point Pleasant, Clermont County, Ohio. It is 3" x 7" high and has very graceful, flowing lines. Archaic period. Courtesy Charles West collection, Ohio.

PLATE 241: *Godar point or blade,* Late Archaic and ca. 2500-500 BC. This piece was found by the owner April 13, 1990, and is 2¼" long. From Kane County, Illinois, it is made of light-colored chert. Courtesy Duane Treest collection, Illinois.

PLATE 240: *Double-groove axe,* Archaic Period, made of a high grade of speckled granite-like hardstone. It measures 2" x 4½" and is from Boyd County, Kentucky. This is not only a very well-made axe, but a rare type as well. Courtesy Charles West collection, Ohio.

PLATE 242: *St. Charles or Dovetail blade,* made of high-grade mottled Flintridge, Early Archaic. Size 1⅝" x 5½", and from Harrison County, Indiana. This piece has fine styling, exceptional workstyle and perfect condition. It is simply a top-of-the-line artifact. Courtesy Charles West collection, Ohio.

PLATE 243: *St. Charles or Dovetail blade,* made of Flintridge material in a very unusual rusty color. It is 1⅝" x 4¾" long, from Franklin County, Ohio. Dovetails are Early Archaic, ca. 7000 BC. Courtesy Charles West collection, Ohio.

PLATE 244: *Indented-base Dovetail,* from the Cumberland Lake area of Kentucky. It is 1⅜" x 4½" long, and very well-made and symmetrical. This is a fine Early Archaic specimen. Courtesy Charles West collection, Ohio.

PLATE 245: *Plummet,* Archaic period, made of mudstone or claystone, compact and fine-grained. This interesting specimen (due to material) is 3½" long, and is from Indiana. The small end is carefully grooved. Courtesy Charles West collection, Ohio.

PLATE 246: *Plummet group,* all of hematite or iron ore, each slightly different in manner of end-grooves. Left and right are from Ohio, while central specimen is from Greene County, Illinois. Courtesy Charles West collection, Ohio.

PLATE 247: *Plummets,* Archaic period, both made of hematite or iron ore. Left example is from Ohio. Right example is a rounded form and is from Illinois. Courtesy Charles West collection, Ohio.

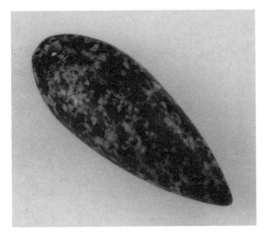

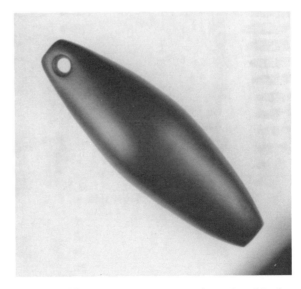

PLATE 248: *Plummet,* Archaic period, made of mottled granite. It is from Calhoun County, Illinois, and is 3⅛" long. This is a fairly uncommon form in that the suspension hole is drilled in the thicker end. Courtesy Charles West collection, Ohio.

PLATE 249: *Plummet,* Archaic period, made of high-grade hematite and very well polished. This piece is 3½" long and it is from Illinois. The state of Illinois has produced a very large number of high-quality hematite plummets. Courtesy Charles West collection, Ohio.

PLATE 250: *Plummet,* hematite, grooved near tip of small end. This was a surface find in Holt County, Missouri. It is from the Late Archaic period. Courtesy Mike George collection, Missouri.

PLATE 251: *Pendant,* glacial slate, 1" x 2". This small example is from the Lynn Farm, Franklin County, Ohio, and is ex-collection of Dr. Gordon Meuser. This may be an Archaic ornament. Lee Fisher collection, Pennsylvania; Anthony Lang, photographer.

PLATE 252: *Pentagonal point or blade,* Archaic, white flint with grey and black inclusions (probably Flintridge), 1½" long. From Ohio, this type is often reworked (resharpened) to a shorter size. Private collection; Del Hetrick, photographer.

PLATE 253: *Full-grooved or ¼ axe,* 7¾ pounds, found in a Holt County, Missouri, creek. Material is brown hardstone and the axe is well-made; Archaic period. Courtesy Mike George collection, Missouri.

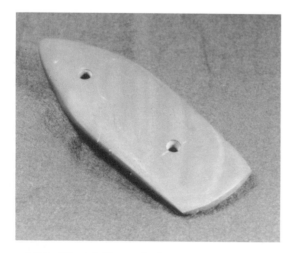

PLATE 254: *Glacial Kame Indian gorget,* two-hole sandal-sole type. It is 5½" long, and made of red banded slate. This piece is from Logan County, Ohio. Late Archaic, Glacial Kame or Gravel Knoll pieces were made in various unusual styles. This artifact is engraved on one face. Courtesy Lee Fisher collection, Pennsylvania; Anthony Lang, photographer.

PLATE 255: *Archaic ¼ grooved adz,* green granite, a very well made and polished piece. This is a rare tool form, 1¾" x 4". Ex-collections of Saunders and Knox, from Hancock County, Ohio. Courtesy Richard E. Jones collection, Ohio.

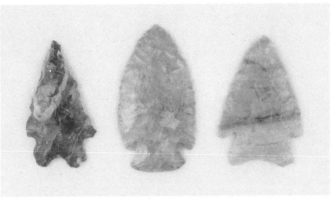

PLATE 256: *Archaic points or blades,* all Ohio. Left, Lost Lake, Flintridge white, 1¾" x 2", ex-collections of Saunders and Good, Franklin County. Middle, Meadowood, Flintridge black with cream veining, 1⅜" x 3¼", ex-collection of Saunders, Wood County. Very high quality flint for type. Right, Decatur or Fractured-base, in Flintridge cream with tan veining, 1⅝" x 2½". Ex-collections of Saunders and Ward, Seneca County. Courtesy Richard E. Jones collection, Ohio.

PLATE 257: *Archaic points or blades,* all Ohio. Left, bifurcate-base, black flint with blue lightning line, 1⅛" x 2". It is ex-collection of Meyer, county unlisted. Middle, St. Charles or Dovetail, made of grey-tan Coshocton flint, 1¼" x 2¼". It also is unlisted as to exact Ohio county; ex-collection of Saunders. Right, concave-base corner-notch, cream and grey striped Upper Mercer, 1⅜" x 2⅛". Found in 1973 in the Buckeye Lake area, it is ex-collection of Meyer and Perry County. Courtesy Christine M. Jones collection, Ohio.

PLATE 258: *Fluted ball bannerstone,* blue and green banded glacial slate, from Hancock County, Ohio. Size is 2" x 2". It is thought that these artifacts were used as Atl-atl or lance-throwing stick balance weights. Fine example, and Archaic in time. Courtesy Lee Fisher collection, Pennsylvania; Anthony Lang, photographer.

PLATE 259: *Slate pendant,* red banded material, from Perry County, Illinois. Since the form is not too well-defined in terms of style, this piece, 2¼" long, may be Archaic. Courtesy Lee Fisher collection, Pennsylvania; Anthony Lang, photographer.

PLATE 260: *St. Charles or Dovetail blades,* Early Archaic. Left, 1¼" x 4", mottled tan and grey flint, Saline County Missouri. Right, tan flint, 1½" x 4", Ross County, Ohio. Courtesy Lee Fisher collection, Pennsylvania; Anthony Lang, photographer.

PLATE 261: *Archaic blades or knives,* all Ohio. Left, Stilwell, frosty white Flintridge with purple veining, 1¼" x 3". Ex-collection of Saunders, Athens County. Middle, Ashtabula, opaque grey Upper Mercer, 1" x 3⅞", ex-collections of Meyer and Barth, Ohio county unknown. Right, St. Charles or Dovetail, Flintridge frosty white with purple and yellow veining. It is 1¼" x 3¼", Licking County, and ex-collections of Meyer and Root. Courtesy Richard E. Jones collection, Ohio.

PLATE 262: *Merom (Riverton cluster) points*, found in Illinois, Indiana, Kentucky and Ohio. Their cultural affiliation is Shell Midden Archaic, technically, but their approximate date of 800 BC places them just inside the Woodland period. Points shown are finds from along the Wabash River, Crawford County, Illinois. Personal finds, from the collection of Don Simmons, Robinson, Illlinois.

PLATE 263: *Loafstone*, probably Archaic, side and bottom views. It is 1³⁄₁₆" wide and 1⅝" long. Material is hematite, artifact is from Ohio, and is ex-collection of Pohler. Private collection; Del Hetrick, photographer.

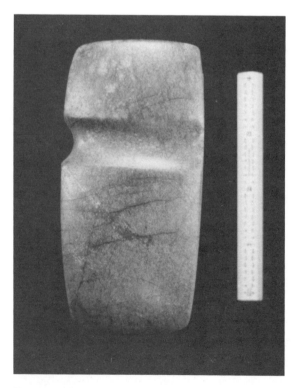

PLATE 264: ¾ *groove axe*, Archaic, from Pettis County, Missouri. Material is a green hardstone with darker veining. This axe has high overall polish and is 1¾" x 2⁹⁄₁₆" x 5⅛" long. Courtesy William Gehlken collection, Illinois; photograph by Bruce Filbrandt.

PLATE 265: *Full-grooved maul*, Butler County, Ohio. It is 9" long and weighs 13 pounds. Large mauls like this were often used in flint quarries to mine flint blocks for tools. The groove suggests this may be an Archaic piece. Courtesy Lee Fisher collection, Pennsylvania; Anthony Lang, photographer.

PLATE 266: ¼ *groove axe,* Archaic period, from Clermont County, Ohio, and ex-collection of Copeland. This fine axe is 6" long and made of a good grade of hardstone. It is nicely polished, and in perfect condition. Courtesy Lee Fisher collection, Pennsylvania; Anthony Lang, photographer.

PLATE 267: *Nebo Hill point,* Late Archaic, and made of tan flint. It is from Des Moines County, Iowa, and is 1½" x 5". Nice specimen of type. Courtesy Lee Fisher collection, Pennsylvania; Anthony Lang, photographer.

PLATE 268: *Archaic axes.* Left, full-groove, hardstone, 3¾" high. It s from DeKalb County, Indiana. Right, three-quarter groove, polished ardstone, good ridges, from Wells County, Indiana. Both pieces are x-collection of Parks. Courtesy Lee Fisher collection, Pennsylvania; nthony Lang, photographer.

PLATE 269: *Pestles,* probably Archaic, both from Ohio. Left, 4" long, fossilized material, Fairfield County. Right, roller-ype, green hardstone, 8¼" long, Franklin County. Courtesy Lee isher collection, Pennsylvania; Anthony Lang, photographer.

PLATE 270: *Mortar and pestle set,* probably Archaic, with pestle 2½" x 7¼" and mortar 3½" x 6". These are from Rowan County, Kentucky. Courtesy Lee Fisher collection, Pennsylvania; Anthony Lang, photographer.

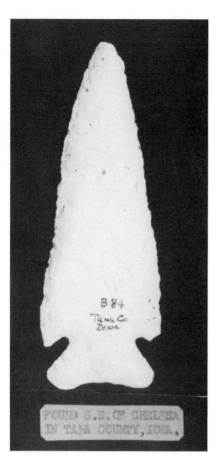

PLATE 271: *Thebes point or blade*, 4" long, made of white chert. It was found southeast of Chelsea in Tama County, Iowa. This is a good, solid Early Archaic piece. Courtesy Verlin Hepker collection, Iowa.

PLATE 272: *Dalton point or blade*, Early Archaic, made of white chert. It is 1½" x 2½", and from Pettis County, Missouri. This piece was probably resharpened down from a longer size. Courtesy Lee Fisher collection, Pennsylvania; Anthony Lang, photographer.

PLATE 273: ¾ *groove axes*, all Geauga County, Ohio, Archaic period. 2" scale shows size. These fine axes are made of high-grade and colorful hardstone, and example on right has raised groove ridges. These are much better than average for Archaic axes. Courtesy Fogelman collection, Pennsylvania.

PLATE 274: *Archaic slate artifacts*, both Geauga County, Ohio; scale, 2". Top, spineback gorget (probably Glacial Kame), drilled, material an olive-green slate with white inclusions. Glacial Kame peoples are noted for their unusual gorget and pendant forms. Bottom, tubular bannerstone, green banded slate, graceful lines. Courtesy Fogelman collection, Pennsylvania.

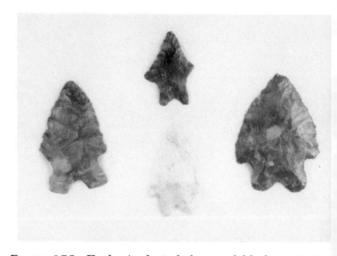

PLATE 275: *Early Archaic bifurcated blades*, all Ohio. Left, 1³⁄₁₆ x 2", black and tan minority Upper Mercer material, Knox County. Upper center, Lake Erie bifurcate, ⅞" x 1⅛", Knox County. Lower Center, Fairfield County, grey-cream Flintridge, 1" x 1¾". Right, 1½" x 2", blue Upper Mercer with tan inclusions, Knox County. This piece before resharpening was likely twice as long. Courtesy Hothem collection, Ohio.

64

PLATE 276: *Surface-found collection,* Iowa, mainly Archaic with a few later examples. Note the wide range of materials, sizes and types. The center point or blade is 4" long. All were found by the owner near the Cedar River in Linn County, Iowa. Courtesy Verlin Hepker collection, Iowa.

PLATE 278: ¾ *and ¼ grooved axes,* all Midwestern and made from a variety of hardstone materials. Note the extra-fine examples second from left and third from right. Courtesy Verlin Hepker collection, Iowa.

PLATE 277: *St. Charles or Dovetail blade,* Early Archaic, made of mixed-colored high-grade chert. This is an excellent artifact, 4" long, and from near Glasford, Illinois. This is an above-average piece with good size, material and workstyle. Courtesy Verlin Hepker collection, Iowa.

PLATE 279: *Surface-found collection,* Iowa, mainly Archaic with a few later examples. The range of materials and types is typical of field finds. All are from near the Cedar River in Linn County, Iowa, and were personal finds by the owner. Courtesy Verlin Hepker collection, Iowa.

PLATE 280: *Points or blades,* possibly Dalton-related and probably Early Archaic. All are made of good-grade cherts, two in light grey and one creamy white. These came from Lewis County, Missouri. Center example is 3" long, and found by Bill Jones. Courtesy Verlin Hepker collection, Iowa.

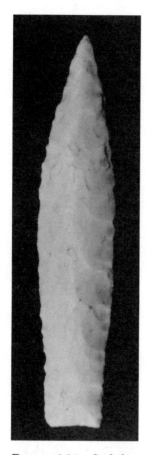

PLATE 281: *Sedalia point,* Archaic, from Banner, Fulton County, Illinois. It is 4¼" long and has very nice flaking for the type. The well-defined flake-scars indicate that the light-colored material is of high quality. Courtesy collection of Russell and Rhonda Bedwell, Illinois.

PLATE 282: ¾ *groove axe,* 3½ pounds, made of a greenstone material. It was found in a creek in Holt County, Missouri, and is highly polished overall. It is from the Archaic period. Courtesy Mike George collection, Missouri.

PLATE 283: *Archaic points and blades,* all Midwestern and all made of quality light-colored cherts in creams and tans. The large Hardin in top row center is 4⅛" long. Fine, quality grouping. Courtesy Verlin Hepker collection, Iowa.

PLATE 284: *Bifurcate points or blades,* Early Archaic period, all Geauga County, Ohio. Most are made of Coshocton or Upper Mercer flints, and types represented include Lake Erie, LeCroy and St. Albans. This is a fine selection of types and materials. Courtesy Fogelman collection, Pennsylvania.

PLATE 285: *Archaic blades,* with one Middle Woodland Snyders point or knife at left in the 9 o'clock position. Various chert and flint materials are represented here; this is a good selection of Midwestern large chipped artifacts. Size is 4" to 7½". All are from Cass County, Illinois. Courtesy Lee Fisher collection, Pennsylvania; Anthony Lang, photographer.

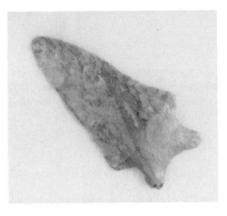

PLATE 286: *Archaic concave-base,* grey and cream mottled Upper Mercer, 1⁹⁄₁₆" x 3³⁄₁₆". It is from Madison County, Ohio, and ex-collection of Bob Champion. This is a sturdy, well-chipped artifact. Hothem collection, Ohio.

PLATE 287: *Palmer corner-notch,* an Early archaic type ca. 6000 BC. Size, 1⅜" x 2⅜". Ohio county is unknown. Material is highly unusual, a medium-grade flint with an orange-buff cast known as Fairfield Orange. This is found in southern Fairfield County, southcentral Ohio. Hothem collection, Ohio.

PLATE 288: *Archaic points or blades,* all Ohio. Left, light grey, blue and cream Upper Mercer, 1¼" x 2¼", ex-collections of F. Meyer and D. Driskoll. Middle, grey hornstone, Darke County, 1½" x 1½", ex-collection of Saunders. Right, Coshocton black and blue with lightning lines, Franklin County, 1¼" x 2⅜", ex-collections of Howard and Seeley. Brian E. Jones collection, Ohio.

PLATE 289: *Bifurcate points or blades,* Early Archaic, all Ohio. Left, Fairfield County, ⅞" x 1⅞", Upper Mercer, ex-collections of Bapst, Good and Potter. Middle, blue-black with cream flint, ¾" x 1½", Marion County, ex-collections of Saunders and Johnson. Right, Upper Mercer black, Scioto County, ⅞" x 1½", ex-collections of Saunders and Lute. Courtesy Brian E. Jones collection, Ohio.

PLATE 290: *Short-tube bannerstone,* brown banded slate, Archaic period, with 2" scale showing size. This is probably a fairly early form as it is not highly developed. Ex-collection of Snodgrass, and from Washington County, Ohio. Courtesy Lee Hallman collection, Pennsylvania.

PLATE 291: *Winged "butterfly" bannerstone,* from central Ohio, with 2" scale indicating size. This is made from attractive banded slate and is a very highly developed Archaic banner type. A very fine specimen. Courtesy Lee Hallman collection, Pennsylvania.

PLATE 292: *Bannerstones,* Archaic, both from Geauga County, Ohio, and ex-collection of White. The two-inch scale indicates size. Left, short-winged banner, banded slate, well-formed. Right, heart-shaped banner, very attractive banded slate. Courtesy Lee Hallman collection, Pennsylvania.

PLATE 293: *Barrel-shaped bannerstones,* Archaic, with dark-brown banding in slate against a tan background. Very attractive material. Two-inch scale shows size, and banner is ex-collection of White. From near Middlefield, Geauga County, Ohio. Courtesy Lee Hallman collection, Pennsylvania.

PLATE 294: *Winged bannerstone,* Archaic, from Geauga County, Ohio. Ex-collection of White, this is probably one of the basic winged forms early in the period. The material is glacial slate with unusual banding. Two-inch scale indicates size. Courtesy Lee Hallman collection, Pennsylvania.

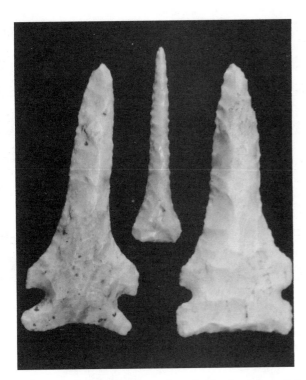

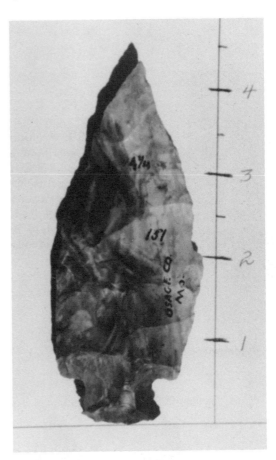

PLATE 295: *Drill grouping,* all probably Archaic, all from Illinois, and Fulton County. Left, Lewistown area, 2¼". Center, expanded-top pin-type, 2" long, fine piece. Right, 2½" long. Courtesy collection of Russell and Rhonda Bedwell, Illinois.

PLATE 296: *Corner-notched blade,* a large and strongly designed piece that has seen extensive knife use. At 4¼" long, it is from Osage County, Missouri. Courtesy Cliff Markley collection, Alabama.

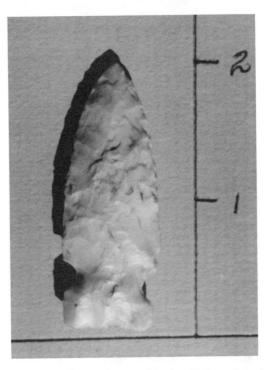

PLATE 297: *Side-notched blade,* probably Archaic, made of high-grade variegated flint. This sturdy and well-made specimen is from St. Louis County, Missouri. Courtesy Cliff Markley collection, Alabama.

PLATE 298: *Godar point or blade,* light-colored flint, Archaic period. It is from Jefferson County, Missouri. Courtesy Cliff Markley collection, Alabama.

PLATE 299: *Archaic knife,* uncertain side-notched type, from Geauga County, Ohio. It is made from a dark black flint, probably Upper Mercer. This is a very fine large blade in top condtion. Courtesy Fogelman collection, Pennsylvania.

PLATE 300: *Smith points or blades,* found in Maries County, Missouri. These are sturdy, serviceable blades with some in-use wear. They are from the Archaic period Photograph by, and collection of, Victor A. Pierce, Missouri.

PLATE 301: *Bifurcated-base blades,* Early Archaic knives, made of eastern Ohio Upper Mercer flints. These are all ex-collection of White and from the Middlefield area of Geauga County, Ohio. Courtesy Lee Hallman collection, Pennsylvania.

PLATE 302: *Humped-back gorget,* Glacial Kame and Late Archaic, banded slate material. Two-holed, this scarce slate form is from Franklin County, Ohio, and measures 2" x 3½". Franklin County is about the southern and eastern extension limit for the type. Courtesy Lee Fisher collection, Pennsylvania; Anthony Lang, photographer.

PLATE 303: *Tube bannerstone,* flattened or fluted one side, partially drilled, and made of banded slate. It is 1½" x 4¾" and is from Butler County, Ohio. Courtesy Lee Fisher collection, Pennsylvania; Anthony Lang, photographer.

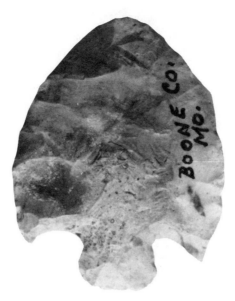

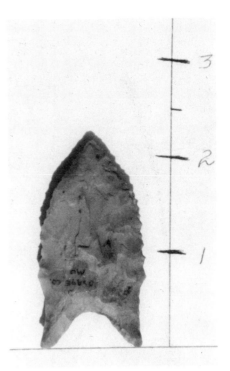

PLATE 304: *Dalton variant,* a point or blade from the Early Archaic. This sturdy and well-designed specimen is made of bi-colored chert and is from Gumbo County, Missouri. Courtesy Cliff Markley collection, Alabama.

PLATE 305: *Earbob Ferry,* a Late Archaic point or blade, made of mottled dark chert. (See Perino, *Selected Preforms, Points and Knives . . .* p 113, for type.) The very excurvate edges and lack of a sharp tip suggest knife use. It is from Boone County, Missouri. Courtesy Cliff Markley collection, Alabama.

PLATE 306: *Dalton point,* Early Archaic, from Osage County, Missouri. This is probably a heavily resharpened (shortened) specimen. Edge-serrations suggest use as a knife. Courtesy Cliff Markley collection, Alabama.

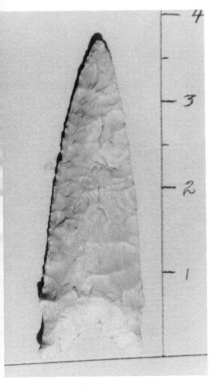

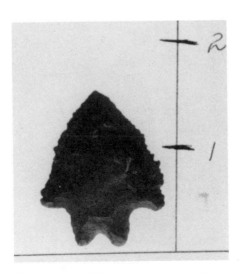

PLATE 307: *Dalton,* Early Archaic, and a large, fine point or blade. This example, from St. Louis County, Missouri, is very well-chipped and in superb condition. Courtesy Cliff Markley collection, Alabama.

PLATE 308: *Bifurcate,* point or blade, from the Early Archaic. Made of a dark, mottled flint, this artifact is from Hamilton County, Ohio. This state alone has several dozen bifurcate types and variants. Courtesy Cliff Markley collection, Alabama.

PLATE 309: *Stilwell point or blade,* Early Archaic, made of dark flint or chert. The dissimilar edges suggest knife use. It is from Putnam County, Illinois. Courtesy Cliff Markley collection, Alabama.

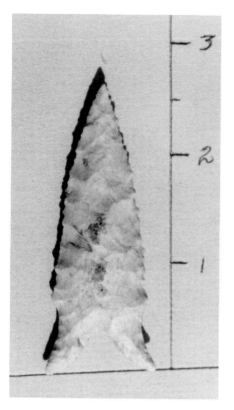

PLATE 311: *Dalton*, Archaic, an unusual variant with expanded blade area above the base. This piece is from Cooper County, Missouri. Courtesy Cliff Markley collection, Alabama.

PLATE 310: *Dalton*, point or blade, Early Archaic, a nicely formed specimen with very extended basal tips. Note the fish-bone like fossil inclusion at left center. This Dalton is from Perry County, Missouri. Courtesy Cliff Markley collection, Alabama.

PLATE 312: *Hidden Valley point o blade*, Middle Archaic. This type i often serrated and barbed. Example i from Jefferson County, Missouri Courtesy Cliff Markley collection Alabama.

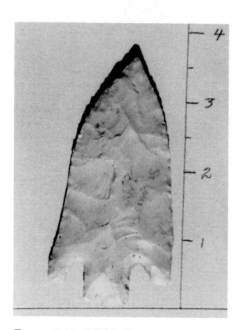

PLATE 313: *Mehlville point or blade*, made of light-colored chert. This large piece is from St. Louis County, Missouri. The type is Archaic, probably late in the period. Courtesy Cliff Markley collection, Alabama.

PLATE 314: *Dalton variant*, Early Archaic, this specimen probably heavily resharpened from knife use. Made of medium-dark chert, it is from Perry County, Missouri. Courtesy Cliff Markley collection, Alabama.

PLATE 315: *Graham Cave point or blade*, made of dark flint or chert, from Marshall County, Illinois. Courtesy Cliff Markley collection, Alabama.

PLATE 316: *Notched/stemmed blade,* probably Archaic, made of light-colored chert. This large, serviceable knife form is from Boone County, Missouri. Courtesy Cliff Markley collection, Alabama.

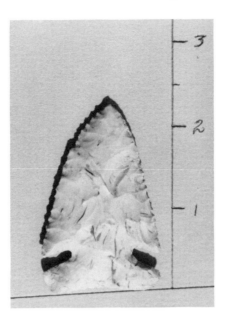

PLATE 317: *Thebes Cache-type blade,* made of a quality light-colored chert. This is an Early Archaic piece, from St. Charles County, Missouri. (See Perino, *Selected Preforms, Points and Knives,* p. 376.) Courtesy Cliff Markley collection, Alabama.

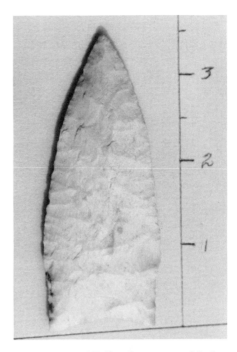

PLATE 318: *Holland point or blade,* Early Archaic, very well-chipped specimen. Judging from the base size and width, this was originally a longer piece that was rechipped or resharpened to the present size. It is from Morgan County, Missouri. This is a fairly rare type. Courtesy Cliff Markley collection, Alabama.

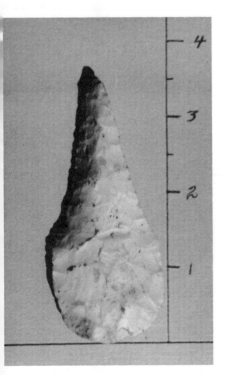

PLATE 319: *Drill or heavily resharpened knife,* from St. Louis County, Missouri. The material is light-colored chert. The beveled sides of the tapered portion are typical of knife-blade resharpening. Courtesy Cliff Markley collection, Alabama.

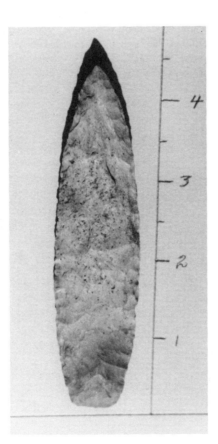

PLATE 320: *Sedalia,* a Late Archaic point, from Benton County, Missouri. Note the general similarity to many Late Paleo points, which can often be confusing. Courtesy Cliff Markley collection, Alabama.

PLATE 321: *Knife,* probably Archaic, a well-made artifact manufactured from mottled flint. It is from Adams County, Illinois. Courtesy Cliff Markley collection, Alabama.

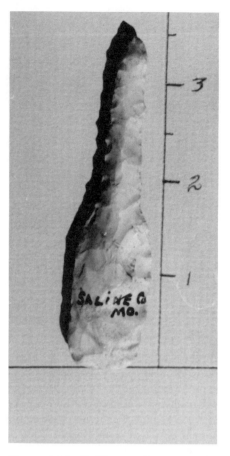

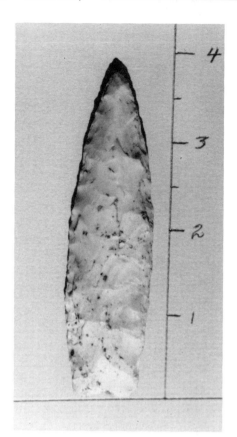

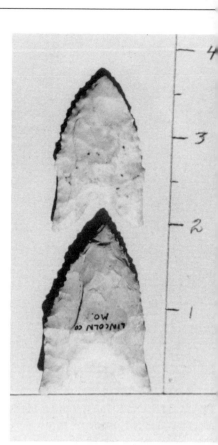

PLATE 322: *Drill or perforator,* probably Archaic, from Saline County, Missouri. It is made of light-colored chert and may have been worked down from what was once a wider blade. Courtesy Cliff Markley collection, Alabama.

PLATE 323: *Late lanceolate,* lightly stemmed, probably Archaic. This large point or blade of light speckled chert is from Morgan County, Missouri. Courtesy Cliff Markley collection, Alabama.

PLATE 324: *Dalton points or blades,* Early Archaic period. Both are heavily used and resharpened specimens made of a quality chert. Top, Adams County, Illinois. Bottom, Lincoln County, Missouri. Courtesy Cliff Markley collection, Alabama.

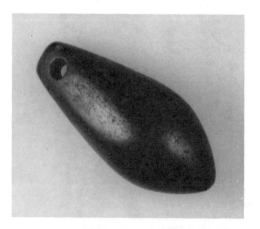

PLATE 325: *Plummet,* Archaic period, this example from Illinois. It is made of mottled granite and is 3⅛" long. Hardstone plummets are a minority form compared with hematite plummets. A scarce type with end-drilled perforation. Courtesy Charles West collection, Ohio.

PLATE 326: *Plummet,* Archaic, made of high-grade hematite or iron ore. This example, 2¾" long, has a large drill-hole at the smaller or attachment end. Despite thousands of plummets having been found in the Midwest, their exact use or purpose is still conjectural. From Dearborn County, Indiana. Courtesy Charles West collection, Ohio.

PLATE 327: *Plummet*, Archaic period, made of rare material for plummets, porphyry. This 3⅞" specimen from Hamilton County, Ohio, is also notable for the suspension hole, which is drilled. Most plummets have grooved ends. Courtesy Charles West collection, Ohio.

PLATE 328: *Plummet*, Archaic, a very fine example made of mottled granite. This piece is very well-shaped and highly polished. The small end is carefully grooved for suspension or attachment. It is 3¾" long, from Pike County, Illinois. Courtesy Charles West collection, Ohio.

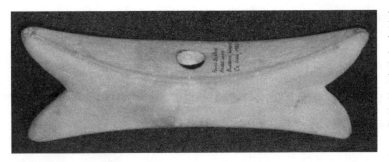

PLATE 329: *Bannerstone*, Archaic, very rare type. It was found by Jack Radke near Burbank, near the Wayne County line, in 1981. Made of very compact fine-grained sandstone instead of the usual slate, the owner has seen only two others, and both were broken. May be a blending form between a reel banner and an elongated double-crescent. Courtesy Steve Puttera Jr. collection, Ohio.

PLATE 330: *Plummet*, Archaic period, made of an unusual and colorful hardstone with highly contrasting inclusions. It is 2" high and was found near Lebanon, Warren County, Ohio. The smaller end is grooved for suspension or attachment. Courtesy Charles West collection, Ohio.

PLATE 331: *Plummet Grouping*, Archaic period, all of tool and ornament grade hematite which accepts a high polish. Left, Clermont County, Ohio; center, Kentucky; right, from Ohio, county unlisted. Despite the similarity in shape, the ends are grooved in three slightly different ways. Courtesy Charles West collection, Ohio.

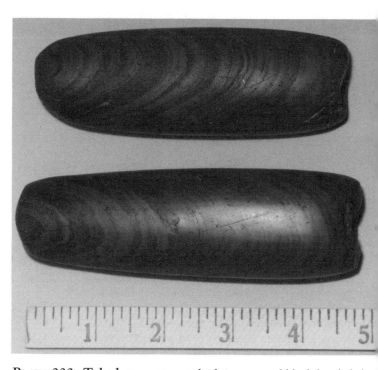

PLATE 333: *Tube bannerstones,* both in grey and black banded slate. Note the similarity in banding design. Archaic era. Top, ex-collection of Sadofsky. Bottom, ex-collection of Perry. Both examples are very highly polished. Courtesy Steve Puttera Jr. collection, Ohio.

PLATE 332: ¼ *groove axe,* 3¼" x 6¼", from Iowa. The fine Archaic specimen is in a good grade of speckled granite. Note the angular outline of this axe, typical of many axes from the Western Midwest. Very nice piece. Courtesy Steve Puttera Jr. collection, Ohio.

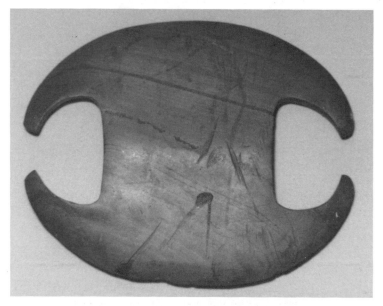

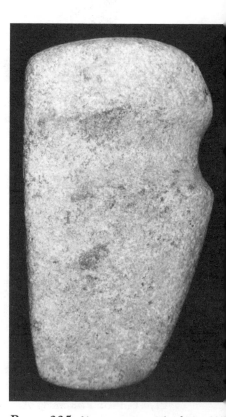

PLATE 334: *Notched ovate bannerstone,* Archaic, nicely banded glacial slate, size 4¼" x 5½". Found southeast of Norwalk, Huron County, Ohio, it was formerly in the collection of Dr. Gordon Meuser (no. 1382 over 5) and ex-collection of Ritter (no. B-105). This superb piece is pictured in *Ohio Slate Types.* Courtesy Steve Puttera Jr. collection, Ohio.

PLATE 335: ¼ *groove axe,* Archaic, 3½ x 6½". This is a well-designed and well made piece, in a high grade of greenish granite material. It is from central Missouri and an above-average specimen. Courtesy Steve Puttera Jr. collection, Ohio.

PLATE 336: *Quartzite Popeyed birdstone*, Archaic, found near Burbank in Wayne County, Ohio. This was found by Mrs. Laura Hodgdon in her garden plot, and the flint points or blades were associated with the birdstone. This is a very rare artifact in highly unusual and scarce material. Private collection, Ohio.

PLATE 337: *Hump-backed adz or gouge*, Archaic, from Pleasant Valley, Iowa; side and bottom views of an extremely rare artifact for the area. A variety with a more pronounced ridge is from Indiana, where it is known as the "Kickapoo celt." This adz was found by an onion farmer named Dodds in 1954. It is 2¼" thick and 7¼" long. Material is spotted high-grade porphyry. Courtesy Bruce Filbrandt collection, Iowa.

PLATE 338: *Plummet*, probably Archaic, made of chlorite. This is a very rare material for artifacts. This piece is from Preble County, Ohio, and about the size of a large egg at 1¼" x 3". Ex-collection of Lawrence E. Hicks. Such fine artifacts were probably more than utilitarian. Courtesy Steve Puttera Jr. collection, Ohio.

PLATE 339: *¾ groove axe*, Archaic period, made of a compact black stone which has taken a high polish. Size 2½" x 5¾", this fine piece was found in the 1960's by Vince Klamert near the confluence of Tinkers Creek and the Cuyahoga River, Cuyahoga County, Ohio. Courtesy Steve Puttera Jr. collection, Ohio.

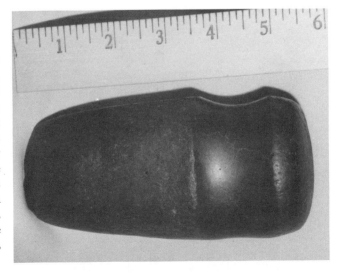

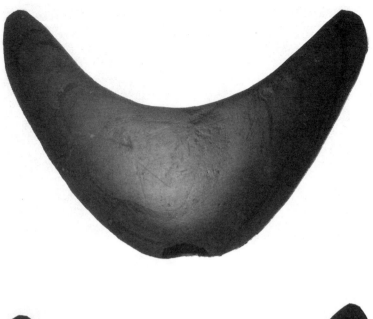

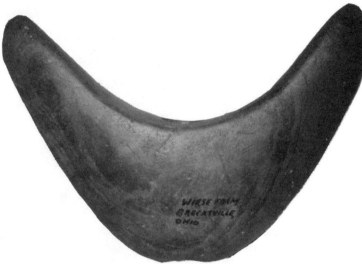

PLATE 340: *Crescent or lunate bannerstone,* Archaic obverse shown. This was found in the town of Brecksville Cuyahoga County, Ohio, ca. 1910 by Ernest E. Wiese, Sr. while clearing land. Courtesy Steve Puttera Jr. collection Ohio.

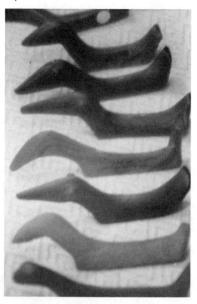

PLATE 343: *Elongated birdstones,* classic Glacial Kame forms, most from Indiana and Ohio. Note the varied treatment in the head region. Courtesy Cameron W. Parks collection, Garrett, Indiana, photo taken 1975. Lar Hothem photo.

PLATE 341: *Crescent or lunate bannerstone,* Archaic, reverse shown. From Cuyahoga County, Ohio, the material is glacial slate in purple and black banding. It is shown in actual size, 1½" x 4". This is a very scarce banner form wherever found. Courtesy Steve Puttera Jr. collection, Ohio.

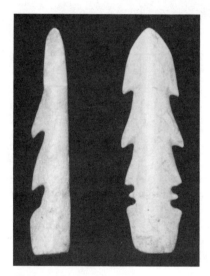

PLATE 344: *Harpoon heads,* socketed-base type, probably Late Woodland or Whittlesey focus (Mississippian). Made of bone or antler, these well-polished artifacts are very scarce and rarely are found. The length is 2" for each specimen. These were found in the 1930's near Independence, Cuyahoga County, Ohio. Courtesy Steve Puttera Jr. collection, Ohio.

PLATE 342: ¾ *groove axe,* Archaic, Cumberland River area of Kentucky. Archaic, it is 9¾" long. This artifact is made of fine-grained hardstone and is very well-shaped and well polished. An excellent piece. Courtesy Rodneyn M. Peck collection, Harrisburg, North Carolina.

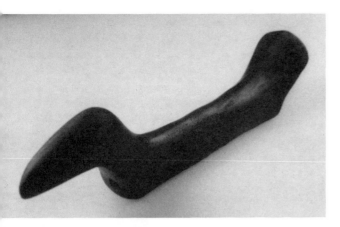

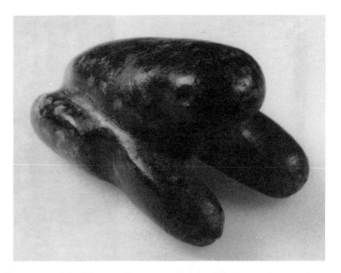

PLATE 345: *Birdstone, elongated type,* Late Archaic Glacial Kame, from LaGrange County, Indiana. Material is a brown ferruginous slate, and length is 6³⁄₁₆". This is a classic Glacial Kame type, and a beautiful piece with excellent and graceful lines. Courtesy Charles West collection, Ohio.

PLATE 346: *Frog effigy,* possible Atl-atl weight, made of hardstone. This is a very unusual early form, probably Archaic, and is from Clinton County, Ohio. Very few effigy forms of this type exist and it is likely one-of-a-kind. Courtesy Charles West collection, Ohio.

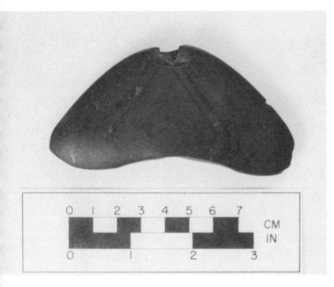

PLATE 347: *Winged bannerstone,* Archaic, from Lewis County, Missouri. Size is 2" x 3⅞", and material is black banded slate. This is a good early piece. Courtesy Rodney M. Peck collection, Harrisburg, North Carolina.

PLATE 348: *Winged bannerstone,* made of banded slate, from Greene County, Ohio. Note how the prehistoric maker worked the material to center the "eye" of the banding at the drill-hole area. Size, 5⅞" wide. Nice early piece, from the Archaic period. Courtesy Charles West collection, Ohio.

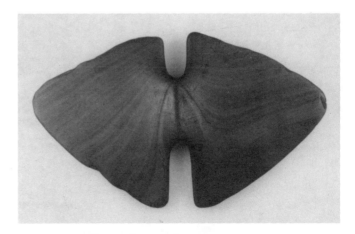

PLATE 349: *Birdstone,* Late Archaic, from Warren County, Ohio. This type has a shortened body, is relatively thick, and has an elongated neck and head region. An attractive piece. Courtesy Charles West collection, Ohio.

PLATE 350: *Butterfly-type bannerstone,* a relatively delicate and graceful banner form from the Archaic. This piece is from Hamilton County, Ohio, and is one of the more advanced forms with double indentations or cut-outs. Courtesy Charles West collection, Ohio.

PLATE 351: *Rounded bar weight,* Archaic period, material a cream-colored quartzite with brown inclusion. It measures 1¼" x 2¹¹⁄₁₆". This is a well-polished artifact, Midwestern, in a rare material. Private collection, Ohio.

PLATE 352: ¾ *groove axe,* Archaic period, from Benton County, Iowa. Material is a very dense tan and green hardstone. The axe is 2" x 2⅝" x 5" inches long, and weight is almost 2 pounds. This is a well-made axe with good lines. Courtesy Jim Roberson collection, Muscatine, Iowa.

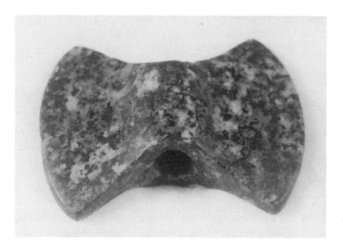

PLATE 353: *Winged bannerstone,* Wisconsin type, from Hamilton County, Ohio. Made of mottled porphyry, it is 2⁷⁄₁₆" x 3⅛". Winged hardstone Wisconsin types are rare from Ohio. A very well-made artifact, Archaic. Private collection, Ohio.

PLATE 354: *Saddle-face prismoidal bannerstone,* Archaic period, from southwestern Indiana. It is made of speckled granite in black and tan and measures 2⅜" x 3" long. Well-formed and nicely finished, this piece has an unusually large hole (⅝" diameter) for size. Private collection, Ohio.

PLATE 355: *Single-ridge prismoidal bannerstone,* from southeastern Ohio, Archaic period. It is made of speckled porphyry, and measures 1¾" x 5⁵⁄₁₆". Porphyry is unusual for this type of artifact, which is well-polished. Good form and finish. Private collection, Ohio.

PLATE 356: *Slant-grooved ¾ axe,* made of grey and green hardstone, from Tama County, Iowa. Ex-collection of Goddard, it is 1⅝" x 2⅜" x 4¾" long. This is a well-made axe with a high degree of polish. Courtesy Jim Roberson collection, Muscatine, Iowa.

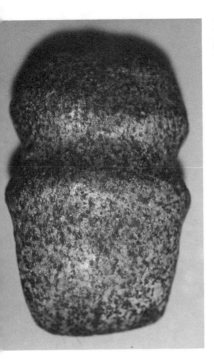

PLATE 357: ¼ *groove axe*, Archaic period, from Louisa county, Iowa. It measures 3" x 4¾", is made of dark speckled hardstone, and has groove ridges. It has good overall polish. Courtesy Gary Klebe collection, Muscatine, Iowa.

PLATE 358: ¾ *groove axe*, Archaic period, made of dark hardstone with light-colored portions below the polished surface. It was found in Marion County, Iowa, and is ex-collections of Watson, DeRosear and Goddard. Sizes is 1⅜" x 2⅛" x 5⅜" long. Courtesy Jim Roberson collection, Muscatine, Iowa.

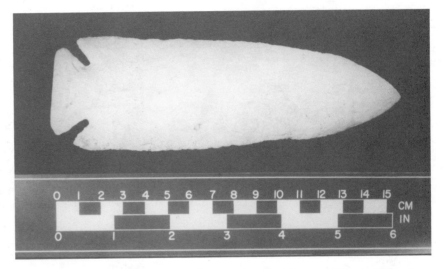

PLATE 359: *Archaic corner-notch,* from St. Clair County, Illinois. This piece is 1⅞" x 6⅛", and material is white chert or flint. This piece may be from early in the Archaic. Courtesy Rodney M. Peck collection, Harrisburg, North Carolina.

PLATE 360: ¾ *groove axe*, 1¾" x 4" long. It is from northwestern Illinois. Both the front and rear face of the poll show the natural stone surface, indicating the poll was made to fit the material. This is a highly unusual axe form in brown hardstone. Courtesy Gary Klebe collection, Muscatine, Iowa.

PLATE 361: *Half-groove Keokuk type axe,* Archaic period, from the Mississippi River Valley in Illinois. It is made of grey and green quality hardstone and is 2½" x 3⅝" x 7½" long; weight is 4¼ pounds. This is a fine axe, well-polished. Courtesy Jim Roberson collection, Muscatine, Iowa.

PLATE 362: *Thebes point or blade,* made from white chert; origin is northeastern Missouri. This is a well-made Early Archaic knife with beveling and is 2⅞" long. Courtesy Gary Klebe collection, Muscatine, Iowa.

PLATE 363: *"Hardove,"* or Hardin-Dovetail, a point or blade with characteristics of both just-named types. It is from Early Archaic times and was found in Mercer County, Illinois. Edges are beveled. The material is very interesting, being fractured chert in shades of light tan and cream. Interesting specimen. Courtesy Lane Freyermuth collection, Muscatine, Iowa.

PLATE 364: *Stilwell point or blade,* from Rock Island County, Illinois. Made of tan-cream chert, it is well-shaped and 3½" long. This is from Early Archaic times. Courtesy Lane Freyermuth collection, Iowa.

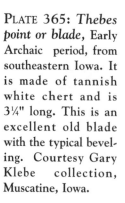

PLATE 365: *Thebes point or blade,* Early Archaic period, from southeastern Iowa. It is made of tannish white chert and is 3¼" long. This is an excellent old blade with the typical beveling. Courtesy Gary Klebe collection, Muscatine, Iowa.

PLATE 366: *Hardin point or blade,* Early Archaic, this example made of a layered chert with cream on brown. It was found in Rock Island County, Illinois, and is beveled. Length, 3⅛" long. Courtesy Lane Freyermuth collection, Iowa.

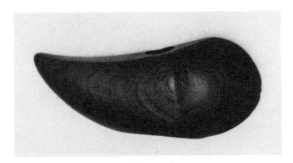

PLATE 367: *Winged bannerstone variant,* Archaic, possibly form salvaged in prehistoric times by reworking. This shape is not one of the average banner classes. Made of banded slate, it is from Warren County, Ohio, and is 3¼" long. Ex-collections of Ward, Driscol and Meuser. Courtesy Paul Rankin collection, Ohio; photograph by Del Hetrick.

PLATE 368: *Pentagonal point or blade,* Late Archaic, a 1989 field-find by Shirley Tyson in Wood County, Ohio. It is made from black, cream and tan flint, and size is 1⅞" long. This is probably a variety of Flintridge striated or striped, the common material for the type. Courtesy Edward Tyson collection, Ohio; photograph by Del Hetrick.

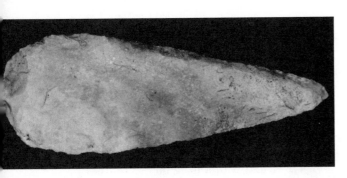

PLATE 369: *Archaic unhafted blade,* this knife form is from Rock Island County, Illinois. Made from a tan and cream chert, the edges are beveled in typical Archaic fashion and it is 5" long. Courtesy Lane Freyermuth collection, Iowa.

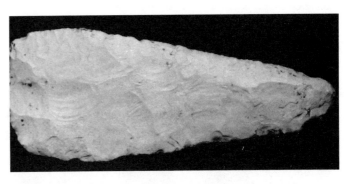

PLATE 370: *Archaic unhafted blade,* this knife made of cream-tan chert. The tip portion was rechipped in prehistoric times, and the piece has edge-beveling. From Rock Island County, Illinois, it is 5⅛" long. Courtesy Lane Freyermuth collection, Iowa.

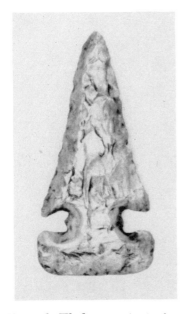

PLATE 371: *E-notch Thebes,* Early Archaic period, sometimes also called a "Key-notch." It is made of grey and black flint and is from the Eastern Midwest. Size is 2¾" long. This fine piece is ex-collection of Paul Rankin. Courtesy Edward Tyson collection, Ohio; photograph by Del Hetrick.

PLATE 372: *Pentagonal,* Late Archaic, a large example made of whitish chert or flint. It is from Knox County, Ohio, ex-collection of Archie Diller. This point or blade is 4¾" long. Courtesy Edward Tyson collection, Ohio; photograph by Del Hetrick.

PLATE 374: ¼ *groove axe*, Rock Island County, Illinois, made of dark speckled hardstone. Size is 2⅝" x 4 x 5½". This axe has a large and well-defined poll area and compared with the smaller blade area evidently has been resharpened many times. Courtesy Lane Freyermuth collection, Iowa.

PLATE 373: *Dovetail blades,* Early Archaic, both from Mercer County, Illinois, and both with beveled edges. Left, 2" long. Right, 2¼" long. Both examples appear to have been heavily resharpened from their original, longer lengths. Courtesy Lane Freyermuth collection, Iowa.

PLATE 375: *Archaic points,* all from Mercer County, Illinois. Center example is a Late Paleo Agate Basin, 2⅝" long, and well made. Left and right, Nebo Hill points with a thick diamond-shaped cross-section, 2½" long. Courtesy Lane Freyermuth collection, Iowa.

PLATE 376: ¼ *groove axe,* Archaic, from Rock Island County, Illinois. A well formed specimen made of mottled hardstone, it is 1¼" x 3⅜" x 5½" long. Courtesy Lane Freyermuth collection, Iowa.

PLATE 377: ¼ *groove axe,* from Rock Island County, Illinois, made in a yellow-tan hardstone. This example has slight grooving on the back-side which has an unusual wavy configuration. Size 2⅛" x 3¼" x 5⅜". Courtesy Lane Freyermuth collection, Iowa.

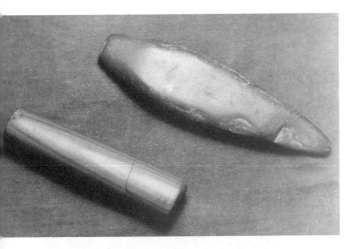

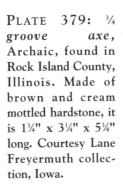

PLATE 378: *Archaic artifacts*, both Ohio. Top right, effigy or lizard stone, atypical in being rather roughly finished though partially polished. It is made of grey slate and size is 1¼" x 4⅞". From Fayette County. Bottom left, tubular pipe fully reed-drilled, ⅞" x 3⅝". Made of banded slate, it is from Hardin County. Hothem collection, Ohio.

PLATE 379: ¾ groove axe, Archaic, found in Rock Island County, Illinois. Made of brown and cream mottled hardstone, it is 1¾" x 3¼" x 5¾" long. Courtesy Lane Freyermuth collection, Iowa.

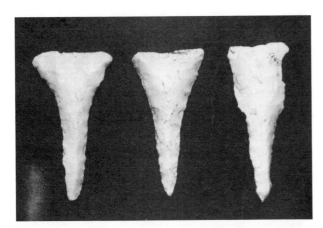

PLATE 380: *Drills*, all possibly Archaic, longest specimens 2⅛". Left and center, Rock Island County, Illinois. Right, with Hardin-like top, from Mercer County, Illinois. Courtesy Lane Freyermuth collection, Iowa.

PLATE 382: *Side-notched point or blade*, Archaic and possibly a Godar, this may have been a renotched artifact. The base appears to have been broken off in early times and another set of more shallow notches put in. The piece is from Illinois and is 3⅛" long. Courtesy Lane Freyermuth collection, Iowa.

PLATE 381: *Tama points or blades*, most found in Rock Island and Mercer Counties, Illinois. Longest specimen here is 1¾". Archaic. Single specimen, bottom right, may be an Early Archaic, and is well-chipped and very thin. Courtesy Lane Freyermuth collection, Iowa.

PLATE 383: *St. Charles or Dovetail blade,* indented base, from Orange County, Indiana. It is made of Indiana hornstone or Harrison County flint, and is 3⅝" long. This piece has very fine workstyle, serrated edges, and is in perfect condition. An Archaic blade, it is ex-collection of Tom Davis. Private collection; photograph by Del Hetrick.

PLATE 384: *Table Rock points or blades,* both from Rock Island County, Illinois. Also called Bottlenecks, these are Archaic. Left, ground stem, 1⅝" long, beveled edges. Right made of a material like quartzite, 2¾" long. Courtesy Lane Freyermuth, collection, Iowa.

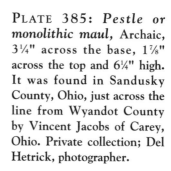

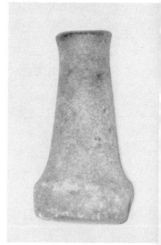

PLATE 385: *Pestle or monolithic maul,* Archaic, 3¼" across the base, 1⅞" across the top and 6¼" high. It was found in Sandusky County, Ohio, just across the line from Wyandot County by Vincent Jacobs of Carey, Ohio. Private collection; Del Hetrick, photographer.

PLATE 386: *Ashtabula point or blade,* Archaic period, a 1935 field-find by Ever Benschoter in Wood County, Ohio. This fine type example is made of multi-colored Flintridge and has quartz inclusions. Courtesy Ed Tyson collection, Ohio; Del Hetrick, photographer.

PLATE 387: *Hardin points or blades,* Early Archaic, all from Mercer County, Illinois. Left, 1⅞", beveled. Middle, 2⅜", very well-chipped specimen. Right 2⅛", beveled. Courtesy Lane Freyermuth collection, Iowa.

PLATE 388: *Sedalia*, Late Archaic, material a tan and grey chert. It is from Mercer County, Illinois, and size is ⅜" x 1⁵⁄₁₆" x 5⅞". This is a large and solid artifact, well-shaped. Courtesy William Gehlken collection, Illinois; Lane Freyermuth, photographer.

PLATE 389: *Archaic side-notched po[...]* form Mercer County, Illinois. Left, 2⅞", [...] upper blade outline. Right 2⅞", creamy-ta[...] black inclusions near the tip. Courtesy L[...] lection, Iowa.

PLATE 391: *Nebo Hill point*, Late Archaic, material a brown and tan chert. It is from Rock Island County, Illinois. Size is ⁵⁄₁₆" x 1" x 5¼". Courtesy William Gehlken collection, Illinois; Lane Freyermuth, photographer.

PLATE 39[...] *[...] or blades* [...] Tama po[...] County, [...] smoke incl[...] Middle, R[...] quality in [...] Right, T[...] County, 1[...] grinding. [...] Freyermut[...]

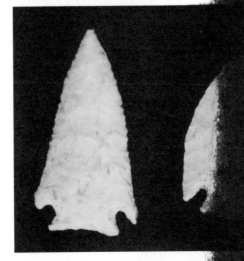

PLATE 392: *Archaic points or blades* [...] white high-grade chert and both from M[...] Left, 2¼", edge-serrations. Right, nic[...] Courtesy Lane Freyermuth collection, Io[...]

PLATE 393: *Dalton points or blades*, Early Archaic. Left, possibly Meserve Dalton, 2¼", Mercer County, Il. Center, Rock Island County, Illinois, 2⅞", with ground lower edges and serrations. Right, Rock Island County, Illinois, 2½", ground basal area and serrated edges. Courtesy Lane Freyermuth collection, Iowa.

PLATE 394: *Thebes blade,* from Mercer County, Illinois. It is 3¼" long and the basal area is heavily ground. As with many Early Archaic types, it has beveled edges. One shoulder tip is missing; material is a creamy white chert. Courtesy Lane Freyermuth collection, Iowa.

PLATE 395: *Archaic points or blades*, both Rock Island County, Illinois. Left, bifurcated form in white chert with rust-like inclusions, 2¾" long. Right, Rice Lobed, well-beveled and resharpened from a larger specimen. Courtesy Lane Freyermuth collection, Iowa.

PLATE 397: *Thebes blade,* Mercer County, Illinois. This artifact is 2⅞" long and the base and notches are well-ground. Material is an unknown chert in striped caramel, unusual. Courtesy Lane Freyermuth collection, Iowa.

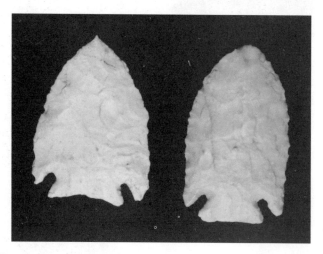

PLATE 396: *Archaic Corner-notched blades*, both from Rock Island County, Il. Left, very thin and with twisted blade, a needle tip, 2¼". Right, rounded blade tip and serrated edges, nicely notched, 2⁷⁄₁₆" long. Courtesy Lane Freyermuth collection, Iowa.

PLATE 398: *Knife blade,* probably Archaic, very thin overall and with the bottom two-thirds very finely chipped along the edges. Material is tan and light brown mottled; this 5¼" specimen is from Rock Island County, Illinois. Courtesy Lane Freyermuth collection, Iowa.

PLATE 399: *Borroughs point,* Late Paleo, reference Morrow, *Iowa Projectile Points.* This is a very well-chipped piece, 2⅞" long, with grinding on the lower side edges. It has a twisted design and red cortex on one side. Found in Rock Island County, Illinois, it may be made of Warsaw chert. Courtesy Lane Freyermuth collection, Iowa.

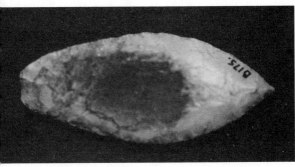

PLATE 400: *Borroughs point,* reverse side, Late Paleo. See obverse for further information.

PLATE 401: *Stanfield blade,* Early Archaic. See Perino, *Selected Preforms, Points and Knives of the North American Indians,* Vol. I, p 360. This example is made of Moline chert and is 4¼" long. Chipping overall is very well done. From Illinois Courtesy Lane Freyermuth collection, Iowa.

PLATE 402: *Sedalia point or blade,* Late Archaic, from Rock Island County, Illinois. It is 4¾" long, and made of cream chert with a basal touch of caramel. Courtesy Lane Freyermuth collection, Iowa.

PLATE 403: *Godar point or blade,* Middle-Late Archaic, from Rock Island County, Illinois. This is a fine, wide specimen with little resharpening. It is 3⅛" long, and from Rock Island County, Illinois. Courtesy Lane Freyermuth collection, Iowa.

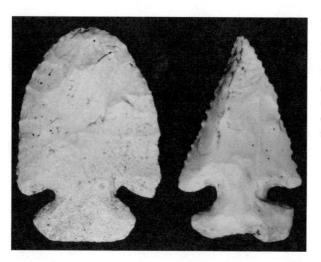

PLATE 404: *Thebes blades*, Early Archaic. Left, rounded-tip specimen with basal and notch grinding, 2⅞" long. It is from Mercer County, Illinois. Right, triangular Thebes with beveled and serrated edges. This specimen was found in the owner's garden. Courtesy Lane Freyermuth collection, Iowa.

PLATE 405: *Short-stemmed Hardin-barbed*, Early Archaic. This is an unusual form, with very good chipping and highly ground stem and base edges. It is from Rock Island County, Illinois, and is 4¼" long. Courtesy Lane Freyermuth collection, Iowa.

PLATE 406: *Archaic artifacts*, both Ohio. Left, bar or loafstone weight, dark red quartzite, 1⅟₁₆" x 2⁹⁄₁₆", Morrow County. Ex-collection of Dr. Meuser, it has a polished concave base on the long axis and is nicely polished. Right, elongated ball bannerstone, of rose, tan and grey banded quartzite. It is 1⅝" x 2⅛", from Shelby County. Reed drilling was begun but not completed. Private collection, Ohio.

PLATE 407: *Loafstones*, probably Archaic (Late) and likely specialized Atl-atl balances. Left, 1½" x 1⅞", tan and cream quartzite conglomerate, ex-collection of A.T. Wehrle, rare material. Right, 1½" x 1¹³⁄₁₆", tan-cream quartzite, from Hardin County. (Both pieces are from Ohio.) It has a cross-groove at 90 degrees to the long axis and main groove. Private collection, Ohio.

PLATE 408: *Missouri knife collection*, most probably Archaic period. This photo offers a good view of different blade types and materials of the kind that are commonly found in Missouri. Average length is 3". Coutesy collection of L.A. Noblett; photograph by Victor A. Pierce, Missouri.

PLATE 409: *Etley blades*, Missouri, Late Archaic period. The longest blade, on left, is 4". These are instructive in showing the style ranges for the type; all are made of different chert materials. Ca. 2000 BC. Courtesy collections of Dake, Noblett and Pierce; photography by Victor A. Pierce, Missouri.

PLATE 410: *Half-groove axe,* this piece found by a Mrs. Brown in Lewis County, Missouri. Mr. Paul Sellers obtained this axe in 1947, and it is pictured in *Who's Who In Indian Relics No. 5,* page 180. This exceptional axe is 4" x 8¼" and weighs 5¼ pounds. It is well-designed and nicely polished. Courtesy Bruce Filbrandt collection, Iowa.

PLATE 411: *Half-groove axe,* from Illinois, county unknown, purchased from the Bob Onken collection. It is made from a dark hardstone, has well-defined features and a very good polish. This fine axe is 3¼" x 7" and weighs about two pounds. Courtesy Bruce Filbrandt collection, Iowa.

PLATE 413: ¾ *groove axe,* light brown granite, 2½" x 5¼", very fine Archaic piece. It was found by Bill Bodine around 1968 in Saline County, Missouri. Axes of this quality are prize field-finds anywhere in the Midwest. Courtesy Steve Puttera Jr. collection, Ohio.

PLATE 412: *Midwestern axes,* a superb grouping of fine Archaic axes, various materials, types and sizes. While these are pictured individually elsewhere in the book, a group photograph of them is of interest. Courtesy Bruce Filbrandt collection, Iowa.

PLATE 414: *Half-groove axe,* one of the largest known of the type, from Van Buren County, Iowa. It is ex-collections of Huff, W. Nelson and Dr. Bunch. Interestingly, this axe was perfectly pecked into shape but was not polished. It is 4½" x 11", 12½" around at the groove, and weighs 9 pounds 12 ounces. The sides are fluted on this large axe. Courtesy Bruce Filbrandt collection, Iowa.

PLATE 415: *Half-groove axe,* Keokuk type, made of speckled greenish hardstone. It was found in Van Buren County, Iowa, and came from the Bob Jenkins collection in 1984. This is a very beautiful axe, and measures 2" x 3" x 6". A fine piece. Courtesy Bruce Filbrandt collection, Iowa.

PLATE 416: *Half-groove axe,* found in Hancock County, Illinois. It is made of a grey-brown hardstone with black specks, and is ex-collection of Larry Van Bibber. It has deep flutes on both sides and is 4¼" x 7⅝", 9⅞" around the groove area. A fine piece. Courtesy Bruce Filbrandt collection, Iowa.

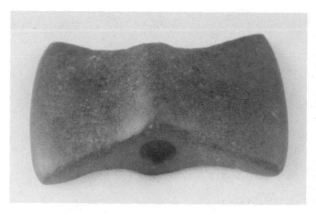

PLATE 417: *Winged bannerstone,* Wisconsin type, made o dark red jasper. It is from Hamilton County, Ohio, and 2⅛" x 3¾". The reed drilling was started at both ends but was no completed. Good form for this scarce Archaic banner type. Private collection, Ohio.

PLATE 418: *Plummets,* Archaic, both Ohio and rare. Left, Hardin County, 1³⁄₁₆" x 3¹¹⁄₁₆", clear quartz crystal and beautifully formed. Top piece. Right, Fairfield County, 1⅛" x 2⁵⁄₁₆", milky to clear quartz crystal, well formed. Superior piece. Private collection, Ohio.

PLATE 419: *Plummets,* Archaic period, left to right; Franklin County, Ohio, 1⅛" x 2¼", ex-collection of E. Good, cavity crystal quartz. Tuscarawas County, Ohio, 1¼" x 3³⁄₁₆", ex-collection of E. Good, cavity crystal quartz. Illinois, grooved, 1¹⁄₁₆" x 1³⁄₄", milky crystal quartz, ex-collection of Floyd Ritter. Private collection, Ohio.

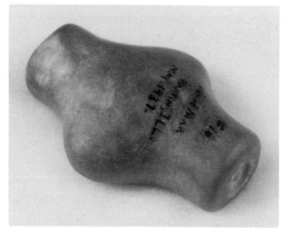

PLATE 420: *Expanded-center bottle bannerstone,* Archaic period, made of rose and white quartzite. From Hardin, Illinois, it is 2⅜" x 3¼". The reed drilling was just started but not completed. Fine coloring for this piece, plus high polish on a rare banner type. Private collection, Ohio.

PLATE 421: *Grooved-end plummet,* Archaic period, made of rare quartzite-jasper conglomerate. From Williams County, Ohio, this piece is 1⅛" x 3½", and is ex-collection of B.W. Stevens. Very fine coloring and contours plus material make this one of the best plummets ever found. Private collection, Ohio.

PLATE 422: *Chlorite pick bannerstone,* one of the most vivid and varied in color from Ohio. It has hues of orange, green, blue and black, and is from Delaware County. Size is 1⅞₁₆" x 3⅞₁₆", and the piece has outstanding aesthetic appeal. Private collection, Ohio.

PLATE 423: *Elongated ball bannerstone,* fluted reverse, Archaic period. It is made of light tan and green chlorite with black mottling. Size, 1½" x 2¼". It is ex-collection of Frank and Merl Sharp, from Putnam County, Ohio. The condition and color make this a very collectible piece. Private collection, Ohio.

PLATE 424: *Loafstone,* Archaic period, material a tan quartzite. This artifact is 1¹¹₁₆" x 2⁹₁₆", and from Fairfield County, Ohio. Loafstones are thought to be a specialized Atl-atl balance weight; in this example, the groove runs completely around the stone, top and bottom. Private collection, Ohio.

PLATE 425: *Chlorite pendant,* possibly Archaic, made of a light olive-green chlorite. It is 1¹¹₁₆" x 2⁹₁₆", and is from the Union-Delaware Counties line, Ohio. This is an oddly shaped artifact with beveled edges. Private collection, Ohio.

PLATE 426: *Humped gorget,* Late Archaic period and Glacial Kame in origin. Material is a tan quartzite and size is 1¾" x 3³₁₆". From Miami County, Ohio, the drilling was begun but not completed on this rare artifact. Private collection, Ohio.

PLATE 427: *Elongated ball bannerstone,* fluted base on reverse, material a rare chlorite in jet black. Size is 1⁷₁₆" x 2⅛". This banner is ex-collection of Max Shipley, and is from Shelby County, Ohio. This piece is well-made and has a few surface scratches that do not detract from appearance. Private collection, Ohio.

PLATE 428: *Elongated ball bannerstone,* fluted base (reverse), Archaic period. It is 1⅝" x 1¹⁵⁄₁₆", from Seneca County, Ohio, and ex-collection of Dr. G.F. Meuser. Material is a very dark brownish green chlorite, nicely colored and highly polished. Rare piece. Private collection, Ohio.

PLATE 429: *Chlorite pick bannerstone,* Archaic, made of light olive green chlorite with tan mottling. This is a large and very fine piece at 1½" x 4⁷⁄₁₆". It is ex-collection of Max Shipley and from Delaware County, Ohio. This is one of the finest chlorite banners to come from the state. Private collection, Ohio.

PLATE 430: *Rounded bar Atl-atl weight,* Archaic period, 1⅜" x 3" long. From Indiana, the material is highly unusual orange and dark red jasper. The chipping marks have all been smoothed and polished away in making this complete artifact in finished form. Private collection, Ohio.

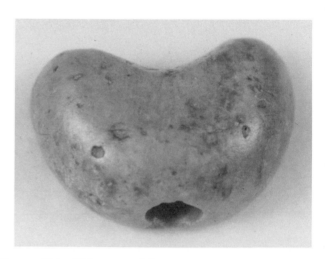

PLATE 431: *Chlorite pick bannerstone,* blunt curved type, Archaic period. It is made of yellowish-tan chlorite and is 1¾" x 2⁵⁄₁₆" long. From Delaware County, Ohio, this artifact is well-made, highly polished and has an unusual shape. Private collection, Ohio.

PLATE 432: *Tubular fluted bannerstone,* Archaic, made of dark green and grey chlorite with tan mottling. It is 1½" x 2⁷⁄₁₆" and from Marion County, Ohio. This piece, ex-collection of Edward Fritch, was found in the year 1900. This interesting weight has a wide flute on the reverse. Private collection, Ohio.

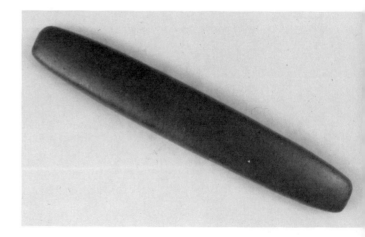

PLATE 433: *Ellipsoidal bar Atl-atl weight,* Archaic period, made of dark red jasper, a form of chalcedony. This is a very rare material for a bar weight, the example shown being 1⅛" x 7" long. It is ex-collection of Phil Kientz and is from Darke County, Ohio. Private collection, Ohio.

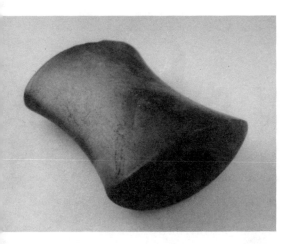

PLATE 435: *Pick bannerstone,* straight type, from the Archaic period. This piece is from Delaware County, Ohio, and measures 1¹⁄₁₆" x 3¹³⁄₁₆". It is ex-collection of A.T. Wehrle and made of a very rare material that appears to be light to dark green nephrite jade. This is a highly polished artifact, fully drilled at center. Private collection, Ohio.

PLATE 434: *Bannerstone,* Archaic, from Gallatin County, Illinois. It is made of rose quartzite and is 3" long. This is a well-colored piece in ultra-hard and attractive material. Hourglass form, here, is one of the more highly developed banners. Courtesy Charles West collection, Ohio.

PLATE 436: *Pebble pendant,* probably Archaic, from Putnam County, Ohio. This curious specimen has characteristics of both a pendant (small hole) and Atl-atl weight (large central hole). It is made of dark tan quartzite and measures ⁹⁄₁₆" x 2³⁄₁₆". Center-hole is about half an inch in diameter. Private collection, Ohio.

PLATE 437: *St. Charles or Dovetail blade,* Early Archaic, made of a lesser Flintridge grade but with some color. This is probably an Ohio artifact and measures 1½" x 3½". It has very good overall form and workstyle. Courtesy Donald E. Shuck collection, Ohio.

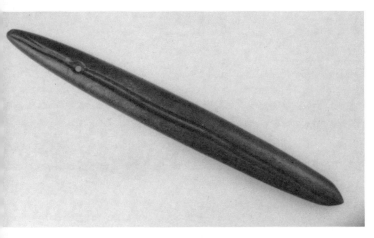

PLATE 438: *Pendant,* possibly Archaic, of highly unusual form. In fact, the term *pendant* is simply the closest descriptive word that can be applied to this one-of-a-kind artifact made of slate. It is from Marion County, Ohio, and is 8½" long. A narrow slot or groove runs the length of the piece. Courtesy Charles West collection, Ohio.

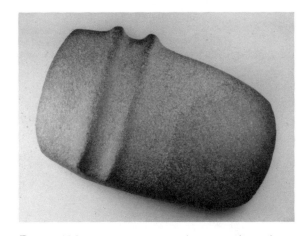

PLATE 439: ¾ *groove axe,* Archaic period, an above average axe in every way. It is made of high-grade green hardstone and came from Clermont County, Ohio. This is a large axe, 6¼" x 9½", with a weight of over nine pounds. It has good grooving, ridging and polish. Courtesy Donald E. Shuck collection, Ohio.

PLATE 440: *Bannerstone,* light blue-grey sandy shale, about 7" long. It may be a blending form of knobbed lunate. Knoblock shows this fine piece on page 155 of the *Bannerstone* book. Ex-collections of Fain King and the Watson Museum; from Hickman County, Kentucky. Courtesy Dale and Betty Roberts collection, Iowa.

PLATE 441: *Archaic knives,* all Flintridge from Licking County, and all Ohio. Left, St. Charles or Dovetail, in cream, tan and blue translucent material, Darke County. Middle, deep-notch Archaic in mainly blue translucent material, heavily resharpened, Medina County, 5½" long. Right, St. Charles or Dovetail in cream and tan material, translucent, Franklin County. Courtesy Dale and Betty Roberts collection, Iowa.

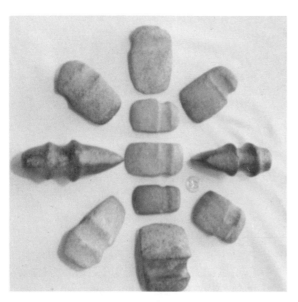

PLATE 442: *Iowa axes,* all found by Dwight Stineman during the period 1984-1985, and all from Louisa County, Iowa. These are a good example of what determined and knowledgeable surface-hunting can still produce. Quarter shows scale. Courtesy Dwight Stineman collection, Wapello, Iowa.

PLATE 443: ¾ *groove axe,* found in the spring of 1953 in Louisa County, Iowa. It is the largest complete ¾ groove axe known to have been found in the state of Iowa. Weight, 26 pounds. This was formerly in the collection of Dwight Stineman. Dwight Stineman photograph, Wapello, Iowa.

PLATE 444: *St. Charles or Dovetail blade,* Midwestern piece, made of black flint with quartz inclusions, probably Upper Mercer material. Length of this fine piece is 4¼". Private collection; photograph by Del Hetrick.

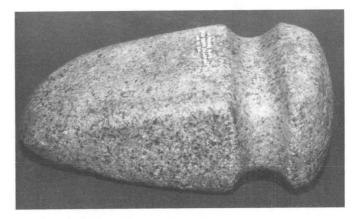

PLATE 445: *Saddle-faced bannerstone*, Archaic, 2⅞" x 3¾". Material is black and white porphyry hardstone and it is from Jasper County, Missouri. This is a superbly made artifact in top condition, well-polished. It is ex-collections of Neusbaum, King, Stephens and Young. Courtesy Dale and Betty Roberts collection, Iowa.

PLATE 446: *Square-back ¾ groove axe*, found in Pike County, Illinois. Ex-collection of Murray, it has excellent groove and lower blade polish, plus overall lighter polish. Material is light brown with dark brown spotting. This very fine piece is 4½" x 8½", 11⅞" around the groove and weighs 7½ pounds. Courtesy Bruce Filbrandt collection, Iowa.

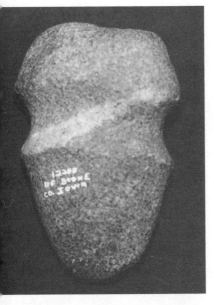

PLATE 447: *Full groove or ¾ axe*, Archaic, found in Boone County, Iowa. It has heavy bit polish, and is an above-average smaller full-groove. It is 3⅛"x 4¾", 7½" around the groove, and weight is about a pound. The diagonal white streak in the grey-green hardstone is of interest. Courtesy Bruce Filbrandt collection, Iowa.

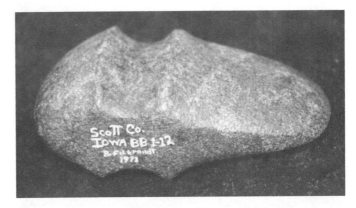

PLATE 448: *¾ groove axe*, Archaic, a personal find by the owner in Le Claire Township, Scott County, Iowa. It is made of dense hardstone in colors of black, green and grey. This axe is 3½" x 6½", about 2 pounds and 8½" around the groove. This is a very fine specimen. Courtesy Bruce Filbrandt collection, Iowa.

PLATE 449: *Half-groove or Keokuk axe*, a personal find by the owner in Pleasant Valley, Iowa, in 1989. A Scott County artifact, it is 2⅛"x 4⅛", with a weight of about half a pound. Material is very dense grey-green hardstone with natural white lines. Side flutes are very deep. A fine small axe. Courtesy Bruce Filbrandt collection, Iowa.

PLATE 450: *Full groove or ¾ axe*, Archaic, and found by an insurance salesman named Smith near New London, Iowa. Material is a black and tan hardstone, and there is a natural fracture or line leading in from the bit. Very high polish is present on this fine axe, 5⅜" x 8¼", 12⅝" around the groove, and with weight of 7 pounds. Courtesy Bruce Filbrandt collection, Iowa.

PLATE 452: *Pine Tree point or blade*, Early Archaic, from central Kentucky. Material is light grey Kentucky flint, and the piece has unusually large serrations for size. It is 1³⁄₁₆" x 2⅛". Courtesy Donald E. Shuck collection, Ohio.

PLATE 451: *St. Charles or Dovetail blade*, Upper Mercer material, this piece from central Ohio. This is a beautiful Early Archaic work, very well made and in top condition, good lines and length, everything. Size is 1½" x 5¼". Courtesy Donald E. Shuck collection, Ohio.

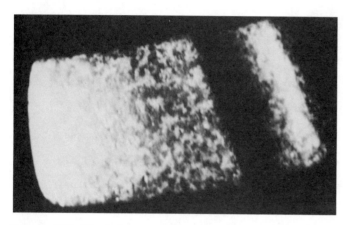

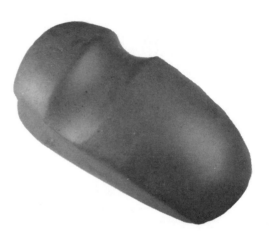

PLATE 453: *Keokuk axe*, Louisa County, Iowa. It was found in the summer of 1945 by the owner, eight years old at the time. This particular axe was the beginning of a lifelong pursuit, hunting for and finding over 300 axes, almost all from Louisa County. Courtesy Dwight Stineman collection, Wapello, Iowa.

PLATE 454: ¾ *groove axe*, Archaic period, material is a light green high-quality hardstone. This axe is very well made, has a fluted back, and is highly polished overall. It won "Best Field Find - 1980" at the Artifact Society meeting and was a personal find by the owner. Size is 3" x 5½"; it is from Brown County, Ohio. Courtesy Donald E. Shuck collection, Ohio.

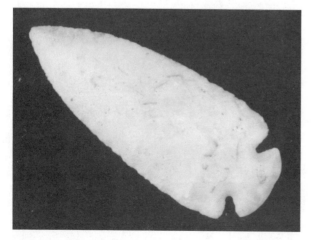

PLATE 456: *Fractured-base Dovetail*, Early Archaic. A rare St. Charles variety with burin-flaking (sliver strike-off) at corners of base-bottom ends. It is made of Kentucky grey flint and is from central Kentucky. Size is 1⅞" x 2¼". Courtesy Donald E. Shuck collection, Ohio.

PLATE 455: *St. Charles or Dovetail blade*, Early Archaic, from Franklin County, Ohio. It is made of Licking County Flintridge in snow-white translucent gem chalcedony, and measures 1⅝" x 3⅞". This is a superior early artifact, very well made and in top condition. Courtesy Donald E. Shuck collection, Ohio.

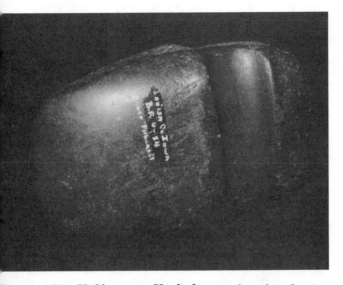

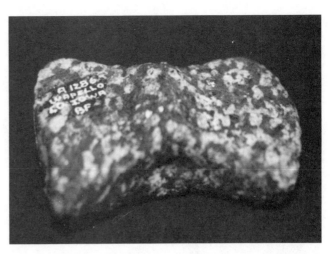

PLATE 457: *Half-groove Keokuk axe,* found in Louisa County, Iowa, by Carl Kemp and purchased at his farm sale in 1984. Material is a dark black and dense hardstone which took a high polish and has much patina. Size is 2¼" x 4½" x 7¼". This is a very fine Iowa axe. Courtesy Bruce Filbrandt collection, Iowa.

PLATE 458: *Bow-tie type bannerstone,* made of a greenish and white hardstone. It was found in Iowa near the Des Moines River in the 1930's. The central drill-hole was just started, but not completed. This is a fine Archaic specimen of a very rare artifact, 1¾" wide at center, 3" wide at ends, and 4" long or wide overall. Courtesy Bruce Filbrandt collection, Iowa.

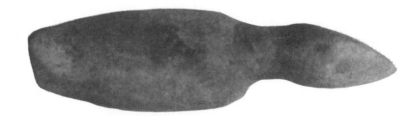

PLATE 459: *Miniature Keokuk axe,* from Muscatine County, Iowa. It was found by Gene Fuller's father, probably in the 1920's. Material is grey-black porphyry with peach-colored inclusions. Size for this fine small Archaic axe is 2" x 3¼". Courtesy Bruce Filbrandt collection, Iowa.

PLATE 460: *Birdstone,* Late Archaic, 4½" long. This was found in 1918 in Crawford County, Indiana. This piece has clean, flowing lines and is made of a coarse granular slate, dark green in color. Private collection, Kentucky.

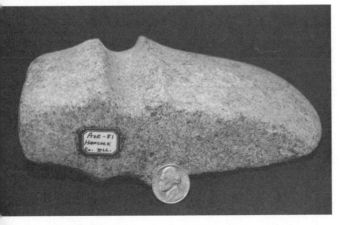

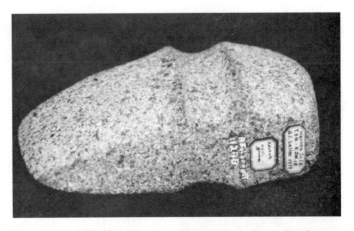

PLATE 461: *Half-groove axe,* found in Hancock County, Illinois. It is light brown in color and is of a good grade of highly speckled hardstone. Size is 2½" x 3½" x 7¼", with overall good polish. This is a superior Archaic axe. Courtesy Bruce Filbrandt collection, Iowa.

PLATE 462: *Half-groove axe,* blue-black and grey hardstone, this artifact found in 1919 in Warren County, Illinois. It has very good polish and good form; size is 2½" x 3¾" x 7½". The finder of this excellent Archaic piece was G.E. Sallee. Courtesy Bruce Filbrandt collection, Iowa.

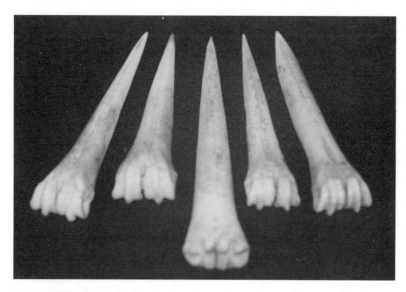

PLATE 463: *Bone awls,* probably Archaic, all from various rock-shelters in Kentucky. The large center awl is 6½" long and was a personal find by the owner in Wayne County, Ky. All awls except the center-piece have a high degree of polish on them. Courtesy Michael Darland collection, Kentucky.

PLATE 464: ¼ *groove axe,* Archaic, this particular axe also shown in the book *Indian Axes,* p 54. The axe was found by the owner on Father's Day 1967, on a rise above the Chaplin River in Washington County, Kentucky. This axe is large and well-made, with exceptionally clean lines. Size, 5" x 7⅝". Michael Darland collection, Kentucky.

PLATE 465: *St. Charles or Dovetail,* Early Archaic, a personal find by the owner, 1967, in Mercer County, Kentucky. The field from which it came had a small cave at one end. Made of a beautiful white mottled flint, the blade is 1½" x 3½" long. Courtesy Michael Darland collection, Kentucky.

PLATE 466: ¼ *groove axe,* Archaic, found in Louisa County, Iowa, near Mediapolis. This was a farm find; it is 4⅛" wide and 6" long, 9" around the groove. Material is black with peach inclusions, very beautiful hardstone. Courtesy Bruce Filbrandt collection, Iowa.

PLATE 467: *Bone gorget,* probably Archaic, from Russell County, Kentucky. This very rare two-hole gorget is ivory-like and highly polished, with 11 incised lines across the face at the ends. Very few similar gorgets have been found. Courtesy Michael Darland collection, Kentucky.

PLATE 468: *Iowa Keokuk axes,* all personally found by the owner in the past 45 years. These fine pieces, made of various high-grade hardstone materials, are but a portion of the Stineman axe collection. Courtesy Dwight Stineman collection, Wapello, Iowa.

PLATE 469: *Hardin point or blade,* Early Archaic, in a very attractive creamy white and brown material. From Perry County, Illinois, this 3½" specimen is the most colorful Hardin seen by David Guy. A superior point or blade in every way. Courtesy the Guy Brothers collection, Illinois.

PLATE 470: *Archaic prehistoric artworks,* all from Iowa. Left, bannerstone, pictured in Knoblock's *Bannerstone* book on page 423, and from Keokuk County. Center, porphyry axe, 2¼" x 5¾", Wapello County, top-grade and rare piece. Right, large ¾ groove axe, 4" x 9¹⁄₁₆", fine design and condition. All items originally from the Julian C. Spurgeon collection, Iowa. Courtesy Dale & Betty Roberts collection, Iowa.

PLATE 471: *Birdstone effigy forms,* Late Archaic period. Note that some specimens are from outside the Midwest as defined in this book, but are included so that the Midwestern items in the photograph can be shown and also so that comparisons can be made with similar artifacts from nearby regions. These are some of the rarest existing artifacts. Top left, yellow and brown porphyry birdstone, Van Buren County, Michigan, 3⅝" long, GIRS (Genuine Indian Relic Society) authentication #I13. Top right, yellow and dark green porphyry pop-eye birdstone, Sandusky County, Ohio. It is 1¾" x 4", GIRS authentication #E11. Center right, banded slate Glacial Kame birdstone, Montgomery County, Indiana. It is 6¼" long and bears GIRS authentication #I15. Lower left, banded slate pop-eye birdstone, Marshall, Michigan. It is 4⅜" long, GIRS authentication #J5. Lower center, banded slate pop-eye birdstone, Oxford County, Ontario, Canada, 4" long. GIRS authentication #I14. Lower right, yellow cream and green porphyry birdstone, pop-eye type, Kent County, Michigan, 3⅜" long. GIRS *Prehistoric Artifacts* p 3. Prehistoric art collection of John Baldwin, West Olive, Michigan.

PLATE 472: *Saddle-faced bannerstone preform,* very rare artifact, from Stark County, Illinois. It has fine color, being a tan and light black spotted hardstone. Center of the face is dished out and the ends are raised or peaked. Size, 3" wide, 3⅜" long. A top Archaic specimen. Courtesy Bruce Filbrandt collection, Iowa.

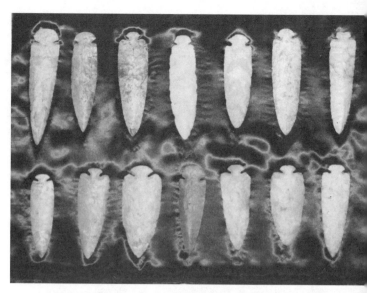

PLATE 474: *St. Charles or Dovetail blades,* Early Archaic, a[l] colorful Flintridge materials and all eastern Midwest. In addition t[o] the fine jewel flint, there is an excellent range of styles or varietie[s] present. Note the different basal configurations. Sizes, 4¼" - 6½"[.] Courtesy Glenn Spray collection, Ohio.

PLATE 473: *Thebes point or blade,* found in Lee County, Iowa, and from the Early Archaic period. This fine point is 4¼" long. The Thebes and related types are found throughout much of the Midwest; they are sturdy knives, with resharpening indicated by the beveling present on most edges. Courtesy Verlin Hepker collection, Iowa.

PLATE 475: *¾ groove axe,* found in Marion County, Iowa. This is a beautiful fully detailed axe with much polish and patina. It is ex-collection of Paul Sellers, and 2½" x 4¼". A very nice Archaic work of prehistoric art. Courtesy Bruce Filbrandt collection, Iowa.

PLATE 476: *St. Charles or Dovetail blades,* Early Archaic, Eastern Midwest, and most made of Flintridge material. Several are o[f] Indiana hornstone and third example from right second row down is probably Carter County flint from Kentucky. Very fine specimens, with the length range 3" - 4⅝". Courtesy Glenn Spray collection, Ohio.

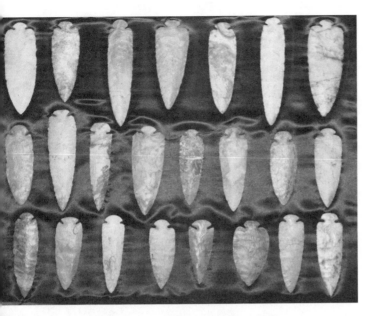

PLATE 477: *St. Charles or Dovetail blades*, Early Archaic, all Ohio pieces. An interesting thing about this tray is that all artifacts have restoration, in some cases very slight. This is a good example of how good materials and an expert touch can result in fine display specimens. Sizes, 3⅜" - 6¼". Most are of Flintridge materials, gem quality. Courtesy Glenn Spray collection, Ohio.

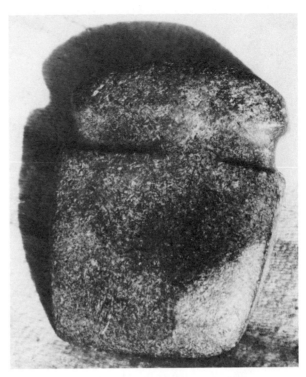

PLATE 478: ¼ *groove axe*, unusually symmetrical, and made from what originally was a fine double-dished grinding plate. In a sense, then, this is a double artifact. Size, 2" x 7" x 8½", with weight 9½ pounds. It is from Louisa County, Iowa. The axe is so unusual that no comparable value figure is available. Courtesy Dwight Stineman collection, Wapello, Iowa.

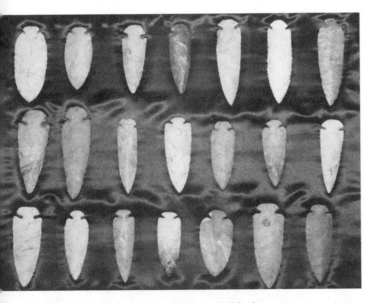

PLATE 479: *St. Charles or Dovetail blades*, Early Archaic, Eastern Midwest and most made of gem Flintridge material. There are probably at least a dozen Dovetail varieties, all related or in the same cluster or family. Sizes, 3¾" - 5⅜". This is a fine type group. Courtesy Glenn Spray collection, Ohio.

PLATE 480: *Keokuk axes*, both Louisa County, Iowa. Left, 2¾" x 4" x 9¾", 7⅝ pounds. This is a beautiful, very well-made specimen. Right, 2¼" x 4¼" x 9¾", 7½ pounds. It was found in the spring of 1981, and is a superb axe, with top value as yet undetermined. Courtesy Dwight Stineman collection, Wapello, Iowa.

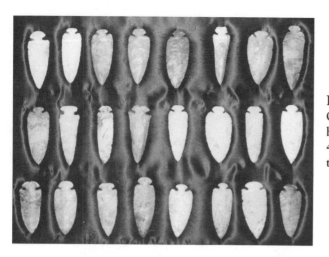

PLATE 481: *St. Charles or Dovetail blades,* Early Archaic, all from Ohio and most made of Flintridge gem material. Note that two specimens have beveled edges, unusual for Ohio Dovetails. Size range here is 3½" 4". Examples with very excurvate edges may not have been resharpened too often. Courtesy Glenn Spray collection, Ohio.

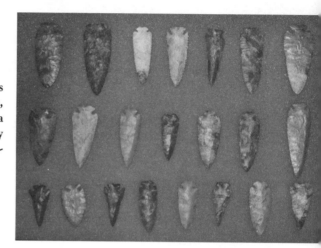

PLATE 482: *Early Archaic blades,* all made of Ohio flints. Types included are St. Charles or Dovetail blades, Notched-base Dove-tails, Notched bases, Unnotched notched-bases, Archaic corner-notched and a Heavy Duty which is second from the right in center row. This fine tray has a excellent range of types and materials. Courtesy Glenn Spray collection, Ohio.

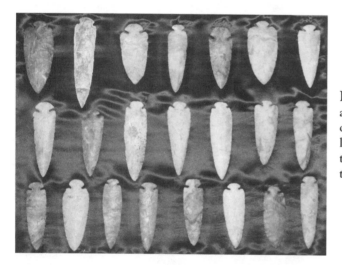

PLATE 483: *St. Charles or Dovetail blades,* Early Archaic, all Ohio and most made of gem Flintridge material. There is an instructive range of styles, from small-base to large-base and varieties in between. Excellent specimens, the sizes are 4" - 6". The second blade from the left, top row, was found on Blennerhasset Island in the Ohio River. Courtesy Glenn Spray collection, Ohio.

PLATE 484: *St. Charles or Dovetail blades,* Early Archaic, all except one made of Nellie or Coshocton flints in blacks, blues and greys. The exception is the top left blade, a very superior specimen, from Missouri. Courtesy Glenn Spray collection, Ohio.

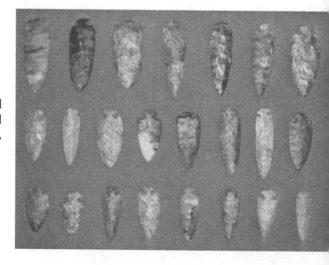

PLATE 485: *Goddard axe collection,* Archaic period, all specimens from Iowa except three from Missouri and one from western Illinois. This is the "heartland" of high-grade axes, as can readily be seen in this remarkable photograph. The large black axe at top center is 11½" long and weighs ten pounds. The little axe beside it is 3¼" long and weighs five ounces. Courtesy Collection of Floyd and Judi Goddard, Wilton, Iowa.

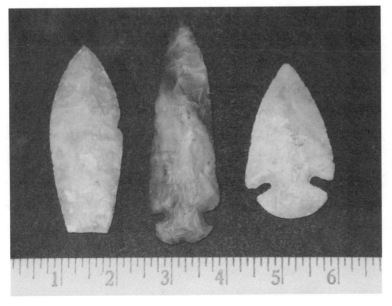

PLATE 486: *Archaic knives and a lanceolate,* Late Paleo, all Ohio. Left to right: Lanceolate, blue-grey Flintridge, Franklin County, found in 1950's. Dovetail, highly colored gem Flintridge, Hancock County, ex-collection of Mike Howard and Billy Ford. Dovetail, reworked in early times from a longer blade, found by Maurice McClay, Stark County. Fine. Courtesy Steve Puttera Jr. collection, Ohio.

PLATE 487: ¼ *groove axe*, a personal find by the owner in Whiteside County, Illinois. This Archaic axe is grey-green hardstone, with extra wide and deep groove. There is heavy overall polish on this piece, which is 3" x 4½" x 7⅛", 10½" around the groove and with weight of about 5 pounds. A very high-quality axe. Courtesy Bruce Filbrandt collection, Iowa.

PLATE 488: *Full groove or ¼ axe*, Archaic, with a very good groove and lower blade polish. Ex-collection of G. Hummel, it is from Pike County, Illinois. Made of light grey-brown hardstone, the axe is 5" x 7", 10⅞" around the groove and has a weight of about 5 pounds. Courtesy Bruce Filbrandt collection, Iowa.

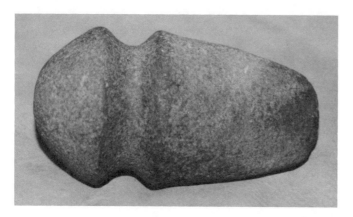

PLATE 489: ¼ *groove axe*, Archaic period, from Tazewell County, Illinois. It is made from an unusual reddish hardstone. Measurements, 2" x 2¾" x 5" long. This is a well-formed and well-shaped specimen. Courtesy William Gehlken collection, Illinois; photograph by Bruce Filbrandt.

PLATE 490: ¼ *groove axe*, Archaic, from DeKalb County, Missouri. It is made of grey hardstone and has good design and a well-polished lower blade area. Size 2¼" x 3⅝" x 6½" long. A good, large Missouri axe. Courtesy William Gehlken collection, Illinois; photograph by Bruce Filbrandt.

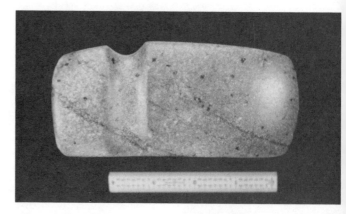

PLATE 491: *Half-groove axe*, no information as to state but probably from the Iowa region. It is well-detailed, and made from mottled greenish hardstone with a good polish. It is 2¾" x 4⅝", has fluted sides and is ex-collections of Burkett and Gerber. Courtesy Bruce Filbrandt collection, Iowa.

PLATE 492: ¼ *groove axe*, Archaic period, from DeKalb County, Missouri. It is made of grey granite with green stripes, a very attractive material. It has good overall polish and is 1½" x 2⅝" x 5¼" long. Courtesy William Gehlken collection, Illinois; photograph by Bruce Filbrandt.

PLATE 493: ¾ *groove axe*, Archaic, from Lee County, Iowa. It is made of grey hardstone, is deeply grooved and has a highly polished lower blade area. Size, 1⁷⁄₁₆" x 2⅜" x 4⅝" long. This is a very well-made Iowa axe. Courtesy William Gehlken collection, Illinois; photograph by Bruce Filbrandt.

PLATE 494: ¾ *groove axe*, Archaic period, from Wapello County, Iowa. It is made of black hardstone, is very deeply grooved and highly polished. This fine example measures 1⅞" x 2⅝" x 5¾" long. Courtesy William Gehlken collection, Illinois; photograph by Bruce Filbrandt.

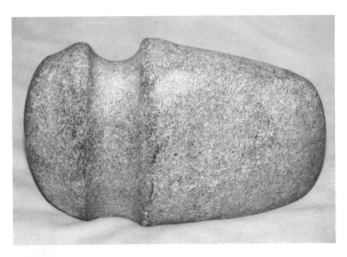

PLATE 496: ¾ *groove axe*, Archaic period, from Mercer County, Illinois. It is made of a quality grey hardstone and the lower blade area was resharpened in prehistoric times. A fine Illinois axe in all aspects, size 2¾" x 5" x 8½" long. Courtesy William Gehlken collection, Illinois; photograph by Bruce Filbrandt.

PLATE 497: *St. Charles or Dovetail blade*, Early Archaic, from Rock Island County, Illinois. This is a good-quality specimen, ³⁄₁₆" x 1¼" x 3½" long. Material is a blackish flint. Courtesy William Gehlken collection, Illinois; Lane Freyermuth, photographer.

PLATE 495: *Basal notch type Dovetail*, Early Archaic knife, made from Carter Cave flint from Kentucky. This artifact is from Barren County, Kentucky, and is 2¾" x 4¾". One ear was broken and reworked anciently. Courtesy Blake Gahagan collection, Tennessee.

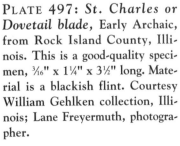

PLATE 498: *Large blade,* probably Archaic period, from Rock Island County, Illinois. It is made from a cream and tan flint, and is ⅞" x 2⅜" x 6⅜" long. This is a fine blade, well-chipped in good material. Courtesy William Gehlken collection, Illinois; Lane Freyermuth, photographer.

PLATE 499: *Large blade,* probably Archaic, from Henry County, Illinois. It is made of mottled tan and brown flint and is ½" x 2⅜" x 7" long. Courtesy William Gehlken collection, Illinois; Lane Freyermuth, photographer.

PLATE 500: *Thebes blade,* Early Archaic, from Rock Island County, Illinois. It is made from cream and brown chert and is ⅜" x 1⅝" x 5" long. This knife is unusually long. Courtesy William Gehlken collection, Illinois; Lane Freyermuth, photographer.

PLATE 501: *Godar point or blade,* from Rock Island County, Illinois, Archaic period. It is made of white chert and measures ⁵⁄₁₆" x 1⅛" x 3" long. This is a solid, good-quality early piece. Courtesy William Gehlken collection, Illinois; Lane Freyermuth, photographer.

PLATE 502: *Archaic side-notch,* probably Early Archaic, made of caramel-cream flint. From Rock Island County, Illinois, this fine specimen is ³⁄₁₆" x 1⁵⁄₁₆" x 5¼" long. It is an exceptionally well-made artifact. Courtesy William Gehlken collection, Illinois; Lane Freyermuth, photographer.

PLATE 503: *Hardin point or blade,* Early Archaic, from Rock Island County, Illinois. It is made of tan chert, and is ¼" x 1¼" x 3¾" long. This is a good-quality early artifact. Courtesy William Gehlken collection, Illinois; Lane Freyermuth, photographer.

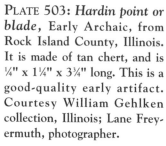

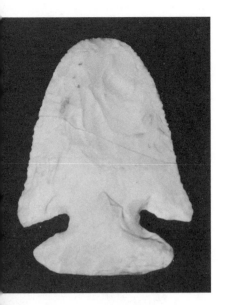

PLATE 504: *Thebes blade*, Early Archaic, made of white flint. It is from Henry County, Illinois, and is ⅜" x 2½" x 3¼" long. Note the rounded tip, indicative of specialized knife use. Courtesy William Gehlken collection, Illinois; Lane Freyermuth, photographer.

PLATE 505: *Thebes blade*, Early Archaic, material a mottled white chert. It is from Tama County, Iowa, and ⁵⁄₁₆" x 1¼" x 3⁵⁄₁₆" long. This is a sturdy and attractive early knife form. Courtesy William Gehlken collection, Illinois; Lane Freyermuth, photographer.

PLATE 506: *Thebes blade*, Early Archaic, Scott County, Iowa. made of tan chert, this wide blade is ⅜" x 2⅛" x 3³⁄₁₆" long. Judging from the excurvate edges, this artifact was not frequently resharpened. Courtesy William Gehlken collection, Illinois; Lane Freyermuth, photographer.

PLATE 507: *Corner-notch blade*, probably Archaic, from Rock Island County, Illinois. It is made of grey and tan flint and is ⁹⁄₁₆" x 2" x 4" long. Courtesy William Gehlken collection, Illinois; Lane Freyermuth, photographer.

PLATE 508: *Hardin Barbed point or blade*, Early Archaic, from Mercer County, Illinois. Made of high-grade tan chert, this piece measures ⅜" x 1½" x 3" long. Courtesy William Gehlken collection, Illinois; Lane Freyermuth, photographer.

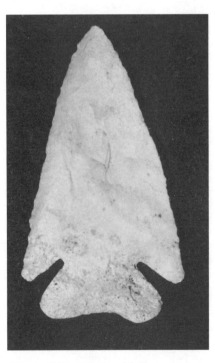

PLATE 509: *Thebes blade*, tan chert material, from Tama County, Iowa. It measures ⅜" x 2⅝" x 4¼" long. This specimen is a well-designed and strong early knife blade. Courtesy William Gehlken collection, Illinois; Lane Freyermuth, photographer.

PLATE 510: *Side-notch point or blade,* Archaic period, with generous notching and edge-serrations. Made of white flint, it is from Rock Island County, Illinois. Size is ¼" x 1⅛" x 3¼". Courtesy William Gehlken collection, Illinois; Lane Freyermuth, photographer.

PLATE 511: *Side-notch point or blade,* Archaic period, from Rock Island County, Illinois. Made of white flint, this measures ⅜" x 1¼" x 3¾" long. Note the tapered tip. Courtesy William Gehlken collection, Illinois; Lane Freyermuth, photographer.

PLATE 512: *Thebes blade,* Early Archaic, tan chert with brown spotting. From Tama County, Iowa, this piece is ⁵⁄₁₆" x 1¾" x 3¾" long. As with most Thebes, it has beveled edges. William Gehlken collection, Illinois; Courtesy Lane Freyermuth, photographer.

PLATE 513: *Sedalia point or blade,* Late Archaic, material a mottled tan chert. It is from Pettis County, Missouri, and ⅜" x 1¼" x 6¼". Courtesy William Gehlken collection, Illinois; Lane Freyermuth, photographer.

PLATE 514: *Sedalia point or blade,* brown and tan chert, from DeKalb County, Missouri. It is ⅜" x 1¾" x 4½" long. Courtesy William Gehlken collection, Illinois; Lane Freyermuth, photographer.

PLATE 515: *Large blade*, probably Archaic, found in Muscatine County, Iowa. It is made of cream and tan chert and is ex-collection of Hirl. Size, ⅜" x 2⅛" x 4¼" long. Courtesy Jim Roberson collection, Muscatine, Iowa.

PLATE 517: *Thebes blade*, Early Archaic, found in Muscatine County, Iowa. It is made of fossiliferous chert, cream-colored, and is ex-collection of Paul. Size is ⁵⁄₁₆" x 2" x 4⅜". This is a large and fine specimen, with the typical family trait, the beveled edge. Courtesy Jim Roberson collection, Muscatine, Iowa.

PLATE 516: *St. Charles or Dovetail points or blades,* from southern Illinois and southern Missouri. These specimens, in light to dark cherts, range in length from 3⅝" to 5⅝". All are excellent regional type examples. Courtesy the Guy Brothers collection, Pickneyville, Illinois.

PLATE 518: *Table Rock or Bottleneck point or blade*, made of a heat-treated multi-colored chert. Late Archaic, it is 1" x 2⅛" and was a personal find by the owner in St. Louis County, Missouri, on March 1, 1987. Courtesy Aaron Rampani collection, St. Ann, St. Louis County, Missouri.

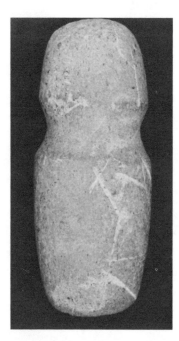

PLATE 519: *Grooved adz*, Archaic, made of a high-grade green granite. It is 2¾" x 6¼", and a very uncommon piece wherever found. This was a personal find by the owner in St. Charles County, Missouri, on March 7, 1990. The specimen is well-made with very good lines. Rare piece. Courtesy Aaron Rampani collection, St. Ann, St. Louis County, Missouri.

PLATE 520: *Half-groove Keokuk axe*, from near the city limits of Muscatine, Iowa. This fine piece was found by Paul Witt, Sr., in 1989. Material is a dark speckled hardstone which took a very high polish. Axe size is 3¼" at the lower blade width, and 5½" long. Weight is about 2½ pounds. Courtesy Paul Donald Witt collection, Barrington, Illinois.

PLATE 521: *Etley point or blade*, Late Archaic, made of tan Burlington chert. It is 1⅜" x 6" long, good length for this classic type piece. Fine work-style adds to beauty. This was found in Lincoln County, Missouri. Courtesy Aaron Rampani collection, St. Ann, St. Louis County, Missouri.

PLATE 522: *Wadlow blade*, made of a tan Burlington chert with good overall patina. A Late Archaic piece, it is 2" x 4½". This fine artifact was a personal find by the owner in St. Charles County, Missouri, on August 22, 1987. Courtesy Aaron Rampani collection, St. Ann, St. Louis County, Missouri.

PLATE 523: *Matanzas point or blade*, made of red chert with good patina. It is a Late Archaic piece, 1" x 2⅝". This was a personal find by the owner on May 28, 1990, in St. Charles County, Missouri. Courtesy Aaron Rampani collection, St. Ann, St. Louis County, Missouri.

Chapter IV
The Mound Builders

Woodland Period (1000 BC - AD 800)

By sometime around the year 1000 BC, 3000 years ago, the Amerind lifeway in the Midwest had changed yet again. Even beyond making full use of natural food supplies, the people to some extent had learned to control and shape nature. The hallmarks of Woodland times in the Midwest are ceramics (pottery) and agriculture, plus to some extent larger, permanent villages, some approaching small towns in size.

Pottery was fairly important, because it allowed new ways to cook food, such as broths and soups. Too, small fish and meat scraps could now be boiled so little food went to waste. However, the main importance of pottery may have been storing food, protecting it from insects and spoilage for the lean times of winter. Of prime significance was the development of agriculture, and beans and squash were widely grown. No doubt as a result of observing plant reproduction cycles, the Woodland folk soon learned to plant, tend and harvest foods that were a more assured harvest than were wild foods alone.

A concentration and emphasis on agriculture meant many things other than a dependable food source, which at first probably only supplemented what was gathered from the wild. Probably, with less time spent hunting and gathering (though these continued) true leisure time seems to have been in abundance. There was an increase in artistic endeavors. Possibly a class society emerged, with certain people or groups of people concentrating on what they did best. And, since proximity to fields was important for regular care (watering, weeding) and protection against hungry birds and animals, hamlets or villages made economic sense. And there was no need or desire to move about frequently, when moving meant leaving productive growing plots. Agriculture, however primitive, not only made possible a fairly sedentary lifeway, but to some degree required it.

The Adena (ca. 800 BC - AD 100) were the first major people of the Woodland period. They constructed sturdy houses and put up conical mounds on higher ground, with such earthworks sometimes containing burials. Mounds built by the Adena, and the Red Ochre people of about the same time or a little before, may have been inspired by the natural knolls that served as cemeteries for the Glacial Kame peoples of the Late Archaic. Another diagnostic Adena earthwork was the small circle, sometimes with a mound at the center, sometimes with an opening or gateway in the circle. There is a theory that some of the circles might have been bases for palisaded walls enclosing important fields or households.

Artifacts of the Adena included hardstone celts or ungrooved axe-heads of several well-made kinds, plus many adz forms. Celts were somewhat narrowed at one end so they would better wedge into the heavy, one-piece hardwood handle. Points and blades were stemmed, and there are half a dozen types, most medium-large in size. As with many prehistoric artifacts of this type, however, size depends partly on how they were originally made and partly on how much they were used and resharpened. Cache blades were made and sometimes deposited in the ground. These were long, unstemmed, and with rounded bases. They are sometimes referred to as leaf-shaped.

The Adena, like the Archaic peoples before them, used the Atl-atl or lance-thrower. This was a wooden stick some 16 to 24 inches long, with a handle at one end and a catch or hook at the other. This hook engaged the butt end of a light lance or javelin. When the lance was thrown, the Atl-atl was retained in the hand and another lance placed in position to throw. The apparatus acted as an extension to the arm and gave more speed and power to the cast. The device may have added about 50 percent to throwing distance, estimated to be 50 to 75 yards. Good accuracy, however, was probably somewhat less.

Other artifacts, today misnamed gorgets, were associated with the Atl-atl in Adena times, as they were in Archaic times. These were usually made of glacial slate, though many other materials were also employed. Gorgets are long, wide and flattish, with a length range of 3 to 7 inches. Most are drilled through the center, with the holes equidistant from the ends. While many examples have two holes, one or three or more are known. A major Adena gorget type was the expanded-center, wide and thick at center and tapering to narrow ends. Many of this type were undrilled, and may have been lashed and/or glued to the Atl-atl.

A characteristic of many Adena gorgets of whatever kind is uniface drilling, done mainly from the flat base or bottom. The emerging hole on the upper face or top was thus relatively small and unobtrusive. Gorgets probably served as counter-balance weights when the lance was held in throwing position.

Adena pipes were mainly tubular forms, in styles

ranging from simple tubes to graceful examples with flared mouth-pieces. Materials were mainly fine-grained sandstone or limestone, but various pipestones were also used. A few effigy tubular pipes were made. Some ornaments of sheet-copper were turned out, and decorative jewelry was made from bone and shell. Many pottery vessels were made, some relatively thick and not as refined as some later ceramics.

The second important people of Woodland times were the Hopewell (ca. 100 BC - AD 500). This people or religion or culture (it has been considered all these things, and more) may have developed from the Adena, or may have gradually produced a distinct lifeway on their own. They too had villages and bark-covered huts with pole frameworks, and practiced agriculture. The Hopewell society must have been strongly led, for no other Native American people before or after them worked so hard to move the earth about, undertaking one massive project after another.

Two different kinds of earthworks were built, and each can be separated into a number of categories. One was the basic mound, erected on higher elevations of river valleys, and some of them served as burial sites. Often Hopewell mounds deviated from the simple conical shape and were oblong, rectangular or of unusual shapes. And while Adena mounds tend to be medium to high, Hopewell mounds were often low to medium height. Such mounds might be single, isolated examples similar to the Adena, or might be set up in small or large interrelated groups.

The second type of earthworks were the gigantic walls, which the old-time writers usually referred to as "fortifications." These in turn seem to have been either ceremonial, or walled hilltops. Some of the former were gigantic, with complexes that covered several square miles. Many of these were put up in the Eastern Midwest, notably Ohio. One of the finest — a series of geometric figures, parallel walls and mounds — exists at Newark, Ohio. Mound City Group National Monument north of Chillicothe, Ohio, is an example of a ceremonial group of mounds enclosed by a wall. Another large earthworks complex across the Scioto River from Mound City has been (September, 1990) acquired and may eventually be open to the public. There are additional Hopewell complexes at Marietta, and elsewhere in Ohio.

The Hopewell Indians, perhaps as their lifeway faded and fragmented into lesser-known groups of the Late Woodland times, built some of the enormous hilltop walls that dot the Eastern Midwest. Again in Ohio, Fort Ancient and Fort Hill are prime examples of sites that were probably both ceremonial and defensive. Finally, in Late Woodland times, small hilltop and blufftop walls were built, probably to protect small villages.

While the Hopewells are known for the elaborate ceremonial artifacts done in copper, mica, pipestone, obsidian and many other materials, everyday artifacts of plainer materials of course predominated. And these, mainly, are what have been surface-found throughout the Midwest for the past two hundred years. The most common artifacts are chipped points and blades, usually with large corner notches, excurvate sides and rounded base bottoms. High-quality cherts and flints were, it seems, purposely selected for such tools and weapons. Long, narrow and thin bladelets were also struck from prepared cores, and these were used as small knives. Wherever these are found they are the craft-mark of Hopewell times.

Celts or ungrooved axes were also made, and many forms have a basic rectangular shape, while others were cylindrical. Adzes were produced as well, and some copied celts in outline. Very many glacial slate ornaments were made, and some sophisticated types developed with the Hopewell. These include the boat- and reel- shaped, and pentagonal or shield-shaped. As with the Adena, many of the pendants are large and finely made. A range of multi-holed gorgets or Atl-atl stones was created, including an expanded-center variety similar to the Adena, but with only one hole at center.

The Hopewell people seem to have faded away around AD 500, at the approximate time that something else happened in the Midwest. That was the advent of widespread bow-and-arrow use. The technology of the bow was a great leap forward in some ways, and certainly made hunting and warfare easier. Whether the coming of the bow and the collapse of the Hopewell are related is still an open question.

After the Hopewells and still in Late Woodland times, a number of minor cultures came and went in the Midwest. Some put up small mounds in or near villages, while others fortified sites easy to defend. The low walls instead of surrounding a large site, often simply meandered along the flat portion of a small bluff, the remaining steep sides apparently enough natural protection.

One very interesting Late Woodland group in the Eastern Midwest was the Intrusive Mound people. They seemed not to have erected their own mounds, but buried their dead in pre-existing Early and Middle Woodland mounds. Their distinctive artifacts — ceremonial picks, raised stem-hole platform pipes, several point types, bone or antler harpoons — only rarely are found on village sites.

In the Woodland era in the Midwest, for the first time, Amerinds probably relied less on hunting and gathering and more on growing plants. They, at least in part, left the forests for the fields.

PLATE 524: *Hopewell point or blade*, Middle Woodland period, and made of an unusual material, Knife River flint. This is translucent amber with cloudy white inclusions. It is 1½" x 2½", and was a personal find by the owner in St. Charles County, Missouri, on September 3, 1989. Courtesy Aaron Rampani collection, St. Ann, St. Louis County, Missouri.

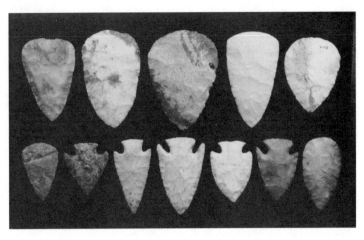

PLATE 527: *North and Snyders blades*, Hopewell period, Middle Woodland. The North (un-notched) may be the preform while the Snyders is the finished blade, with larger corner notches. These pieces are from Indiana, Illinois and Missouri, and material is heat-treated chert. Smallest blade is 1¼" x 2½", the largest 3⅜" x 4½". Courtesy Aaron Rampani collection, St. Ann, St. Louis County, Missouri.

PLATE 525: *Waubesa point or blade*, tan Burlington chert, found in St. Louis County, Missouri. It is 1¼" x 3⅛"", and Middle Woodland ca 100 BC - AD 350. This is a superbly made piece with good lines, and in a quality material. Courtesy Aaron Rampani collection, St. Ann, St. Louis County, Missouri.

PLATE 528: *Snyders blades*, Hopewell and Middle Woodland, these examples made of heat-treated cherts and Indiana hornstone or Harrison County flint. Examples are from Indiana, Illinois and Missouri. The smallest is 1¾" x 2⅞", the largest 2¾" x 4⅛". Courtesy Tom Razmus collection, Georgetown, Illinois.

PLATE 526: *Pendant*, banded slate, Woodland period. This was a personal field-find by the owner in the spring of 1989. Size is 1⅝" x 3¼", and the artifact is nicely shaped, marked and drilled. When found in the field, there was a root growing through the pendant hole. This came from Vermillion County, Indiana. Courtesy Tom Razmus collection, Georgetown, Illinois.

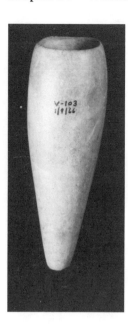

PLATE 529: *Tubular pipe*, Adena culture of the Early Woodland, carefully crafted from what may be high-grade limestone. This was a personal field-find by the owner in Vermillion County, Indiana, on January 9, 1966. Size is 1⅜" x 4⅜" for this fine and rare piece. Courtesy Tom Razmus collection, Georgetown, Illinois.

PLATE 531: *Decorative artifacts*, recovered during a salvage operation in northern Ohio in 1950. Of interest are the beads, cannel-coal objects, whelk shell pendant or gorget and whelk or conch large drilled beads. Ca. Late Woodland. Courtesy Steve Puttera Jr. collection, Ohio.

PLATE 530: *Hopewell double-notched blade*, Middle Woodland period. This came from Vermillion County, Indiana, and is made of snow white chert; size is 1¼" x 7¾". The find was made in two sections. The base was found by Stanley Razmus on June 4, 1975, while the point section was recovered by Tom Razmus on June 6, 1975. This is a very rare blade type. Courtesy Tom Razmus collection, Georgetown, Illinois.

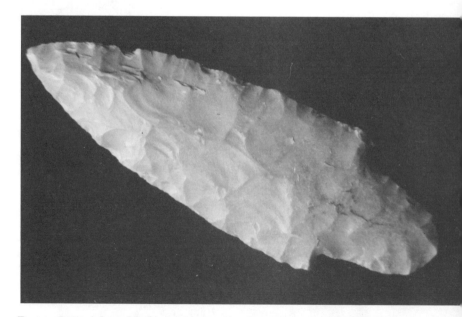

PLATE 532: *Adena blade*, Early Woodland period, from Vermillion County, Indiana. It was a personal field-find by the owner in the spring of 1990. Size is 1¼" x 3⅞" and material is Indiana grey hornstone or Harrison County flint. Courtesy Tom Razmus collection, Georgetown, Illinois.

PLATE 533: *Adena slate artifacts*, Early Woodland, and all from one site near Lake Erie in Ottawa County, Ohio. These were found in a two-year period, 1985-1987. There is a wide range of types and materials, mostly glacial slate. All were found by Steve Puttera Sr. and Steve Puttera Jr. Courtesy Steve Puttera Jr. collection, Ohio.

PLATE 536: *Pendants*, Late Woodland affiliation, found on the west bank of the Cuyahoga River, Cuyahoga County, Ohio. Left, miniature form that is grooved on both faces. Right, miniature form that has engraving on both faces. Courtesy Steve Puttera Jr. collection, Ohio.

PLATE 534: *Black Creek blade*, preform to the Mason point or blade, Early Woodland and ca. 1000-500 BC. This very large blade, size 3" x 8", is made of black Zaleski flint and is from Washington County, Ohio. Ex-collections of B.W. Stephens, Gray LaDassor, Jim Carskadden, Dave Howard and Paul Sellers. Reference, Perino, *Selected Preforms, Points and Knives...*pp 37, 243. Courtesy Steve Puttera Jr. collection, Ohio.

PLATE 537: *Quadri-concave gorget*, Adena (Early Woodland) period, found near the confluence of Tinkers Creek and the Cuyahoga River, Cuyahoga County, Ohio. Material is maroon and black slate, and size is 2½" x 3¼". Courtesy Steve Puttera Jr. collection, Ohio.

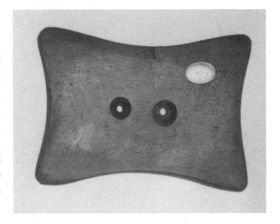

PLATE 535: *Celts*, Woodland period, both Ohio. Left, granite, socketed type with slight grooving on both upper faces. Size, 3" x 6¼", northern Ohio and ex-collection of William Bush. This is a superb piece with high polish. Right, pink and black speckled granite from near Chardon, Geauga County. It is 2½" x 6⅛", collected by C.T. Crocker in 1938. Courtesy Steve Puttera Jr. collection, Ohio.

PLATE 538: *Hardstone adz,* probably Woodland period, the material here a dark green granite. The adz is from Lewis County, Missouri, and is 1¾" x 5⅝". One face is rounded and the opposite face is flat; it has good use-polish in the blade area. A nicely made specimen. Courtesy collection of Bob Rampani, Bridgeton, St. Louis County, Missouri.

PLATE 540: *Bell-shaped pendant,* from Summit County, Ohio. This was collected by Mr. Belden in the 1920's. This has beautiful form and the banded slate is in purple, black and grey. All edges are tally-marked, and there are about 189 tallies. This is a superb piece in every way. Adena. Courtesy Steve Puttera Jr. collection, Ohio.

PLATE 541: *Full groove axe,* found by D. Dennison near the Spoon River in Stark County, Illinois. It is hard to explain the very high degree of polish on this axe. Size, 5½" x 7½", and weight is about six pounds. Courtesy Bruce Filbrandt collection, Iowa.

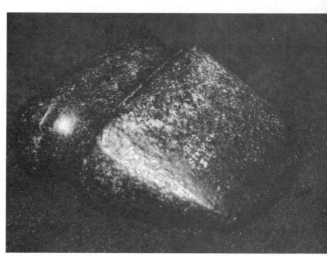

PLATE 539: *Celt,* Woodland period and possibly Hopewell, a personal find by the owner on Feb. 28, 1988. It came from near U.S. 61 in Muscatine County, Iowa. This celt has fluted sides and spots, possibly porphyry, and is a beautiful artifact. Well-polished, the celt is 2½" x 5", and is 1½" thick. Courtesy Virginia Filbrandt collection, Iowa.

PLATE 542: *Celt,* probably Woodland period, from Henry County, Illinois. It is made of colorful spotted hardstone and is 1⅞" x 3½" x 9¼" long. This is a very fine specimen in all important ways. Courtesy William Gehlken collection, Illinois; photograph by Bruce Filbrandt.

PLATE 543: *Adena Leaf-shaped blade*, Early Woodland period, a very unusual blade for area of finding. It was a personal find by the owner, 1983, in Louisa County, Iowa. Material is Burlington chert in white, tan and grey with crystal inclusions. Blade size is ½" x 2⁹⁄₁₆" x 6" long. It has two opposing pairs of shallow side notches, also unusual. Courtesy Jim Roberson collection, Muscatine, Iowa.

PLATE 544: *Jersey Bluff pipe*, reddish pottery, Late Woodland period. This is ca. AD 450-1200 and is from Jersey County, Illinois. Courtesy Gregory L. Perdun collection, Illinois.

PLATE 545: *Hopewell platform pipe*, Middle Woodland period, found near Phills Creek, Jersey County, Illinois. Even though heavily damaged, this pipe is a rare form. Courtesy Gregory L. Perdun collection, Illinois.

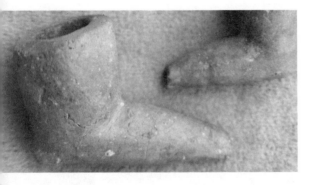

PLATE 546: *Pottery pipes*, elbow-type, Late Woodland period. These grit-tempered examples are from Calhoun County, Illinois. Courtesy Gregory L. Perdun collection, Illinois.

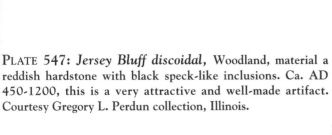

PLATE 547: *Jersey Bluff discoidal*, Woodland, material a reddish hardstone with black speck-like inclusions. Ca. AD 450-1200, this is a very attractive and well-made artifact. Courtesy Gregory L. Perdun collection, Illinois.

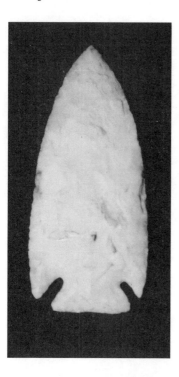

PLATE 548: *Corner-notch,* possibly a fairly rare Hopewell blade (Middle Woodland) sometimes found in caches. It is made of white flint, is from Rock Island County, Illinois, and size is ¼" x 1¼" x 2¾". Characteristics include deep, careful notching, overall fine workstyle and thinness. Courtesy William Gehlken collection, Illinois; Lane Freyermuth, photographer.

PLATE 551: *Creased-poll celt,* probabl[y] Woodland, from Rock Island County, Illinois. I[t] is made of very colorful mottled hardstone an[d] has a well-polished bit. Size is 2" x 3⅞". Thi[s] uncommon celt form has one or more shor[t] incised lines or creases at or near the poll top[.] Courtesy William Gehlken collection, Illinois[;] Lane Freyermuth, photographer.

PLATE 549: *Celt,* probably Woodland, made of a highly unusual celt material, porphyry. It is a well-made piece, from Rock Island County, Illinois. Size is 3" x 4⅞" long. Courtesy William Gehlken collection, Illinois; photograph by Bruce Filbrandt.

PLATE 550: *Waubesa point or blade,* Middle Woodland period. From Louisa County, Iowa, it is 4⅞" long and made from a fossiliferous chert material. Note the unusual extended shoulder tips that may be the result of heavy upper blade resharpening, or original design. Courtesy Gary Klebe collection, Muscatine, Iowa.

PLATE 552: *Quadriconcave gorget,* Adena and Early Woodland, material a red stone. It is from Mercer County, Illinois, and measures ¼" x 2" x 2¼". Courtesy William Gehlken collection, Illinois; Lane Freyermuth, photographer.

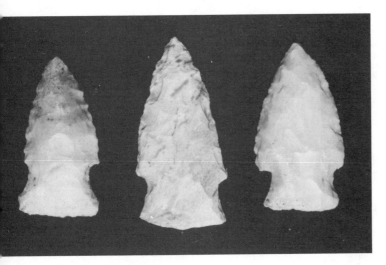

PLATE 553: *Steuben points*, Middle-Late Woodland period, all found in Rock Island County, Illinois. Length range is 1¾" to 2⅛". Material is cream-colored chert with occasional dark shading. Courtesy Lane Freyermuth collection, Iowa.

PLATE 554: *Squared-stem Adena points or blades*, Early Woodland. Left, Rock Island County, Illinois, 2⅞". Middle, 2⅞", Allamakee County, Iowa, colorful material. Right, Rock Island County, Illinois, 2⅝" long. Courtesy Lane Freyermuth collection, Iowa.

PLATE 556: *Celt*, Woodland period, found in Mercer County, Illinois. Size is 1¼" x 2⅛" x 4¼", and material is a dark mottled hardstone. Courtesy Lane Freyermuth collection, Iowa.

PLATE 555: *Stemmed Adena points or blades*, Early Woodland period. All are from Rock Island County, Illinois, and range in size from 2¼" to 2½" long. There is a wide range of colorful material here. Courtesy Lane Freyermuth collection, Iowa.

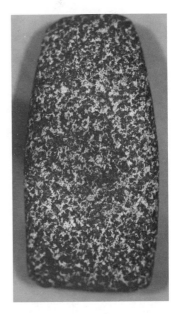

PLATE 557: *Celt*, probably Woodland period, found in Rock Island County, Illinois. Size is 1⅛" x 2½" x 5⅛" long. Material is a speckled hardstone. Courtesy Lane Freyermuth collection, Iowa.

PLATE 560: *Adz*, probably Woodland, found in Mercer County, Illinois. Dimensions are 1" x 1¾" x 5" long. Courtesy Lane Freyermuth collection, Iowa.

PLATE 558: *Celts*, Woodland period, both from Mercer County, Illinois. Left, 1" x 1⅝" x 3½", with a shallow groove on one side. Right, 1" x 1⅞" x 3¾", with expanded bit. Courtesy Lane Freyermuth collection, Iowa.

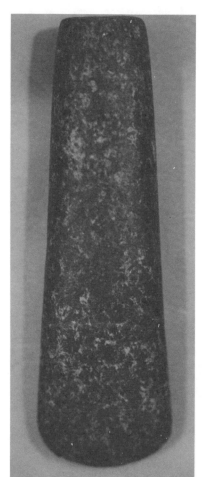

PLATE 561: *Dickson point or blade*, Woodland period, material a cream-colored chert. It is from Henry County, Illinois, and size is ¼" x 1¾" x 3⅞". This piece is quite thin for size, and edges appear to have had use. Courtesy William Gehlken collection, Illinois; Lane Freyermuth, photographer.

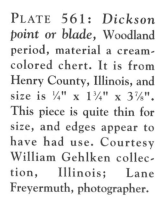

PLATE 559: *Spud-like celt*, possibly Late Woodland, found in Iowa. It is made of high-grade mottled hardstone and is ¹⁵⁄₁₆" x 1⅝" x 5½" long. Courtesy Lane Freyermuth collection, Iowa.

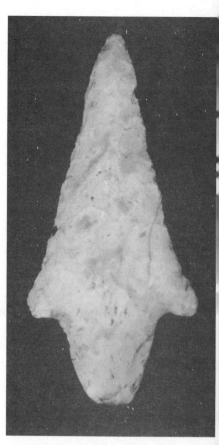

PLATE 562: *Dickson point or blade,* Woodland period, from Henry County, Illinois. It is made of white flint and size is ⅟₁₆" x 1½" x 3¾" This extremely thin artifact has good lines and indented stem base found on some varieties. Courtesy William Gehlken collection, Illinois; Lane Freyermuth, photographer.

PLATE 563: *Dickson point or blade,* Woodland period, from Henry County, Illinois. Material is pink-grey-cream chert for this highly colored artifact. Size is ⅜" x 1¾" x 4¾". Courtesy William Gehlken collection, Illinois; Lane Freyermuth, photographer.

PLATE 566: *Copper celt,* probably Woodland era, the only one the owner knows to be from the area of finding, Clinton County, Iowa. It is a well-made piece pounded from raw copper. Size 2" x 2½", and the bit area is well-worn and/or polished. Courtesy Bruce Filbrandt collection, Iowa.

PLATE 564: *Hopewell celt,* Middle Woodland, made of green speckled porphyry. Size, 3" x 5¾", found by Bill Bodine near the Lamine River, Cooper County, Missouri, in 1972. Courtesy Steve Puttera Jr. Collection, Ohio.

PLATE 565: *Peisker Diamond blades,* a cache found near Loami in Sangamon County, Illinois. (See Perino, *Selected Points and Blades...*p 294.) These are Black Sand from the Early Woodland, ca. 500-150 BC. The longest blade of this rare grouping is 6". Courtesy Eldon Launer collection, Illinois.

PLATE 567: *Ceremonial pick,* Late Woodland Intrusive Mound people, a very rare artifact from Boone County, Iowa. Material is a black diorite-like stone and it has good patina and polish. Size, 1⅜" x 9" long. The hafting area (lighter-color ring) is of interest. A highly unusual and high-grade artifact wherever found in the Midwest. Courtesy Bruce Filbrandt collection, Iowa.

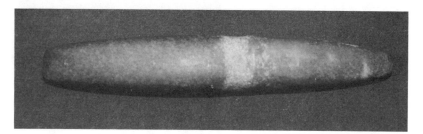

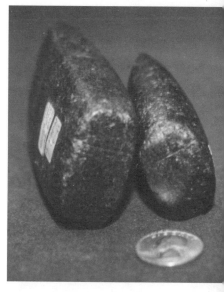

PLATE 570: *Creased-poll celts,* a rare form probably from Woodland times. The small lines are visible on left example about one-third distance from top corner, and on right about one-forth distance from the top corner. No one knows what the marks were used for. Both are from Fulton County, Illinois. Small, 1¼" x 3⅜"; large, 2½" x 5⅛". Courtesy Bruce Filbrandt collection, Iowa.

PLATE 568: *Celt,* probably Woodland, a very high grade piece. This is believed to be the finest celt to come from Peoria County, Illinois, and is ex-collection of Marion Knotts. The celt was found in 1949 and a .22 rifle was traded for it. The material is black hardstone with a tan-white inclusion. Size, 1¼" x 3" x 7⅜" long. Superb celt. Courtesy Bruce Filbrandt collection, Iowa.

PLATE 571: *Square-sided celt,* a personal find by the owner in 1971 near Le Claire, Iowa. It is black and grey in color, and has very high polish. This Woodland artifact measures 2½" x 5½". Courtesy Bruce Filbrandt collection, Iowa.

PLATE 569: *Square-sided celt,* probably Woodland, found in 1956 in Scott County, Iowa. The example is from a site on the Mississippi River. Material is a dense black hardstone and sides, faces and bit area are well-polished. The celt is 2¼" wide at bit, 3¼" wide at midsection, and 7¼" long. Courtesy Bruce Filbrandt collection, Iowa.

PLATE 572: *Knife blade*, possibly Woodland, a personal find by the owner on March 5, 1976. It came from a rise above the Salt River in Mercer County, Kentucky. This blade is made of high-grade multicolor flint and is 2¼" x 4⅞" long. Courtesy Michael Darland collection, Kentucky.

PLATE 573: *Adena pendants*, Early Woodland, both found on April 19, 1985, in Ottawa County, Ohio. Left, biconcave type, grey and black banded slate, 4½" high, found by Stephen Puttera Sr. Right, rare effigy-like form, grey and black banded slate, 1⅝" x 2¾", found by Steve Puttera, Jr. Courtesy Steve Puttera Jr. collection, Ohio.

PLATE 574: *Hopewell celt*, Middle Woodland, 2½" x 7¼". Material is an attractive and durable granite in hues of black, green and pink. It was found in the spring of 1984 along Killbuck Creek in Holmes County, Ohio, by Larry Blyland on his first trip surface-hunting. Courtesy Steve Puttera Jr. collection, Ohio.

PLATE 575: *Pipe*, probably Late Woodland period, found in Summit County, Ohio. This is a nicely shaped artifact, made of grey Ohio pipestone. Size, 2" x 3½" and collected by a Mr. Belden from Akron, prior to 1930. Courtesy Steve Puttera Jr. collection, Ohio.

PLATE 576: *Adena slate artifacts*, Ottawa County, Ohio. Left, found March 26, 1986, dark slate material, quadriconcave type, 2½" x 3¾". Center, found April 19, 1985, shown elsewhere in book. Right, biconcave gorget in black and maroon slate, 2½" x 4", found March 28, 1986. All three pieces found by Stephen Puttera Sr. Courtesy Steve Puttera Jr. collection, Ohio.

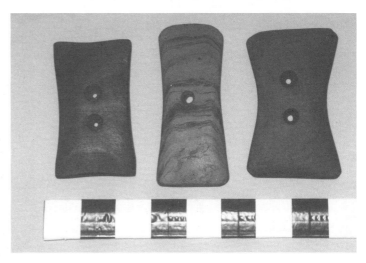

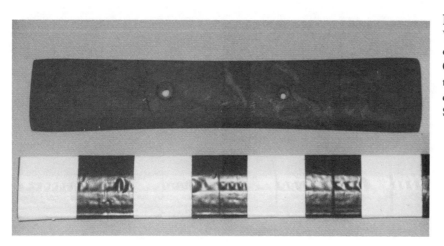

PLATE 577: *Bar-type gorget,* probably Woodland, with Adena-type drilling done from one side or face only. It is from Huron County, Ohio, and 1¼" x 6¾" long. Material is an attractive purple slate with white streaks. Ex-collection of John Sarnovsky. A very fine piece. Courtesy Steve Puttera Jr. collection, Ohio.

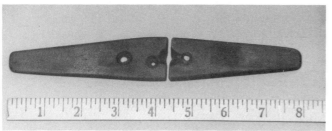

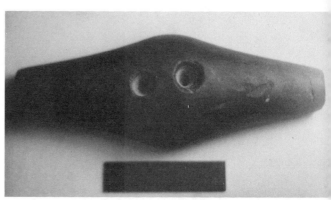

PLATE 578: *Adena gorget,* Early Woodland, rare elongated expanded-center type. It is 8" long and made of fine-grained polished sandstone. From Ohio, and ex-collections of Hovan and Tackett. Note the break through the original hole and the salvage drilling operation to either side. Courtesy Steve Puttera, Jr. collection, Ohio.

PLATE 580: *Adena expanded-center gorget,* probably from central Ohio, with 2" scale showing size. This piece, from the Early Woodland period, is nicely drilled but with unusually large holes on the obverse. Material is glacial slate with very light banding. Courtesy Lee Hallman collection, Pennsylvania.

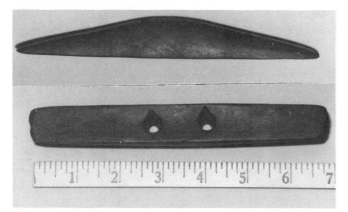

PLATE 579: *Boatstone or keeled gorget,* fine-grained black slate, side (top) and bottom (lower) views. This fine piece is 7" long and probably Woodland. From northern Ohio, it was collected by Archie and Pete Diller from the Fry collection, Sandusky, Ohio, in the early 1960's. An outstanding and scarce type. Courtesy Steve Puttera, Jr. collection, Ohio.

PLATE 581: *Bar amulet,* Early Woodland and possibly Red Ochre. These unusual elongated artifacts may have been the result of birdstone design. The 2" scale show size. This is a fine end-drilled piece in banded slate; provenance is simply "Ohio." Courtesy Lee Hallman collection, Pennsylvania.

PLATE 582: *Edged tool*, made of cannel coal, an unusual material. Probably a Woodland-era piece, it is ½" x 2" x 3¾" long. The artifact is well-polished, and from Seneca County, Ohio. Courtesy Marguerite L. Kernaghan collection, Colorado; photo by Marguerite & Stewart Kernaghan.

PLATE 585: *Pipe*, steatite, from Wabash County, Illinois. Woodland period, size is 1" x 2" x 4¾" for this Late Woodland example. It is ex-collection of Chalmer Lynch. Courtesy Marguerite L. Kernaghan collection, Colorado; photo by Marguerite & Stewart Kernaghan.

PLATE 583: *Celt*, probably Woodland period, made of mottled slate. It is ¾" x 2" x 5¾" long. This is a well-finished piece, and lighter-colored area is probably the hafting region. It is from Ohio. Courtesy Marguerite L. Kernaghan collection, Colorado; photo by Marguerite & Stewart Kernaghan.

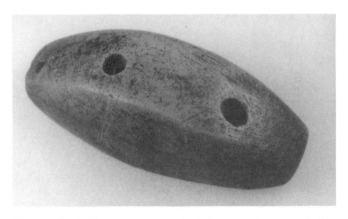

PLATE 586: *Boatstone*, two-holed gorget form, probably Woodland. It was found near Eagle Creek, Brown County, Ohio, and was a personal find by the owner. It is made of Ohio pipestone, is well-polished and drilled, and lightly engraved. Size is 1³⁄₁₆" x 2". A fine piece. Courtesy Donald E. Shuck collection, Ohio.

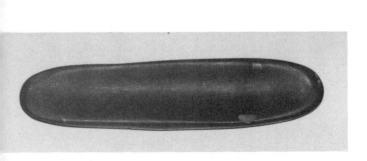

PLATE 584: *Boatstone*, undrilled, Woodland period. This example is from Livingston County, Kentucky, and is made of slate with pyrite inclusions. Size is 1" x 5". This artifact is ex-collection of B. Faith. Courtesy Marguerite L. Kernaghan collection, Colorado; photo by Marguerite & Stewart Kernaghan.

PLATE 587: *Rectangular celt*, probably Hopewell and Middle Woodland, from northern Campbell County, Kentucky. Material is a high grade of dark green hardstone, and size is 2" x 4¾". This celt was a personal find by the owner. Courtesy Donald E. Shuck collection, Ohio.

PLATE 588: *Ceremonial pick,* very nicely shaped specimen with an unusual angled blade and squared bit and tapered poll end. The material is diorite and the pick is 14½" long. This very rare piece is from the Newark, Ohio, area and is ex-coll. Dr. Meuser. Courtesy Charles West collection, Ohio.

PLATE 589: *Ceremonial pick,* Intrusive Mound culture, late Woodland. This fine specimen is made of highly polished dark hardstone and is 1⅛" x 12⅛" long. From Darke County, Ohio, it is ex-collection of Dr. Meuser. Courtesy Charles West collection, Ohio.

PLATE 590: *Celt,* probably Woodland and possibly Hopewellian, it is a finely shaped artifact made of speckled hardstone. This celt is from Clermont County, Ohio, and is 1¾" x 5" long. Courtesy Charles West collection, Ohio.

PLATE 591: *Tapered-poll celt,* Woodland period, made of near-black high-grade hardstone. It came from southern Adams County, Ohio, and measures 2½" x 5½". This fine piece with good polish was a personal find by the owner. Courtesy Donald E. Shuck collection, Ohio.

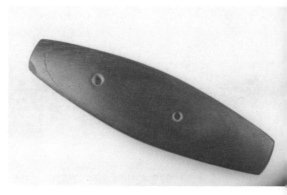

PLATE 592: *Gorget,* probably Woodland period, from Johnson County, Indiana. This is a very well-made piece, fully polished, accurately drilled. Material is unusual, red slate, and the gorget is 6⅝" long. Courtesy Charles West collection, Ohio.

PLATE 593: *Hardstone gorget,* material with slight banding or striations that are angled across the face. This artifact is from Scioto County, Ohio, and is 6⅜" long. The piece has well-placed and nearly matching holes, which add to symmetry and value. Courtesy Charles West collection, Ohio.

PLATE 594: *Cones,* Woodland period, top example of hardstone and from Clermont County, Ohio. Left, hematite cone, Boone County, Kentucky. Right, hematite, from Ohio, county unknown. Despite the fact that cones are fairly widespread finds in the Midwest, their actual purpose or use has never been certain. Courtesy Charles West collection, Ohio.

PLATE 595: *Hematite cones,* Woodland period, this material being various solid grades of natural iron ore. Bottom left and right specimens were highly polished. Top, Butler County, Ohio; left, Phelps County, Missouri; right, Clermont County, Ohio. Courtesy Charles West collection, Ohio.

PLATE 596: *Cone,* 1⅛" x 1⁷⁄₁₆", Woodland period. It is made of a very rare material, dark green nephrite jade. From Clinton County, Ohio, it is ex-collection of A.T. Wehrle. This is an attractive artifact with good polish. Private collection, Ohio.

PLATE 597: *Elongated ball bannerstone,* Archaic period, fluted on the base along the longitudinal axis. Material is an attractive olive-green banded hardstone or durable slate, and size is 1¹⁵⁄₁₆" x 2⅝". It is from Wood County, Ohio, and highly collectible. Private collection, Ohio.

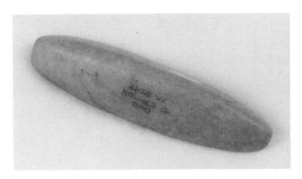

PLATE 598: *Boatstone,* or boat-shaped gorget, probably Woodland period, made of golden tan quartzite. This piece is 1⁷⁄₁₆" x 5⅜", and from Holmes County, Ohio. Ex-collection of A.T. Wehrle, it is undrilled but appears complete. This is an attractive artifact with polish. Private collection, Ohio.

PLATE 599: *Cone,* Woodland period, made of a pink quartzite. It is ¹⁵⁄₁₆" x 1¾", and has a deeply concave base (bottom or base shown in photo). From Ohio. Private collection, Ohio.

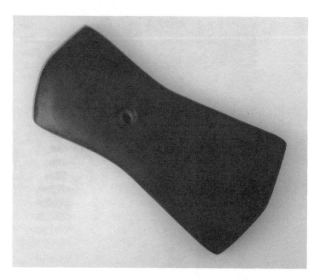

PLATE 600: *Pentagonal pendant,* Hopewell Indian (Middle Woodland), from Warren County, Ohio. It is made of slate and is 5⅝" long. This is a well-shaped piece, with nicely centered suspension hole in the upper portion. Courtesy Charles West collection, Ohio.

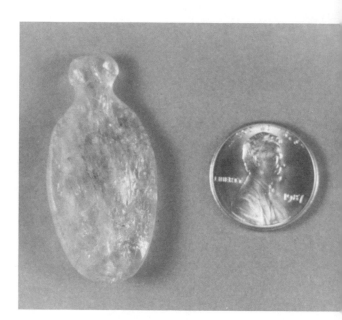

PLATE 602: *Knobbed pendant,* possibly Woodland, an unusual shape in an even more unusual material—clear crystal quartz. It is only ⅛" thick, and ¾" x 1½". It came from the Grove City area of Franklin County, Ohio, and is a delicate, sparkling little decoration. Private collection, Ohio.

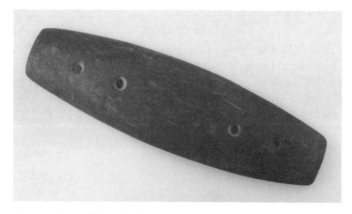

PLATE 601: *Four-hole gorget,* slate, from Russell County, Kentucky. Any gorget with other than the most common two holes (one, three, four, five, etc.) is unusual. This is a large (at 6½" long) and well-made artifact. Courtesy Charles West collection, Ohio.

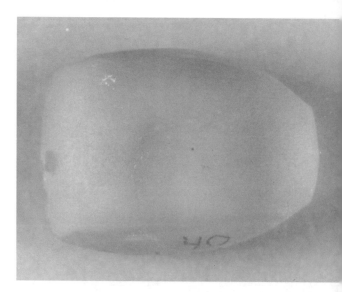

PLATE 603: *Celt or adz blade,* Woodland period, material a clear quartz crystal. It is 1⅛" x 1½" long, ex-collection of C.T. Love; it is from Hardin County, Ohio. Though small, the workstyle and especially the material make this a fine piece. Private collection, Ohio.

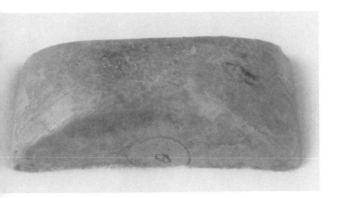

PLATE 604: *Semi-keeled gorget*, Adena and Early Woodland, made of tan-colored quartzite. It measures 1⅞" x ⅛" and is from Preble County, Ohio. The hole-drilling was started but not completed, not uncommon in such ultrahard material. Private collection, Ohio.

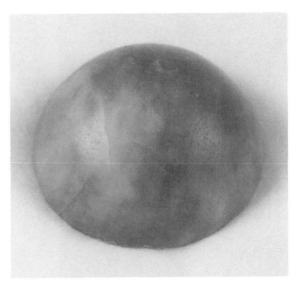

PLATE 606: *Cone*, or hemisphere, Woodland period, from Bond County, Illinois. It is made of rose and cream quartzite, a rare material for cones, and measures 1" x 2⁵⁄₁₆". There is a shallow indentation or pit in the polished base; this piece has fine polish and excellent coloring. Private collection, Ohio

PLATE 607: *Turkeytail point or blade*, Early Woodland (may also go back into Late Archaic), in grey Kentucky flint. From Butler County, Kentucky, this is the finest example from a cache of 25 found. It is 7½" long, with GIRS (Genuine Indian Relic Society) authentication #117. This is a superb example of a scarce Midwestern artifact type. Prehistoric art collection of John Baldwin, West Olive, Michigan.

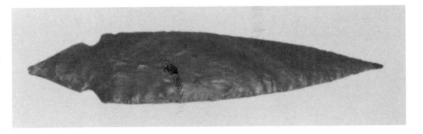

PLATE 605: *Convex gorget*, probably Woodland period, from Montgomery County, Ohio. It is made of speckled gneiss in black and cream; size is 1¹³⁄₁₆" x 4⅛". This hard-stone gorget is well-shaped and highly polished, with holes started but not completed. Ex-collection of Frank Williams. Private collection, Ohio.

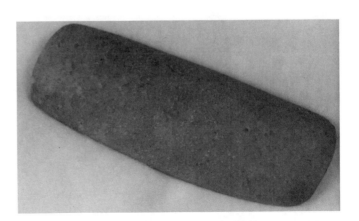

PLATE 608: *Rectangular gorget*, probably Woodland, this material is golden tan quartzite. It measures 1⅞" x 4⅞" and is from Hamilton County, Ohio. Though this piece is undrilled, it has some polish and may in fact be a fully finished piece. Private collection, Ohio.

PLATE 609: *Dickson point or blade,* Middle Woodland period. This is very similar to the Early Archaic Hidden Valley type, but the latter usually has strongly barbed shoulders and edge-serrations. This is a well-made example in a high-grade light-colored chert. Collection of Scott Dake; photograph by Victor A. Pierce, Missouri.

PLATE 612: *Rice Side-notch,* Late Woodland period, made of high-grade white chert. This is a very well-made example, in fine condition. Collection of Scott Dake; photograph by Victor A. Pierce, Missouri.

PLATE 613: *Turkeytail blade,* Early Woodland period, from Montgomery County, Ohio. It is made from Indiana hornstone or Harrison County Flint. This is a fine specimen, 4⅝" long. Courtesy Paul Rankin collection, Ohio; Del Hetrick, photographer.

PLATE 610: *Knife blade,* probably Woodland period, found in the bottomland along the Gasconade River in Missouri. This is a fine large example in quality light-colored chert. Collection of Scott Dake; photograph by Victor A. Pierce, Missouri.

PLATE 614: *Missouri points or blades,* mainly Woodland period. There is a very good range of types and materials here, typical of surface finds throughout the Midwest. Most examples are about 3" long. Collection of Dake, Noblett and Pierce; photograph by Victor A. Pierce, Missouri.

PLATE 611: *Missouri points or blades,* Woodland period. Left and right, Dickson knives; center, Rice Side-notched. All are late in the Woodland timeframe. Center, 2½". Collection of Scott Dake; photograph by Victor A. Pierce, Missouri.

PLATE 615: *Hopewell celts,* rounded-poll types, Middle Woodland period, both Ohio. Top, 1⅝" x 4¼", greenish hardstone, high polish, Darke County. Bottom, 2⅜" x 9", brownish hardstone, medium polish, Tuscarawas River Valley of Coshocton County. This is a large and well-made piece. Hothem collection, Ohio.

PLATE 618: *Bar amulet,* by Red Ochre people of the Early Woodland, this example from Ohio. It is 2⅞" long and made of Ohio pipestone from the lower Scioto Valley. Bar amulets have drilling at each end similar to that of most birdstones from the Late Archaic. Courtesy Charles West collection, Ohio.

PLATE 616: *Boatstone,* Woodland period, from Hardin County, Ohio. Material is a rare grey-beige translucent quartzite. This interesting and well-finished piece measures 1⅛" x 4¼" long. Two holes were started but not completed, and base bottom is concave and polished. Very collectible. Private collection, Ohio.

PLATE 619: *Two-hole gorget,* probably Woodland, from Owen County, Kentucky. It is 5¼" long, and made of a dense black slate. Of major interest is the presence of 48 tally-marks on the edges of the long sides near the ends of the gorget. The reason for such markings is unknown, but may have been primarily decorative. Courtesy Charles West collection, Ohio.

PLATE 617: *Cones,* or hemispheres, Woodland, Ohio. Left, tan-cream colored quartzite, 1⅛" x 1¹⁵⁄₁₆", from Franklin County, attractive coloring. Right, cream-colored quartzite, 1¹⁵⁄₁₆" x 2", Ross County, an irregular base but well-finished. Private collection, Ohio.

PLATE 620: *Adz*, Adena and Early Woodland period, one of the finest adzes to come from the state of Ohio. It is from Hamilton County and measures 3" x 7" inches. Material is a dark speckled granite-like hardstone, and the artifact is well-polished overall. Beautiful piece. Courtesy Charles West collection, Ohio.

PLATE 622: *Trapezoidal pendant*, probably Woodland period, from Lula County, Kentucky. It is 1⅜" across the base and 2³⁄₁₆" long. Material is a red slate with green banding. Attractive form and workstyle, ex-collection of Tom Davis. Private collection; photograph by Del Hetrick.

PLATE 623: *Celt grouping*, probably Woodland, all from Wyandot County, Ohio. Length range is from 2½" to 5", and all are made of good grades of hardstone. Private collection; photograph by Del Hetrick.

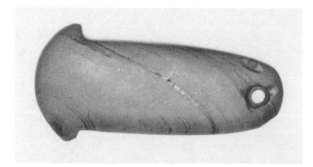

PLATE 621: *Anchor-type pendant*, Woodland period, 1½" at base and 3³⁄₁₆" long. Material is olive-green slate with banding. From Anderson County, Indiana, it is ex-collection of Tom Davis. A good type example. Private collection; Del Hetrick, photographer.

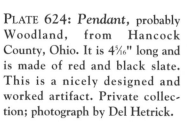

PLATE 624: *Pendant*, probably Woodland, from Hancock County, Ohio. It is 4⁵⁄₁₆" long and is made of red and black slate. This is a nicely designed and worked artifact. Private collection; photograph by Del Hetrick.

PLATE 625: *Celt,* or ungrooved axe, probably Woodland era, made of medium-dark hardstone. It is 3⅞" high and from Ohio. Ex-collection of Norm Dunn. Private collection; photograph by Del Hetrick.

PLATE 628: *Flared celt or spud-like axe,* Late Woodland, Jersey Bluff culture. It is well-made of ultra-hard diorite and is from Jersey County, Illinois. A very fine specimen. Courtesy Gregory L. Perdun collection, Illinois.

PLATE 626: *Jersey Bluff pipe,* Late Woodland period, made of Niagra Limestone. This elongated specimen is from Jersey County, Illinois. Courtesy Gregory L. Perdun collection, Illinois.

PLATE 627: *Jersey Bluff pottery,* terminal phase, from Fulton County, Illinois. This is a rare form, being four-lobed, smoothed over cord-marking, and with split and notched rim. It also is in superb condition. Courtesy Gregory L. Perdun collection, Illinois.

PLATE 629: *Pottery human effigy,* facial features put in, Middle Woodland period. It is from Lincoln County, Missouri, and ca. 100 BC - AD 400. Courtesy Gregory L. Perdun collection, Illinois.

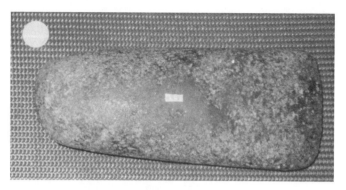

PLATE 630: *Celt,* probably Woodland period, a large and fine specimen. It was found in Pike County, Illinois, and is 8½" long. Celts of this size are rarely picked up anymore, at least without damage from farming implements. Courtesy Eldon Launer collection, Illinois.

PLATE 632: *Adena points or blades,* all Ohio. Left, Flintridge cream with tan veining, 1¾" x 3¼". From Marion County, it is ex-collections of Kill and Johnson. Middle, translucent Flintridge with smoky grey and white inclusions, 1½" x 2¾". Ex-collections of Saunders and Spires, from Fairfield County. Right, Flintridge grey with white specks, 1¾"x 3¾". This was found by D.W. Jones in the 1940's, Van Wert County. Courtesy Richard E. Jones collection, Ohio.

PLATE 633: *Anchor pendant,* green banded slate, Adena or Early Woodland. This undrilled example is from Franklin County, Ohio, and measures 2" x 4¼". It has some scratches from farming implements, common signs on much field-found slate in the Midwest. Courtesy Lee Fisher collection, Pennsylvania; Anthony Lang, photographer.

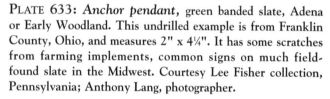

PLATE 634: *Hopewell point or blade,* probably Flintridge, black with white and rose quartzite inclusion near tip. From Warren County, Ohio, it is Middle Woodland and 3⅝" long. Ex-collections of Cain and Hetrick. Courtesy Tyson-Holman collection, Ohio; Del Hetrick, photographer.

PLATE 631: *Waubesa point or blade,* from the river bottoms of Pike County, Illinois. This is a Middle Woodland piece, probably Hopewell, and in fact came from a Hopewell site. This is a fine, large piece with excellent chipping, in light-colored chert. Size, 4⅜" long; a personal find by Mr. Launer. Courtesy Eldon Launer collection, Illinois.

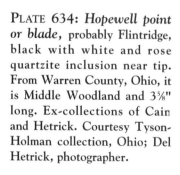

PLATE 635: *Cone,* Woodland period, ½" high and 1¼" across the bottom. The material is quartzite, and this piece is from Jefferson County, Ohio. Private collection; Del Hetrick, photographer.

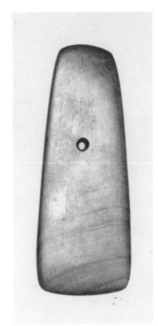

PLATE 636: *Pendant,* trapezoidal form, probably Woodland period. Material is a red slate with dark banding. This well-shaped piece is 6" high and from Wyandot County, Ohio. Private collection; Del Hetrick, photographer.

PLATE 637: *Woodland rectangular poll adz,* in tan, cream, brown and green hardstone. Ex-collections of Good and Potter, it measures 1¾" x 2¾". This is a nicely shaped and polished adz, and provenance is only listed as Ohio. Courtesy Richard E. Jones collection, Ohio.

PLATE 638: *Adena point or blade,* from Ohio, material a dull white flint with rind or inclusion on the left edge (darker area). This large artifact is from a state that does not usually produce very large flint artifacts. Outstanding specimen. Woodland era. Courtesy Fogelman collection, Pennsylvania.

PLATE 639: *Adena rectangular celt,* Early Woodland, made of dark green granite. It is 1¾" x 4", and was found by D. William Jones in Van Wert County, Ohio. Polish on the sides indicates the hafting area. Nice piece. Courtesy Richard E. Jones collection, Ohio.

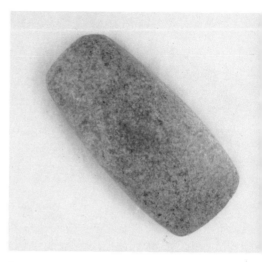

PLATE 642: *Woodland rectangular poll adz,* grey and light-dark brown granite, 1½" x 3¼". This is heavily polished, ex-collection of Meyer and from Stark County, Ohio. Courtesy Richard E. Jones collection, Ohio.

PLATE 640: *Adena tapered poll adz,* made from a dark, close-grained material, possibly diorite. Size, 2" x 4½", ex-collections of Saunders and Johnson. It is from Hardin County, Ohio. It has excellent shape and workstyle, nicely polished. Courtesy Richard E. Jones collection, Ohio.

PLATE 643: *Woodland rectangular poll adz,* tan, with black and green specks and spots, 1¾" x 3¼". The material is quite unusual and high-grade, well-polished. Ex-collection of Ward, found by Shawn Higgins in 1978; from Delaware County, Ohio. Courtesy Richard E. Jones collection, Ohio.

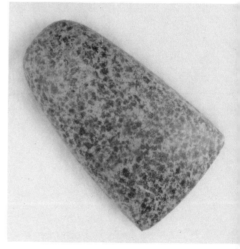

PLATE 641: *Adena adz,* from Indiana, in green and brown granite. It is 2¼" x 3¾", and ex-collections of Mear and Hoffman. This piece, with excellent polish, was found along the Tippecanoe River. Courtesy Richard E. Jones collection, Ohio.

PLATE 644: *Adena tapered poll adz,* made of black and white speckled granite. It is 2½" x 4½", and is ex-collections of Gebhart and Saunders; from Mercer County, Ohio. This piece has good overall polish. Courtesy Richard E. Jones collection, Ohio.

PLATE 645: *Glacial slate artifacts*, a small portion of the collection of Cameron W. Parks and most specimens from the Eastern Midwest. Left, animal-form birdstones; center, preforms and partial birds; right, bar amulets that are believed related to birdstones. Photo taken 1975. Lar Hothem photo.

PLATE 646: *Adena tubular pipe*, fully drilled length-wise, made of steatite. It measures 1" x 4", and is from Logan County, Kentucky. This is a fine example of a scarce pipe form. Courtesy Charles West collection, Ohio.

PLATE 648: *Hopewell point or blade*, Middle Woodland period, made from the classic material, Flintridge from Ohio's Licking County. This piece is from Ohio and measures 2" x 5½". Courtesy Charles West collection, Ohio.

PLATE 647: *Adena rounded-poll adzes*, both Ohio. Left, green and brown granite, 1½" x 3", ex-collection of Ahlstrom, Lake County. Well-polished piece. Right, brown and white granite, 1¾" x 3". Ex-collections of Potter and Good, this Franklin County specimen is well made and polished. Courtesy Richard E. Jones collection, Ohio.

PLATE 649: *Hopewell point or blade,* Indiana hornstone, 1½" x 5⅞". This is a Middle Woodland piece, with good size, fine workstyle and in top condition. It is from Spencer County, Indiana. Courtesy Charles West collection, Ohio.

PLATE 652: *Adena point or blade,* Early Woodland made of mottled jewel Flintridge. It is 2" x 5⅞" long from Greene County, Ohio. Blades of this size are rarely found unbroken and blades of this quality are rarely found. Courtesy Charles West collection, Ohio.

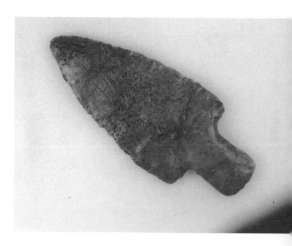

PLATE 650: *Celt,* made of very dense slate, size 1¾" x 4½". Probably Woodland period, it is from Kosciusko County, Indiana. This is a finely shaped and polished artifact, ex-collection of Parks. Courtesy Charles West collection, Ohio.

PLATE 653: *Adena point or blade,* Early Woodland period, made of high quality Flintridge material. It is 2⅛" x 5¼", from Warren County, Ohio. This is one of the better Ohio blades from this timeframe. Courtesy Charles West collection, Ohio.

PLATE 651: *Turkeytail point or blade,* Red Ochre culture, Early Woodland period. It is 1⅛" x 3¾", and is from Clermont County, Ohio. Turkeytails are infrequently solitary finds, as many have been found as caches or in groups, buried in the ground. Courtesy Charles West collection, Ohio.

PLATE 654: *Adena adz,* Early Woodland, made of dark, speckled granite. It was found in Clermont County, Ohio, in 1987 and is 2⅝" x 4½" long. This is a good, attractive tool. Courtesy Charles West collection, Ohio.

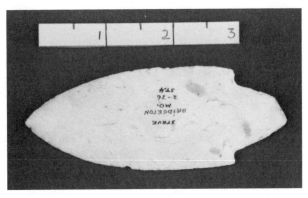

PLATE 657: *Dickson point or blade,* Middle Woodland Hopewell, late BC centuries to early AD centuries. Material is heat-treated glossy pink and orange Crescent chert. Size, 1½" x 3⅞". It was found by Steve Rampani in February of 1976 in St. Louis County, Missouri. This is a fine, large piece. Collection of Bob Rampani, Bridgeton, St. Louis County, Missouri.

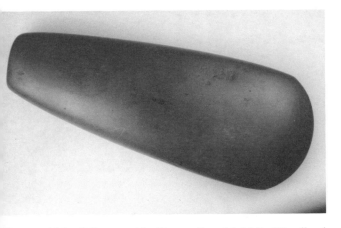

PLATE 655: *Celt,* possibly Hopewell and Middle Woodland, made of dense, dark slate. It is from Illinois, and 3½" x 9½" long. This is a very large and fine specimen, well-shaped and polished to a glossy finish. An exceptional celt. Courtesy Charles West collection, Ohio.

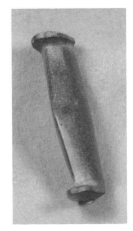

PLATE 658: *Bar amulet,* Red Ochre culture of the Early Woodland period, 1" x 3⅟₁₆". Made of hardstone, it has birdstone-like drilling at each end and has a beautiful polish. This fine piece was found along Brush Creek in Adams County, Ohio. Courtesy Lee Fisher collection, Pennsylvania; Anthony Lang, photographer.

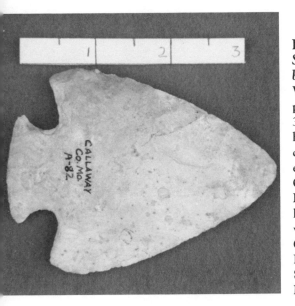

PLATE 656: *Snyders point or blade,* Middle Woodland Hopewell period. It is 2⅝" x 3⅝", and is made of heat-treated red chert. A fine type example, it is from Callaway County, Missouri. Extra-large size here is very much a plus. Collection of Bob Rampani, Bridgeton, St. Louis County, Missouri

PLATE 659: *Celts,* Woodland period, all from Porter County, Indiana. These all came from the same site and were found one a week for three weeks. Private collection of Kenneth Spiker.

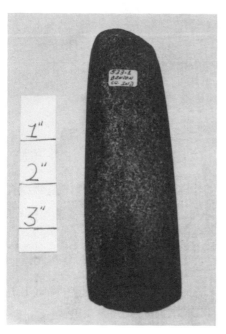

PLATE 660: *Celt*, ungrooved axe from Woodland times, found in Benton County, Indiana. It is 2" x 6¼", and a well-made example. Private collection of Kenneth Spiker.

PLATE 663: *Adz*, may be Hopewell and Middle Woodland period, made of dark, high-grade granite-like material. It is 2¾" x 6¼", and has an unusual squared configuration and tapered profile. This is a fine piece from Posey County, Indiana. Courtesy Charles West collection, Ohio.

PLATE 661: *Celt*, possibly Woodland period, 2¾" x 7½" x 1¾" thick. This hardstone example has well-ground blade area and is a fine piece from an old-time local collector in Kane County, Illinois. Courtesy Duane Treest collection, Illinois.

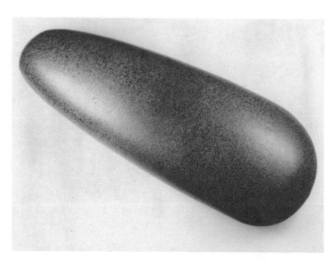

PLATE 662: *Ceremonial celt*, Hopewell, Middle Woodland, from Spencer County, Indiana. It is one hundred percent polished and has no signs of actual use. Material is a dark, close-grained hardstone. Size is 3¾" x 10¾" for this rare artifact. Courtesy Charles West collection, Ohio.

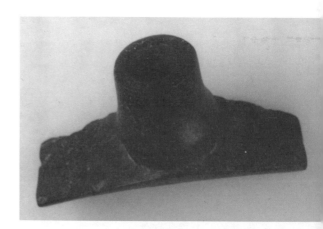

PLATE 664: *Hopewell platform pipe*, made of dark, close-grained stone. This rare pipe, Middle Woodland, would be ca. AD 300. This is the classic plain Hopewell style, and very few such pipes are in private collections. This example is from Hancock County, Illinois. Courtesy Charles West collection, Ohio.

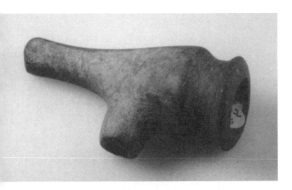

PLATE 665: *Jersey Bluff handled pipe*, made of polished limestone, from Jersey County, Illinois. It measures 1¾" x 3⅝". The Jersey Bluff is Late Woodland, ca. AD 650 - 950, and the pipe is typical of the type. (Ref. Gordon Hart, *Hart's Prehistoric Pipe Rack*, 1978, pp 124-126.) A fine specimen, ex-collections of Dr. Letterington, Meek, and Dr. Hawes. Courtesy Charles West collection, Ohio.

PLATE 668: *Hopewell squared-poll celt*, Middle Woodland period, made of a dark high-grade hardstone. This piece has the classic form and clean lines, with a very artistic blade edge. It is from Ross County, Ohio (Hopewell "heartland" of Ohio) and measures 2¾" x 6⅛". Courtesy Charles West collection, Ohio.

PLATE 666: *Adena adz*, Early Woodland period, made of a compact, dark hardstone that took a high polish. This piece in addition to superb workstyle has exceptional size, being 3⅛" x 7⅞" long. It is from Dearborn County, Indiana. Top-grade piece. Courtesy Charles West collection, Ohio.

PLATE 669: *Celt*, made of dark hardstone, from Dearborn County, Indiana. The squared poll area and slightly flared bit area suggest a Hopewell form, Middle Woodland period. This is a fine, large example at 2⅞" x 7¼". Courtesy Charles West collection, Ohio.

PLATE 667: *Celt*, probably Woodland period, made of a colorful conglomerate material. This interesting specimen is from Boyle County, Kentucky, and is 1¾" x 4½" long. Courtesy Charles West collection, Ohio.

PLATE 670: *Celt,* probably Woodland period, made of fine porphyry hardstone with the typical inclusions of lighter color. This well-designed and highly polished piece is from Henry County, Ohio, and measures 3¼" x 7¼". Very fine, top-of-the-line specimen. Courtesy Charles West collection, Ohio.

PLATE 673: *Adz,* Woodland period, with very artistic lines. Material is dark, speckled high-grade hardstone, and size is 3⅛" x 6⅛". From Miami County, Ohio, this specimen is especially interesting because both the large and small ends were worked into adz bits. Specimens of double-ended adzes are very unusual. Courtesy Charles West collection, Ohio.

PLATE 671: *Celt,* probably Woodland period, made of medium-dark hardstone. This is a fine large piece with interesting side treatment; both sides are grooved or fluted. Size, 4" x 8¾"; this excellent piece is from Noble County, Indiana. Courtesy Charles West collection, Ohio.

PLATE 674: *Celt,* made of speckled hardstone, from Dearborn County, Indiana. This piece is probably Woodland, and is a well-made celtiform axe. Size, 2¼" x 7¾". Courtesy Charles West collection, Ohio.

PLATE 672: *Hopewell celt,* squared-poll type, Middle Woodland period. It is made from high-grade green hardstone which accepted a high degree of overall polish. It is from Ohio County, Indiana, and is 2⅜" x 6" long. This is an exceptional artifact. Courtesy Charles West collection, Ohio.

PLATE 675: *Snyders point or blade*, Middle Woodland, 3⁵⁄₁₆" x 2". Material is pink and white high-grade chert; found in Holt County, Missouri. Courtesy Mike George collection, Missouri.

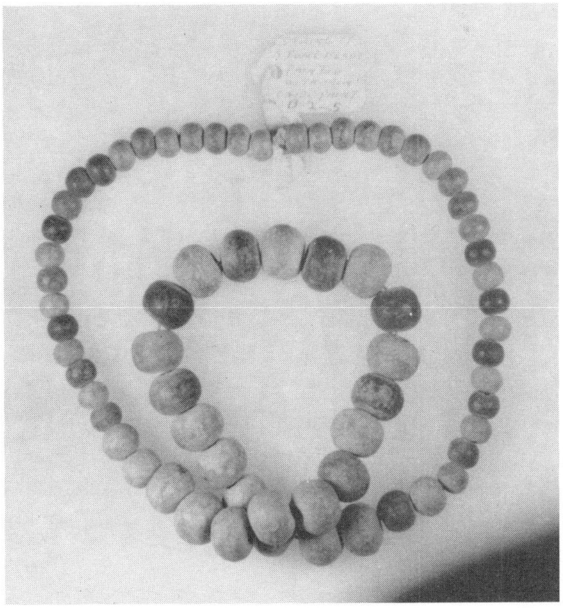

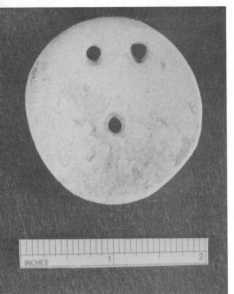

PLATE 676: *Three-hole shell gorget*, Woodland period, found at the Pool Site, Pike County, Illinois. It is approximately 2" in diameter, and is in excellent condition. Tim & Patty Wiemers collection, Edwardsville, Illinois.

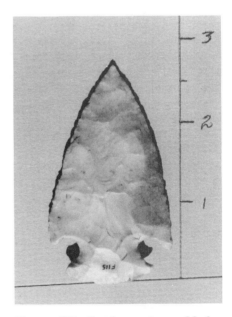

PLATE 678: *Necklace,* probably Woodland, made of graduated-size stone beads. The old tag states the beads were painted with iron oxide paint, probably hematite. An unusual and interesting decorative set, from Spencer County, Indiana. Courtesy Charles West collection, Ohio.

PLATE 679: *Snyders point or blade,* light mottled high-grade chert. This well-made piece is from Lincoln County, Missouri. It is Middle Woodland in time. Courtesy Cliff Markley collection, Alabama.

PLATE 677: *Celt,* probably Hopewell rectangular poll and Middle Woodland. This has the rare flared bit; material is a quality granite-like hardstone and the lower areas are highly polished. This piece, from Ohio, measures 3" x 5¼". Courtesy Charles West collection, Ohio.

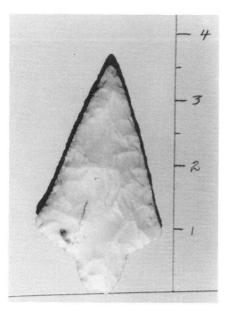

PLATE 680: *Dickson broad-blade*, Middle Woodland, made from light-colored chert or flint. This is a fine, large knife or point, more common to Western Midwest than to Eastern. This example is from Fort Bellefontain, Missouri. Courtesy Cliff Markley collection, Alabama.

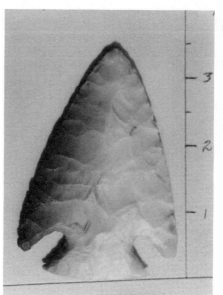

PLATE 683: *Snyders point o blade,* intermixe high-grade cher very well chippe and good size to t piece. It is fro Lawrence Count Ohio, and Middl W o o d l a n (Hopewell) in or gin. Courtesy Cli Markley collectio Alabama.

PLATE 681: *Quadriconcave gorget,* Adena and Early Woodland, undrilled, made of nicely banded slate. Size is 2" x 3"; it is from Summit County, Ohio. Lee Fisher collection, Pennsylvania; Anthony Lang, photographer.

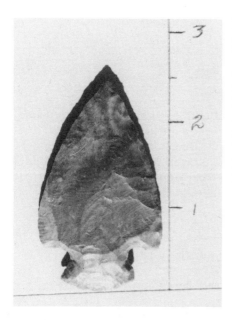

PLATE 682: *Snyders point or blade,* Middle Woodland, made of a dark and striated material. This nicely marked specimen has the typically large and smooth corner notches. It is from Franklin County, Illinois. Courtesy Cliff Markley collection, Alabama.

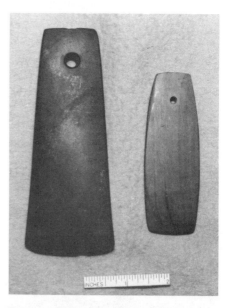

PLATE 684: *Woodland pendants,* both Geauga County, Ohio. Left, pendant-celt, made of dark grey-green banded slate, unusual material for celts. Right, pendant of olive-green banded slate, made very thin. Excellent lines and symmetry. Courtesy Fogelman collection, Pennsylvania.

PLATE 685: *Celt*, Woodland era, made of an unusual conglomerate material which is light grey-green with brownish-yellow inclusions. A well-formed specimen in a scarce stone. Courtesy Fogelman collection, Pennsylvania.

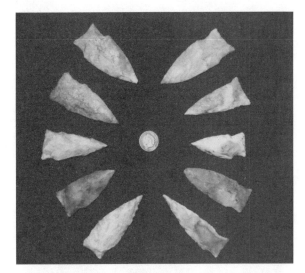

PLATE 687: *Rice shallow side-notched points or blades*, from the counties of Maries and Osage, Missouri. The excellent range of sub-types is partly due to original design and partly the result of resharpening from use. Woodland era. Collection of L.A. Noblett and Victor A. Pierce; photograph by Victor A. Pierce, Missouri.

PLATE 686: *Woodland-period blades*, various chert materials, all pieces found in the counties of Maries and Osage, Missouri. Note the variety of workstyles and materials, typical for authentic field-found chipped artifacts. Collection of L.A. Noblett and Victor A. Pierce; photograph by Victor A. Pierce, Missouri.

PLATE 688: *Dickson points or blades*, Woodland period, and found in counties of Maries and Osage in Missouri. Note the good range of size, styles and high-grade cherts used for the type. Collection of L.A. Noblett and Victor A. Pierce; photograph by Victor A. Pierce, Missouri.

PLATE 689: *Woodland-era blades*, all from the counties of Maries and Osage, Missouri. There is a wide variety of chert materials for the group, and center blade is 4⅝" long. Photograph by, and collection of, Victor A. Pierce, Missouri.

PLATE 691: *Woodland-era blades*, all Ohio. Left, Shelby County, 1¼" x 2½", black Upper Mercer flint, ex-collections of Potter and Killkenny. Middle, mottled grey with cream unknown flint, 1⅜" x 3", Coshocton County, ex-collections of Beer and Saunders. Right, Upper Mercer blue-black, Richland County, 1¼" x 2¼", ex-collections of Beer and Saunders. Courtesy Richard E. Jones collection, Ohio.

PLATE 690: *Hopewell points or blades*, all Ohio. Left, Flintridge translucent grey with cream tip, Defiance County, 1¼" x 2¼", ex-collection of Potter. Center, Flintridge pink with light blue, Licking County, 1" x 2¼", ex-collections of Saunders and Yerian. Right, translucent light grey with cream, Fairfield County, 1" x 2¼", ex-collections of Saunders and Yerian. Courtesy Christine M. Jones collection, Ohio.

PLATE 692: *Hopewell points or blades*, all Ohio. Size comparison, bottom center piece is 1" x 1½". Collections represented here include Beer, Potter, Champion, Saunders and Lute. Top left, Flintridge, Ashland Co. Top right, Flintridge, Knox Co. Bottom, left, Flintridge, Marion Co. Bottom, center, U. Mercer, Ohio. Bottom, right, Flintridge, Scioto Co. Courtesy Christine M. Jones collection, Ohio.

PLATE 693: *Hopewell blades*, all Ohio, Middle Woodland. Left, Flintridge light amber with cream inclusion, Licking County, 1¼" x 2¼". Ex-collections of Johnson, Bondley and Saunders. Middle, Flintridge cream with pink, from Hardin County, 1¼" x 2⅜", ex-collections of Potter. Right, Flintridge cream with tan, Ross County, 1⅛" x 2½". Ex-collections of Meyer and Driskoll. Courtesy Richard E. Jones collection, Ohio.

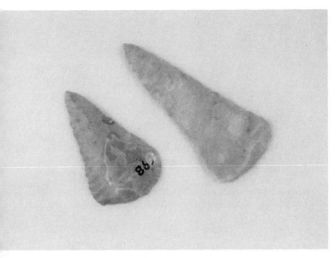

PLATE 694: *Woodland-era blades*, both Ohio. Left, light grey with white streaks, Ross County, 1⅛" x 1¾". Ex-collections of Meyer and Driskoll. Right, Flintridge mottled cream flint, Scioto County, 1" x 2½". Ex-collections of Shipley and Seeley. Courtesy Richard E. Jones collection, Ohio.

PLATE 696: *Adena blades*, Early Woodland, all Ohio. Left, Flintridge cream with light blue and lavender, Licking County, ex-collections of Saunders and Potter, 1½" x 2¾". Center, Flintridge plum-colored with crystals, Wyandot County, 2⅛" x 3⅛". Ex-collections of Johnson and Saunders, fine and superior example. Right, Flintridge cream with purple streaks and crystal at middle, Licking County, 1⅜" x 2⅞", ex-collections of Potter and Saunders. Courtesy Richard E. Jones Collection, Ohio.

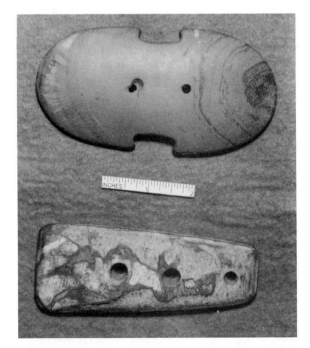

PLATE 695: *Woodland artifacts*, of slate, both Geauga County, Ohio. Top, indented gorget (Adena) of green banded slate, with unusual gouging or scooping at one obverse end. A rare gorget form. Bottom, three-hole gorget or pendant, probably Woodland, with materials that may be brown and white indurated shale. Courtesy Fogelman collection, Pennsylvania.

PLATE 697: *Late Woodland blades*, both Ohio. Left, black Zaleski flint, ex-collection of Spires and Saunders, Licking County, ⅞" x 2⅜". Right, light cream Flintridge with touches of pastel lavender at base, ex-collection of Len Weidner. Size, 1" x 2½", from Wood County. Courtesy Richard E. Jones collection, Ohio.

PLATE 698: *Celt*, probably Woodland, 3½" x 7¼". In excellent condition, this was found on a campsite in Holt County, Missouri. The lower blade or bit is highly polished. Courtesy Mike George collection, Missouri.

PLATE 699: *Celts*, probably Woodland period, all made of banded glacial slate. The grouping shows a good range of size for celts. All are from Geauga County, Ohio. Nice specimens. Courtesy Fogelman collection, Pennsylvania.

PLATE 701: *Snyders points or blades*, Middle Woodland in time, and all found in Benton County, Indiana. The largest example on left is 2¼" x 2½". Private collection of Kenneth Spiker.

PLATE 700: *Hematite cone*, Woodland period, from Franklin County, Ohio. These artifacts were once known as hemispheres; their use has never been determined with certainty. Courtesy Lee Fisher collection, Pennsylvania; Anthony Lang, photographer.

PLATE 702: *Fulton Turkeytail*, Early Woodland, from Spencer County, Indiana. It is made of grey mottled flint (probably Harrison County) and is 1" x 4". Sometimes these artifacts are found in caches or underground deposits. Courtesy Lee Fisher collection, Pennsylvania; Anthony Lang, photographer.

PLATE 703: *Adena tubular pipe*, Early Woodland [P]eriod, from Wood County, Ohio. Made of a compact [d]ark stone, this pipe was once in the collection of the [f]amous collector, A.T. Wehrle of Newark, Ohio. It [m]easures ⅞" x 2¾". Courtesy Charles West collection, [O]hio.

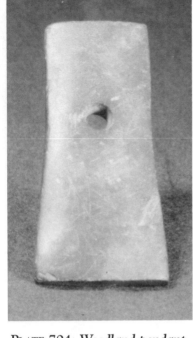

PLATE 704: *Woodland pendant,* Adena bell-shaped, 4" high. This piece is from Allen County, Indiana. This is the typical Early Woodland form, with single large hole near the smaller end, and relatively thick and well-finished. Courtesy Lee Fisher collection, Pennsylvania; Anthony Lang, photographer.

PLATE 705: *Adena blocked-end [p]ipe,* this tubular form so-called [b]ecause the mouthpiece end (top [l]eft) has a much smaller hole (and [s]ometimes an interior plug) than [t]he opposite end. This fine speci[m]en of dark hardstone is from [R]oss County, Ohio, and measures [ ]" x 3½". The blocked-end is a [h]ighly developed form of the tubu[l]ar variety. Charles West collec[t]ion, Ohio.

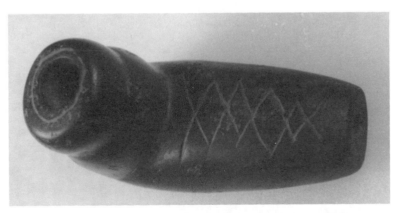

PLATE 706: *Elbow pipe,* probably Late Woodland and ca. AD 650, made of a compact dark hardstone that is well-polished. Size is 1¾" x 2¼", and it is from Hardin County, Illinois. Note the criss-crossed line decoration on the upper surface of the stem. Courtesy Charles West collection, Ohio.

PLATE 707: *Hopewell platform pipe,* Middle Woodland period, ca. AD 300. This is the classic pipe form, made of Ohio pipestone; it measures ⅞" x 2⅜". The pipe is from Ross County, Ohio, and is ex-collections of Archie Diller and D. Burton. Courtesy Charles West collection, Ohio.

PLATE 708: *Celt,* probably Woodland period, from Champaign County, Illinois. It is made of quality speckled hardstone and is 9½" long. The lower blade area is nicely polished. Courtesy Dale Richter collection, Illinois.

PLATE 709: *Copper rings and tubes,* Ohio Hopewell Indian, Middle Woodland period. Copper artifacts from this period and region tended to be mainly decorative and ornamental, as opposed to copper tools. The Ohio Hopewell made a few copper celts or adzes of utilitarian size, but this use was very restricted. Scale is in cm. Courtesy E. Neiburger/Andent, Inc.

PLATE 710: *Ceremonial celt,* believed to be the largest prehistoric copper artifact in North America. The celt is from Ohio, Hopewell culture and Middle Woodland. Weight is 17.7 kg (about 39 pounds) and dimensions are 4.5 x 13 x 61 cm. Courtesy E. Neiburger/Andent, Inc.

PLATE 711: *Apple Creek points or blades*, a scarce type from the Middle Woodland, ca. AD 350 - 550; see Perino, *Selected Preforms...*p 19. Left, grey-brown hornstone, 1¼" x 2½", ex-collections of Saunders and McGreevy. It is from Montgomery County, Ohio. Right, tan-grey hornstone, ex-collections of Lute and Saunders, from Scioto County, Ohio. The type is uncommon in Ohio and is usually found more to the west, toward Illinois. Courtesy Richard E. Jones collection, Ohio.

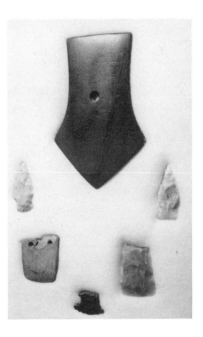

PLATE 713: *Shield-shaped pendant*, Late Woodland period, from Delaware County, Ohio. It was found with the associated minor artifacts. The shield-shape is just over 5" long, with obverse slightly convex and reverse slightly concave. This is a rare form in large size and top workstyle and perfect condition. Private collection.

PLATE 712: *Late Woodland points*, all Ohio, sizes ⅞" to 2⅜". Materials include hornstone, Upper Mercer flints, and pebble cherts in grey and off-white. This fine assemblage of scarce complete point types (these are often found broken) is from various collections. Included: Decore, Beer, Shipley, Alkire, Johnson, Ward, Knoll, Smith, Saunders, Lute, Potter, Goode and Davis. Courtesy Richard E. Jones collection, Ohio.

PLATE 714: *Large classic Adena blades*, Early Woodland period, one specimen from outside the Midwest but shown for comparative interest. These are rare chipped artifacts. Left, cream, gold and blue Flintridge material, from Ohio. It is ex-collection of W.K. Moorehead, 3½" x 8¼", with GIRS (Genuine Indian Relic Society) authentication #J3. Left center, cream, white and blue Flintridge stemmed Adena blade, from Kent county, Delaware. It is 3" x 9½", and the longest known Ohio Flintridge stemmed blade. GIRS authentication #I18. Center right, clear chalcedony Flintridge with green and yellow spotting, Adena blade, from Licking County, Ohio. It is 2⁷⁄₁₆" x 5½", GIRS *Redskin* pp 6-7. Right, blue, cream and gold Flintridge blade, from Steuben County, Indiana. It is 4" x 8", with GIRS authentication #J4. One of the largest known Adena blades. Courtesy Prehistoric art collection of John Baldwin, West Olive, Michigan.

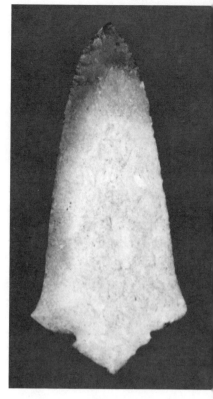

PLATE 715: *Hopewell platform pipes*, Middle Woodland period. Though one example is from outside the Midwest as that region is defined in this book, it is shown here as a matter of comparative interest. Top left, unusually large platform pipe, Ross County, Ohio, size 2¼" x 6" long, well polished. Top right, Ohio pipestone platform pipe, Franklin County, Ohio, 1⅞" x 4½", GIRS authentication #L4. Center right, Wood-duck effigy platform pipe, Ohio pipestone, Kent County, Michigan. It is 2¹⁄₁₆" x 4⅛" and bears GIRS authentication #P1. A very rare specimen. Lower left, Ohio pipestone platform pipe, St. Louis County, Missouri, size 1¾" x 4¼". GIRS authentication #L2, well-polished specimen. Lower right, frog effigy platform pipe, claystone material. It is from Lincoln County, Missouri, size 1⅞" x 2⅞". Prehistoric art collection of John Baldwin, West Olive, Michigan.

PLATE 717: *Hopewell blade*, a rare form, from Middle Woodland times. It is made of an unusual chert in tan and dark brown to black. This has excellent workstyle and superior design. Size, 5" long. Courtesy the Guy Brothers collection, Illinois.

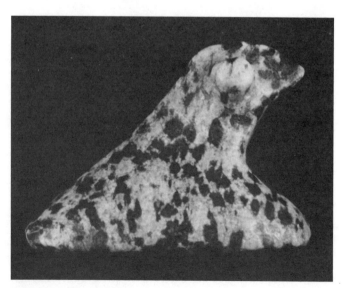

PLATE 716: *Bust-type birdstone*, Woodland period, and found in central Kentucky in the early 1960's. It is 1½" x 2¼" long, and is made from colorful hardstone. The bust-type bird is one of the rarest forms, and few apparently were ever made. Private collection, Kentucky.

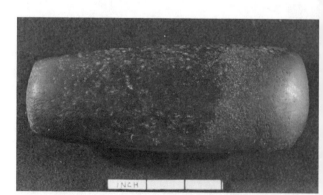

PLATE 718: *Celt*, or ungrooved axe, from Madison County, Illinois. It is made of a high grade of dark granite and is 7½" long. This celt has good lines and high polish, and is in perfect condition. It may be Hopewell or Middle Woodland. Courtesy Tim & Patty Wiemers collection, Edwardsville, Illinois.

Chapter V
The Farmers

Mississippian Period (AD 800 – AD 1650)

After the growth of the Adena in Early Woodland, the flowering of Hopewell in Middle Woodland, and the apparent decline of culture in the Late Woodland, a new era arrived. Sometime several centuries before AD 1000, a vigorous lifeway perhaps originating in and flowing from the Southern U.S. arrived in the Midwest. These were the Mississippian peoples, and there were various sub-groups.

The Eastern Midwest had Fort Ancient and Whittlesey plus others, while the Western Midwest had New Madrid and others. These various sub-groups mainly followed the Mississippian lifeway, which was solidly centered around village and town life. Permanent groups of dwellings were possible now because much food was raised in nearby fields.

One of the characteristics of most major sites of this period is that they were located in river valleys. This is probably because the level floodplains made good fields, which were periodically enriched by flooding. It is known that squash and beans were raised, and native plants like sunflower were probably cultivated as well. And, for the first time on a large scale, corn or maize was grown.

Another characteristic of the Mississippian in the Midwest is the growth of a huge pottery industry. Ceramics were made in many shapes and sizes, from salt-rendering pans to typical water vessels to storage jars to fine effigy forms depicting animals, birds or people.

It all fit together: The settled lifeway allowed large-scale farming, farming allowed surplus food to be stored, and long-term food storage allowed a settled lifeway. The circle of seasons was complete.

Domesticated crops provided only a part of the diet, which was supplemented with wild game of all kinds. River mussels and fish were favorite foods, plus deer and other smaller animals. The Mississippians had long had the bow and arrow, and the chert and flint points were quite simple. The most common form was a triangle without stems or notches, and with edges smooth or serrated. Collectors once called them "warpoints," but they were all-purpose and equally suitable for hunting or hostilities. Another type had side-notches, sometimes with a third notch at the baseline center.

Some other chert or flint objects were chipped into shape. These include a wide range of knives, again many made in triangular forms but larger and much longer. Bi-pointed knives were fairly common, and some drills were duo-tipped, with a working tip at each end. Hoes and spades, often notched, were used in fairly large numbers and both are typical of the Mississippian period.

In addition to the many utilitarian objects chipped into final form, a range of large ceremonial artifacts was created. Here, chipping was the first stage and often the objects were further ground and polished to become very beautiful. These include the so-called scepters with handle-shafts and expanded tops. These may have been symbols of authority or rank. Maces or ceremonial clubs were also made. Some examples were so highly ground and polished that all traces of chipping scars were removed in the process.

Hardstone was worked into a range of celt or ungrooved axe forms, from very small to very large. Two celt-like objects, both probably ceremonial upon occasion, were the spatulates and spuds. Spatulates have long and narrow tapered handles (some extend for 18 inches) and an abruptly expanded blade and bit end that may be notch-decorated. More common are the spuds, made sometimes in hardstone but more frequently in chert or flint. Long and narrow, the widest portion is the flared or extended lower blade section. Again, some examples are heavily polished, either in the blade area or overall.

Glacial slate was used to some extent for pendants and most of these were basic, elongated types with a hole near one end. Slate (and other stone) was sometimes made into rounded or tubular beads, and small effigies. One interesting thing is that the Mississippian people did not seem to make or use gorgets, at least not in large numbers. This is indirect proof that these bow-and-arrow users had no need for the throwing-stick weights or decorations.

Many objects were made of antler, bone and shell. These included conical arrowheads (antler), beads and hairpins and whistles (bone), and necklace elements and rounded pendants (shell). Some pendants had intricate designs of birds, spiders or humans, outlined by incising and sometimes by openwork. A favorite motif was the weeping eye, done on pottery, pipes and pendants.

The Mississippian people also had several unique artifacts that had never before been made in the Midwest. One was the discoidal, a round and flattened or concave-faced stone. Some were holed in the center or had drill-marks or incised decorations. A few were beautifully made of near-gem material like rose quartzite. These apparently were rolled along the ground in a game or contest called "chunkey," and there are numerous early historic reports of the activity.

Another very rare artifact is called a spool because of the shape. These are like short, thick cylinders, usually smoothly concave in the center. Most have deeply incised lines on the rounded surface, and sometimes they have shallow holes at the middle of the sides. The use of spools was long a mystery, but present thought is that they were used with paint for body decorations. Rolled, for instance, in a paste of powdered red hematite and bear grease, and held with a forked stick, spools could very quickly add strips of paint designs to arms and legs. Most were made of porous sandstone, which again aided the process. They were quite an innovation for their time.

The flowering of Midwestern Mississippian culture reached a peak at the great Illinois ceremonial and population center known as Cahokia. This was probably the largest true urban center in prehistoric North America, and it coursed with life for half a thousand years. The best dates available assign Cahokia to the period AD 900 - 1400. The largest mound of the complex is known as Monks Mound. It is about 100 feet high, was built up in four terraced levels, and the huge base covers approximately 16 acres.

At one time, a large structure was situated atop the highest level of the mound, its purpose unknown. One reason for Cahokia's being may have been as an administrative and trading center, meeting the requirements of many smaller satellite towns up to several hundred miles distant. At Cahokia and in the immediate vicinity, perhaps thirty thousand people may have lived and worked. Other aspects of Cahokia included smaller mounds carefully sited (perhaps for astronomical purposes), many fields, dwelling sites, and an enormous stockade or city wall.

No one knows precisely why the vigor faded from Mississippian times in general or Cahokia in particular. One could just as easily ask the same question about the 500-year span of the Hopewell Indians, or the brief time of the Red Ochre people, and many others. All across the Midwest, for a certain time and in a special place, distinctive ways of life developed and were practiced and disappeared.

For various reasons and with dates averaged-out, prehistoric times ended in the Midwest about AD 1650. About then, historic times began. Of course, more than a precise date, it was a drawn-out and gradual change. The meaning was that traditional ways of doing things clashed with innovative objects and materials and concepts, and the new outweighed the old. Historic times brought the magic of the written word, with journals and reports and observations and documents. When historic times arrived, the Midwest changed dramatically and forever.

PLATE 719: *Mississippian pottery*, both pieces Pemiscot County, Missouri. Left, red and white painted greyware breast effigy hooded water bottle, 4" diameter, 5" high. Right, red and white painted human head effigy with child-like features, 4¼" diameter, 4¼" high. Vessels were found together, perhaps made by the same potter. Courtesy Blake Gahagan collection, Tennessee.

PLATE 722: *Pottery vessel*, four knob handles, Mississippian period, from Kentucky. Size is 2½" x 6" for this greyware bowl. Courtesy Marguerite L. Kernaghan collection, Colorado; photo by Marguerite & Stewart Kernaghan.

PLATE 720: *Mississippian pottery*, unusual little frog effigy jar. It combines Parkin Punctuated with Campbell Applique on a buff-color finish. This fine ceramic piece is 5" diameter and 3" high. It is from Pemiscot County, Missouri. Courtesy Blake Gahagan collection, Tennessee.

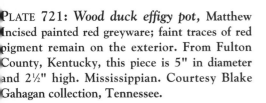

PLATE 721: *Wood duck effigy pot*, Matthew Incised painted red greyware; faint traces of red pigment remain on the exterior. From Fulton County, Kentucky, this piece is 5" in diameter and 2½" high. Mississippian. Courtesy Blake Gahagan collection, Tennessee.

PLATE 723: *Pottery vessel*, shell-tempered Mississippian piece, with two of the four handles missing. With punctuated decoration, size 3½" x 5". It is from Henderson County, Kentucky, and ex-collection of Chalmer Lynch. Courtesy Marguerite L. Kernaghan collection, Colorado; photo by Marguerite & Stewart Kernaghan.

PLATE 724: *Pottery vessel*, Mississippian period, from Henderson County, Kentucky. It is shell-tempered and one of the four handles is missing. Size is 3" x 5"; ex-collection of Chalmer Lynch. Courtesy Marguerite L. Kernaghan collection, Colorado; photo by Marguerite & Stewart Kernaghan.

PLATE 725: *Pottery vessel,* Mississippian, shell-tempered. From Henderson County, Kentucky, size is 2½" x 4". This is almost a miniature form, and ex-collections of Pavlonis and Lynch. Courtesy Marguerite L. Kernaghan collection, Colorado; photo by Marguerite & Stewart Kernaghan.

PLATE 728: *Effigy pot,* the image probably representing the prairie chicken, from Pemiscot County, Missouri. Size is 6¼" x 10¼". Effigy forms of this type are quite rare. A fine Mississippian vessel. Courtesy Marguerite L. Kernaghan collection, Colorado; photo by Marguerite & Stewart Kernaghan.

PLATE 726: *Pottery vessel,* shell-tempered, Mississippian period, from Henderson County, Kentucky. Size is 2" x 4" and the piece is ex-collection of Chalmer Lynch. Courtesy Marguerite L. Kernaghan collection, Colorado; photo by Marguerite & Stewart Kernaghan.

PLATE 727: *Effigy pot,* probably the image of a deer, from Henderson County, Kentucky. It is shell-tempered and holes are punched in the top of the thick rim. Size is 2" x 5½". Courtesy Marguerite L. Kernaghan collection, Colorado; photo by Marguerite & Stewart Kernaghan.

PLATE 729: *Flint hoe or adz,* probably Mississippian period, made of polished brown flint. It is from Marshall County, Kentucky, and is 2" x 2¾". Ex-collection of B. Faith. Courtesy Marguerite L. Kernaghan collection, Colorado; photo by Marguerite & Stewart Kernaghan.

PLATE 730: *Pottery vessel*, Mississippian, wide-mouthed footed bottle. Three of the four small handles are present and the base is slotted. Provenance is listed as Ohio. Size is 5¼" x 5¾"; a partial dark glaze remains. Ex-collection of Chalmer Lynch. Courtesy Marguerite L. Kernaghan collection, Colorado; photo by Marguerite & Stewart Kernaghan.

PLATE 733: *Mississippian artifacts*, all from Illinois. Left, pipestone pendant, St. Clair County. Center and right, pottery owl and shell gorget, both from Madison County. These are interesting and unusual artifacts. Courtesy Gregory L. Perdun collection, Illinois.

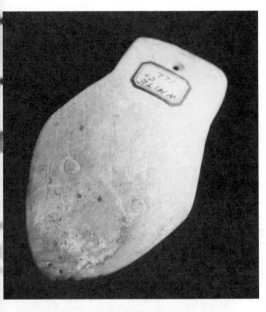

PLATE 731: *Effigy pendant*, possibly Mississippian, made of shell. It represents a snake head, as seen by the triangular configuration, cross-hatching that may represent scales, eyes and nostrils. This excellent and very rare piece is from White County, Illinois, and ex-collection of Earl Cheeseboro. Courtesy Dale & Betty Roberts collection, Iowa.

PLATE 734: *Effigy pipe*, human face, Mississippian or proto-historic, made from a fine-grained grey stone. It came from Rock Island County, Illinois. The pipe is about 3" long and 1½" high. Courtesy Bruce Filbrandt collection, Iowa.

PLATE 735: *Oval spade*, Mississippian culture, found in St. Louis County, Missouri. It is 3¼" x 9" long and made of Mill Creek chert. This is a fine, large specimen in top condition. Collection of Bob Rampani, Bridgeton, St. Louis County, Missouri.

PLATE 732: *Salt River discoidal*, Mississippian, made of a very attractive cream-white and black hardstone. Well-made and polished, this example is from Green County, Illinois. Courtesy Gregory L. Perdun collection, Illinois.

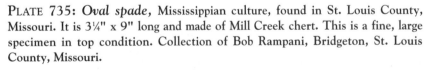

PLATE 736: *Pottery vessel*, Mississippian, Fortune Noded type. It was found in Pemiscot County, Missouri, and is decorated with protruding nodes and strap handles. It is 5½" high and 7¼" in diameter. Courtesy collection of Bob Rampani, Bridgeton, St. Louis County, Missouri.

PLATE 739: *Salt River type discoidal*, made of a rare material, hematite or dark natural iron ore. Mississippian, it is 1½" x 3½", and from Brown County, Illinois. Note the edged circumference and dimpled top and side. Fine piece. Courtesy collection of Bob Rampani, Bridgeton, St. Louis County, Missouri.

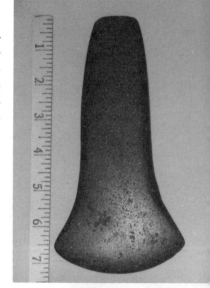

PLATE 737: *Compound pottery bottle*, Mississippian era, the rare "Love Bottle" form. It was found in Pemiscot County, Missouri, and is 6¼" high and 7" in diameter. It is painted in Old Town Red, and is a nicely formed work. Courtesy Collection of Bob Rampani, Bridgeton, St. Louis County, Missouri.

PLATE 740: *Spud or spatulate*, probably Mississippian, in high-quality dark granite. It is 3¼" (at flared bit) and 7¼" high. From Miami County, Ohio, it is ex-collection of George C. Kiefer. This rare piece is very thin and well made, with a high degree of polish. Courtesy Steve Puttera Jr. collection, Ohio.

PLATE 738: *Double-bitted hoe*, found in St. Louis County, Missouri. It is 2⅞" x 8⅛" and is made of white Kaolin chert. The piece has good polish on both ends. Ex-collections of Linton D. Fosterling and Ben Thompson. This is a Mississippian piece. Collection of Bob Rampani, Bridgeton, St. Louis County, Missouri.

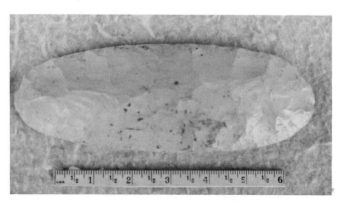

PLATE 741: *Flared-bit celt or spud*, Mississippian period, found in the 1930's near the Des Moines River in Iowa. This is a well-shaped piece, made of diorite, and highly polished. Note the poll end where the lack of polish indicates the hafted portion. Size, 2¾" across at bit, 1¾" across at poll, 5¾" long. Courtesy Bruce Filbrandt collection, Iowa.

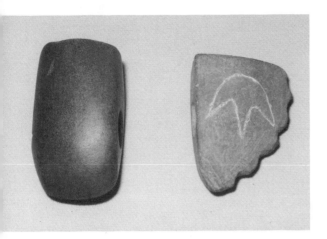

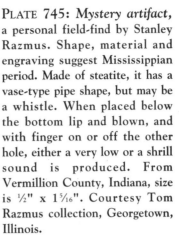

PLATE 745: *Mystery artifact,* a personal field-find by Stanley Razmus. Shape, material and engraving suggest Mississippian period. Made of steatite, it has a vase-type pipe shape, but may be a whistle. When placed below the bottom lip and blown, and with finger on or off the other hole, either a very low or a shrill sound is produced. From Vermillion County, Indiana, size is ½" x 1⅝". Courtesy Tom Razmus collection, Georgetown, Illinois.

PLATE 742: *Ohio pipes,* late prehistoric, pipe on right shown elsewhere in book. Left, unusual celt-effigy pipe form, from Tuscarawas County, Ohio. It is made of a brownish fine-grained material. Mississippian period. Courtesy Steve Puttera Jr. collection, Ohio.

PLATE 743: *Engraved pipe,* obverse and reverse sides, pictures 75% size. This was found on the west bank of the Cuyahoga River, Cuyahoga County, Ohio, by Stephen Puttera Sr., in 1983. Made of grey slate, it is Whittlesey and ca. AD 1100 - 1450, Mississippian. Classed as a keel-shaped pipe, this is a scarce form. Courtesy Steve Puttera Jr. collection, Ohio.

PLATE 746: *Pottery vessel,* Mississippian, Cahokia focus and ca. AD 900 - 1200. It was found in Madison County, Illinois, in 1968, and is 5" high and 7¾" in diameter. Style is either Powell Plain or St. Clair Plain, and exterior has fire-clouds. Courtesy collection of Bob Rampani, Bridgeton, St. Louis County, Missouri.

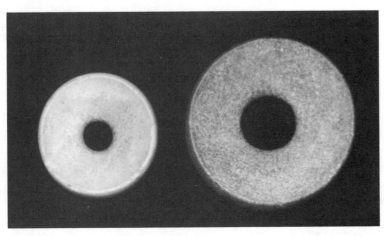

PLATE 744: *Perforated-center discoidals,* Mississippian, both Ohio, both very rare artifacts. Left, yellow quartzite, 2½" in diameter, Adams County, ex-collection of Dr. Meuser (no. 5035 over 5). Right, green granite, 3½" in diameter, Clermont County, ex-collections of Copeland and Klamert. Courtesy Steve Puttera Jr. collection, Ohio.

PLATE 747: *Pottery vessel*, Mississippian, Parkin Punctate style, AD 1200 - 1600. It was found in Pemiscot County, Missouri, and is 4⅞" high and 5½" in diameter. Decorations are punctated sides and four strap handles. This is a very good greyware piece. Collection of Bob Rampani, Bridgeton, St. Louis County, Missouri.

PLATE 750: *Celt*, probably Mississippian period, from Madison County, Illinois. It is made of quality speckled hardstone, black with white particles. This flared-bit example is 3¼" x 6½" long. Courtesy William Gehlken collection, Illinois; photograph by Bruce Filbrandt.

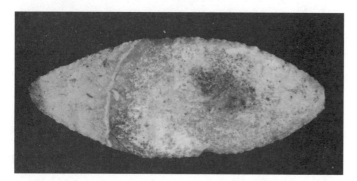

PLATE 748: *Bi-pointed knife*, probably Mississippian, made of unusual mottled and veined chert. Size is 2⅜" x 6"; it was found in Rock Island County, Illinois. Courtesy Lane Freyermuth collection, Iowa.

PLATE 749: *Bi-pointed blade*, probably Mississippian period, from Louisa County, Iowa. It is 2⅜" x 6" long and unusually thin for size. This well-made specimen was done in a cream-tan chert of high quality. Courtesy Gary Klebe collection, Muscatine, Iowa.

PLATE 751: *Spade*, Mississippian period, from Rock Island County, Illinois. Material is a brown chert and there is heavy bit polish. Size is ¾" x 5" x 8½". Courtesy William Gehlken collection, Illinois; Lane Freyermuth, photographer.

PLATE 752: *Discoidals*, all sandstone, Mississippian period, and all from Mercer County, Illinois. Note incised lines on each. Top left, ½" x 2⅜". Lower center, 1⅛" x 1⅝". Top right, ⅞" x 2½". Courtesy William Gehlken collection, Illinois; Lane Freyermuth, photographer.

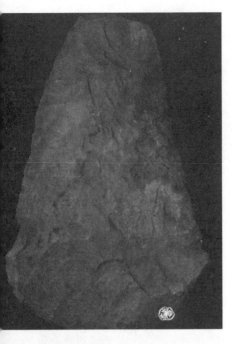

PLATE 753: *Spade,* Henry County, Illinois; it is Mississippian period. Material is a grey chert and there is lower blade or bit polish. Size is ¾" x 5¼" x 8" long. Courtesy William Gehlken collection, Illinois; Lane Freyermuth, photographer.

PLATE 756: *Human effigy,* found in 1920 north of Grimes, Iowa. It is made of taconite, a fine-grained sedimentary rock with magnetite, hematite and quartz inclusions. Size, 2½" to 6½" in diameter, 13½" tall. Weight, 22 pounds. It was purchased from the King Family estate by the owner in 1990. Courtesy Dwight Stineman collection, Wapello, Iowa.

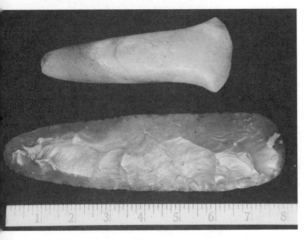

PLATE 754: *Mississippian-era artifacts,* both from Illinois. Top, Cahokia type polished flint spud, 2¼" x 5¾", Madison County. Bottom, polished flint spade from southern Illinois, Kaolin flint, 2¼" x 8"; it is ex-collection of Floyd Ritter. Courtesy Steve Puttera Jr. collection, Ohio.

PLATE 757: *Discoidal,* nearly 2" in diameter and from southern Illinois. This is a Mississippian piece and Cahokia type. Made of quartzite, this small discoidal has some damage. Courtesy collection of Russell & Rhonda Bedwell, Illinois.

PLATE 755: *Pottery vessel,* Whittlesey Focus, ca. AD 1100 - 1450, Mississippian period. It was found in 1984 by the owner in a refuse pit, Cuyahoga County, Ohio. When recovered, the vessel was only two-thirds complete and was restored by the owner. Size, 8" x 10½" high. Ohio ceramics of any period are quite rare. Courtesy Steve Puttera Jr. collection, Ohio.

PLATE 758: *Pottery effigy,* a rare form found at Cahokia Mounds, Illinois. The length is 1¾", and it is Mississippian period. Courtesy Tim & Patty Wiemers collection, Edwardsville, Illinois.

PLATE 759: *Effigy pipe,* human face profile and bowl head, made of fine-grained sandstone that took a good polish. Size is 3" x 4⅛", and it is from Mason County, Kentucky. The face is so detailed that the nose has drilled nostrils. An unusual specimen, and from Mississippian times. Courtesy Charles West collection, Ohio.

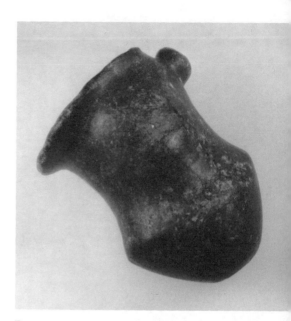

PLATE 762: *Effigy pipe,* vase-form, made of steatite that has been well-polished. It measures 2¼" x 3¼" high, and is Mississippian in time. This is a nicely crafted pipe, from Trumbull County, Ohio. Courtesy Charles West collection, Ohio.

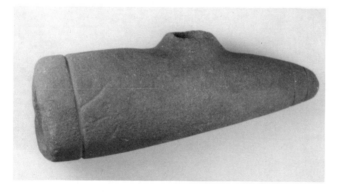

PLATE 760: *Fort Ancient pipe,* unusual form, made of fine-grained sandstone. It is 1⅞" x 6" long, with incised decorations at each end of the tubular body. This pipe is from Logan County, Ohio. Courtesy Charles West collection, Ohio.

PLATE 761: *Elbow pipe,* an interesting artifact made from fine-grained sandstone. It is 2½" x 3½" and has a faceted or paneled stem and a rounded bowl. It was found at the Cahokia Site in Illinois and is Mississippian in time. Courtesy Charles West collection, Ohio.

PLATE 763: *Effigy pipe,* red Catlinite, very late Mississippian/proto-historic period, with wolf or dog effigy. Size, 2½" x 7¼". This fine piece was found during terrace construction near Forest City, Missouri, in Holt County. Courtesy Mike George collection, Missouri.

PLATE 764: *Disc-bowl pipe*, Catlinite, 2⅜" long and 2¼" across the disc. It was a surface-find after heavy rains in Holt County, Missouri. This is a late piece, Mississippian. Courtesy Mike George collection, Missouri.

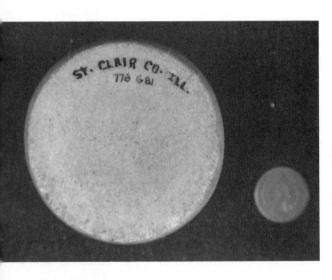

PLATE 767: *Triangular point or blade*, Mississippian period, Pickaway County, Ohio. Made of near-black Zaleski flint, it is 1½" x 2½". Ex-collections of Shipley and Saunders. Courtesy Richard E. Jones collection, Ohio.

PLATE 768: *Bi-pointed blade*, Mississippian period, from Kentucky. Material is a brown Kentucky flint with blue-grey inclusions. Size, 1⅝" x 8½". This fine piece was found in the late 1940's by D. William Jones. Courtesy Richard E. Jones collection, Ohio.

PLATE 765: *Cahokia type discoidal*, Mississippian period. This excellent artifact was found at Cahokia Mounds, Illinois. It is 2½" in diameter and is made of well-polished light-colored granite. Courtesy Tim & Patty Wiemers collection, Edwardsville, Illinois.

PLATE 769: *Mississippian bi-points*, both Ohio. Left, Carter County (KY) material, from Ashland County, 1" x 3". Right, Kentucky blue flint, ¾" x 2½". Ex-collections of Beer and Saunders. Courtesy Richard E. Jones collection, Ohio.

PLATE 766: *Celt*, tapered-poll type, probably Mississippian. It is 2⅛" x 5½" and was found in Holt County, Missouri. Material is black hardstone and it has high polish overall. Courtesy Mike George collection, Missouri.

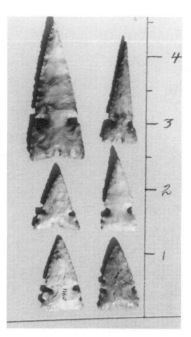

PLATE 770: *Cahokia points,* various flints and cherts, with various notching arrangements. All points shown are from St. Clair County, Illinois. They are Mississippian period. Courtesy Cliff Markley collection, Alabama.

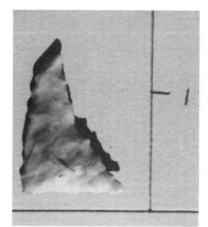

PLATE 773: *Cahokia Sharktooth,* Mississippian period, designed for insetting into a club or sword. This rare artifact is from St. Clair County, Illinois. (See Perino, *Selected Preforms, Points and Knives...*p 61.) Courtesy Cliff Markley collection, Alabama.

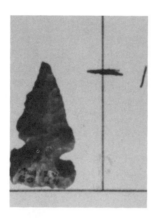

PLATE 771: *Schugtown point,* a small fairly thick true arrowhead. These are Mississippian in time. The example is from Madison County, Illinois. Courtesy Cliff Markley collection, Alabama.

PLATE 774: *Hooded human effigy water bottle,* Mississippian period, from Trigg County, Kentucky. This is a well-made ceramic vessel in a scarce form. It is 8" high. Courtesy Charles West collection, Ohio.

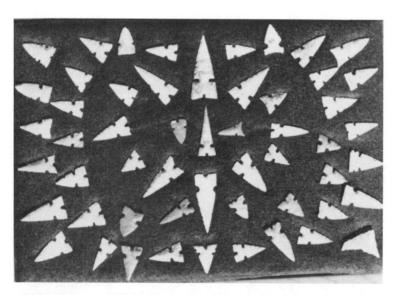

PLATE 772: *Cahokia points,* late true arrowheads from the Mississippian period. These are shown in one and two-paired notchings as well as the classic triple-notch type. They are all from St. Clair County, Illinois. Courtesy Cliff Markley collection, Alabama.

PLATE 775: *Pottery Bowl*, Mississippian period, from Butler County, Ohio. This is a finely formed utilitarian ceramic vessel; Ohio pottery is quite scarce. Size, 2½" high and 3⅞" in diameter. Courtesy Charles West collection, Ohio.

PLATE 778: *Columella bead*, made from the central structure of a conch shell. It is drilled full-length, and is almost 3" long. From Illinois, it was a surface find by Tim Wiemers. Mississippian period. Courtesy Tim & Patty Wiemers collection, Edwardsville, Illinois.

PLATE 776: *Pottery Bowl*, Mississippian period, from the Kentucky Lake region, Marshall County, Kentucky. It is 2½" high and 4½" in diameter, and is a well-made plain vessel. Courtesy Charles West collection, Ohio.

PLATE 779: *Spud*, Mississippian period with narrow shaft and very flared blade and very excurvate bit. It is from Pike County, Illinois, and measures 3" x 7¼". Material is porphyry with light-colored inclusions. Courtesy Charles West collection, Ohio.

PLATE 777: *Pottery Bowl*, Mississippian period, with decorated rim exterior. It is from Trigg County, Kentucky, and measures 2½" high and 4½" in diameter. Courtesy Charles West collection, Ohio.

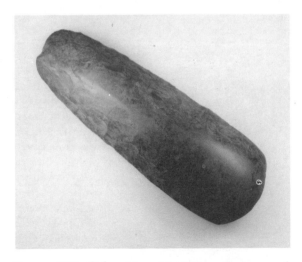

PLATE 780: *Celt*, chipped into general shape and ground into final form, Mississippian period. This is a fine celt, made of Dover flint, which is usually in brownish hues and from the Tennessee area. Size is 3¼" x 9½". Courtesy Charles West collection, Ohio.

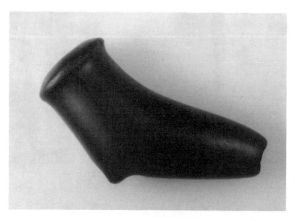

PLATE 781: *Modified elbow pipe*, probably northern Mississippian (Erie?), made of slate. It is 2¼" x 4", and from Seneca County, Ohio. It is ex-collection of C. Theler. This is a well-shaped and highly polished example. Courtesy Charles West collection, Ohio.

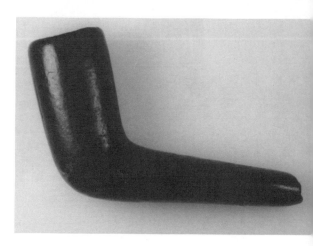

PLATE 784: *Elbow pipe*, Erie, ca. AD 1300 - 1600. It is very well made from black steatite and is highly polished. This piece measures 1½" x 4", and is from Tuscarawas County, Ohio. Ex-collections of Meek, Theler and Wachtel. Courtesy Charles West collection, Ohio.

PLATE 782: *Vase-type pipe*, Late Mississippian, polished dark hardstone, size 1½" x 2¾". It is from the Fort Ancient Madisonville Site, from Hamilton County, Ohio. While the vase pipe is a relatively simple form, this is an outstanding specimen. Courtesy Charles West collection, Ohio.

PLATE 785: *Disc pipes*, or sun-disc pipes, ca. AD 1200 - 1600, and Mississippian period. Both are well-made from Catlinite or Minnesota red pipestone. Top example, Brown County, Ohio. Bottom, from Henderson County, Kentucky. Courtesy Charles West collection, Ohio.

PLATE 783: *Vase-type pipe*, Mississippian period, made of black steatite. It measures 1¾" x 3½", and is from Fayette County, Ohio. The vase form is one of many late prehistoric pipe varieties. Nice example, very well made. Courtesy Charles West collection, Ohio.

PLATE 786: *Disc pipes*, or sun-disc pipes, Mississippian, made of Catlinite. Top example is from Cumberland County, Kentucky. Bottom example is from Henry County, Missouri. This pipe style was a favorite late prehistoric form over much of the Midwest. Courtesy Charles West collection, Ohio.

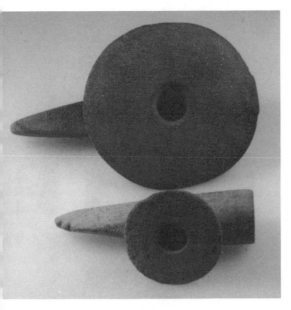

PLATE 787: *Disc pipes*, sometimes called sun-disc pipes, Mississippian, ca. AD 1200 - 1600. Top specimen is sandstone, from Posey County, Indiana. Bottom, limestone, from Henderson County, Kentucky. Courtesy Charles West collection, Ohio.

PLATE 790: *Midwestern drills*, all Illinois and all from an Upper Mississippian site. The longest piece shown is 1½". Ca. AD 800 - 1600, and found by the owner in Kane County. Courtesy Duane Treest collection, Illinois.

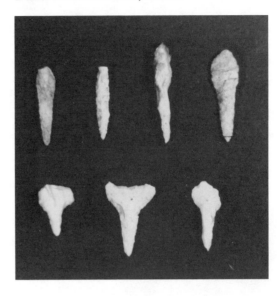

PLATE 791: *Double-bitted celt*, probably Mississippian, made of hardstone. At bottom right is a large sharpened blade, at top left is a similar but smaller blade edge. Size, 1½" x 5"; this piece is from Pike County, Illinois. An interesting and unusual chisel-like celt. Courtesy Charles West collection, Ohio.

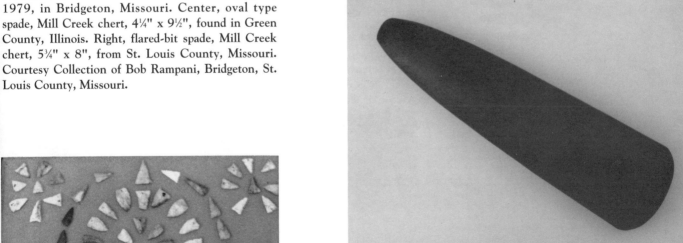

PLATE 788: *Mississippian agricultural implements.* Left, double-bitted hoe, white chert, 2½" x 7¾", good polish. Personal find by Steve Rampani, 1979, in Bridgeton, Missouri. Center, oval type spade, Mill Creek chert, 4¼" x 9½", found in Green County, Illinois. Right, flared-bit spade, Mill Creek chert, 5¾" x 8", from St. Louis County, Missouri. Courtesy Collection of Bob Rampani, Bridgeton, St. Louis County, Missouri.

PLATE 789: *Madison points*, Mississippian period, all from Benton County, Indiana. The top center example is 1" x 1½". This collection shows the varied types of Indiana flints and cherts. Private collection of Kenneth Spiker.

PLATE 792: *Hairpin*, probably Mississippian, from Kentucky. This is a well-designed and finely made specimen, with large decorated terminal. Made of polished bone, it is 4½" long. Courtesy Charles West collection, Ohio.

PLATE 793: *Pendant, bead or disc*, central hole, incised track-like markings radiating out from the center. This piece is probably Mississippian, 2⅝" in diameter, and from Mason County, Kentucky. The material is well-polished cannel coal. Courtesy Charles West collection, Ohio.

PLATE 795: *Engraved pendant*, found on an Upper Mississippian site in Kane County, Illinois. This may be ca. AD 800 - 1600. Found December 4, 1983 by the owner; length is 2½". All marks on the front and back appear intentional. It has engraving above the groove that may be a face and the base may represent a cloak-covered body. Very unusual piece. Courtesy Duane Treest collection, Illinois.

PLATE 794: *Human effigy mask*, Fort Ancient aspect of the Mississippian culture, with the diagnostic weeping-eye motif. It is made of cannel coal and is 4" wide and 4½" high. The rare mask is from Bracken County, Kentucky. Courtesy Charles West collection, Ohio.

PLATE 796: *Ft. Ancient knife*, Mississippian period, from Geauga County, Ohio. It has edge-serrations, is quite thin, and material is dull black flint. This fine specimen has the diagnostic squared basal configuration. Courtesy Fogelman collection, Pennsylvania.

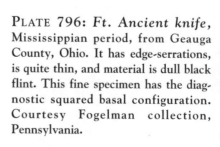

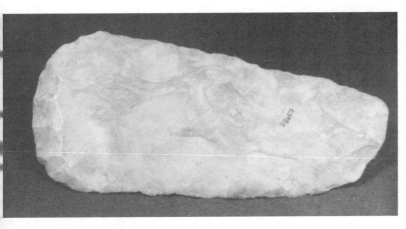

PLATE 797: *Chipped spade,* highly polished chert, from Sangamon County, Illinois. This Mississippian agricultural tool is 4½" x 9" long. Courtesy Lee Fisher collection, Pennsylvania; Anthony Lang, photographer.

PLATE 800: *Pottery vessel,* grey base with some remaining dark paint, found near Glasford, Fulton County, Illinois. It is probably Middle Mississippian plain ware (see Griffin *Archaeology of Eastern United States,* 1952, figure 151-5). This is a nice piece of utilitarian ceramics. Courtesy Eldon Launer collection, Illinois.

PLATE 798: *Chipped celt,* found near Waverly, Scott County, Illinois. Material is brown mottled chert and length is 4⅜". This is likely a Mississippian piece. Courtesy Eldon Launer collection, Illinois.

PLATE 801: *Mississippian chalice,* opposing lug handles built into the rim, very graceful overall form. This fine example is from Schuyler County, Illinois. Courtesy Gregory L. Perdun collection, Illinois.

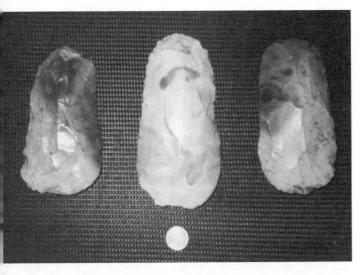

PLATE 799: *Chipped hoes,* probably Mississippian, from near Winchester, Scott County, Illinois. All are made of colorful chert, with longest 6¾". Courtesy Eldon Launer collection, Illinois.

PLATE 805: *Bear effigy bowl,* Mississippian period. This is a well-made effigy form, and from Schuyler County, Illinois. Courtesy Gregory L. Perdun collection, Illinois.

PLATE 802: *Spoon River vessel,* Mississippian, from Fulton County, Illinois. This is a well-made pot with bold and flared rim. Courtesy Gregory L. Perdun collection, Illinois.

PLATE 803: *Mississippian pipe forms,* various materials. Top left, limestone frog effigy pipe, Jersey County, Illinois. Top right, Catlinite disc-bowl pipe, Jersey County, Illinois. Bottom, pottery projecting-stem pipe, St. Genevieve County, Missouri. Courtesy Gregory L. Perdun collection, Illinois.

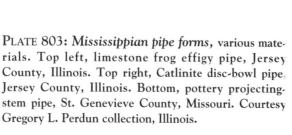

PLATE 804: *Effigy pipe,* Niagra limestone, effigy of a frog under a lily pad or water plant. This interesting Early Mississippian pipe is from Jersey County, Illinois. Courtesy Gregory L. Perdun collection, Illinois.

PLATE 806: *Wood-duck effigy bowl,* Mississippian period, from Madison County, Illinois. Effigy forms often depict birds of various kinds, sometimes animals and humans. This vessel is from Madison County, Illinois. Courtesy Gregory L. Perdun collection, Illinois.

PLATE 807: *Plainware,* Mississippian, with two strap handles. This well-formed and top condition vessel is from Pulaski County, Illinois. Courtesy Gregory L. Perdun collection, Illinois.

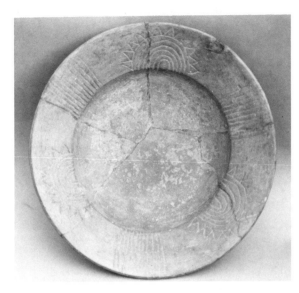

PLATE 810: *Pottery,* Mississippian, Wells Incised, plate form. It has alternate straight lines and sunbursts for design. This piece is from Brown County, Illinois. Courtesy Gregory L. Perdun collection, Illinois.

PLATE 808: *Plainware,* Mississippian, from Fulton County, Illinois. This is a well-formed container in very fine condition. Courtesy Gregory L. Perdun collection, Illinois.

PLATE 811: *Tippetts bean pot,* or beaker, Mississippian, and from the Cahokia Mound area. The upturned handle is interesting, being an image of a paw. This example is ca. AD 1000 - 1500. See Hathcock, *Ancient Indian Pottery of the Mississippi River Valley,* 2nd edition, p 53. Courtesy Gregory L. Perdun collection, Illinois.

PLATE 809: *Mississippian artifacts,* including triangular and notched arrowheads and a very rare Cahokia shark-tooth flint blade. These were inset into wooden clubs to make what were probably ceremonial weapons. It is from St. Genevieve County, Missouri, and is the only known example not to have come from the Cahokia Mounds proper. Courtesy Gregory L. Perdun collection, Illinois.

PLATE 813: *Discoidal,* Mississippian period, from Calhoun County, Illinois. It is made of a dark granite-like material and is scooped and polished. Size, 2" x 4½". Courtesy Charles West collection, Ohio.

PLATE 812: *Discoidal,* Mississippian period, from Madison County, Illinois. It is made of a dark, speckled granite-like hardstone that is quite attractive. This piece is nicely polished and measures 2½" x 4". Courtesy Charles West collection, Ohio.

PLATE 814: *Discoidal,* Mississippian period, from Schuyler County, Illinois. Material is an attractive light-colored granite with dark inclusions. This is a well-made and polished example, 1⅝" x 3¼" in diameter. Courtesy Charles West collection, Ohio.

PLATE 815: *Discoidal,* Mississippian period, a fine and large example made of light-colored granite-like hardstone. It is well scooped and polished, from Brown County, Illinois, and measures 2½" x 4½" in diameter. Courtesy Charles West collection, Ohio.

PLATE 816: *Discoidal,* Mississippian period, made of highly polished hardstone. It is 1¾" x 5¼", and is from Miami County, Ohio. This is a large and well-made example, ex-collection of H. Wachtel, who was one of the major oldtime Midwestern collectors. Courtesy Charles West collection, Ohio.

PLATE 817: *Scooped discoidals,* Mississippian period, both from Kentucky. Left, ½" x 2", Calloway County. Right, ½" x 1⅞", Trigg County. Both are made from high-grade hardstone and are heavily polished. Courtesy Charles West collection, Ohio.

PLATE 820: *Discoidal,* Mississippian period, from Moline, Illinois. It is made of fine dark granite-like hardstone and is well-polished. Size is 3" x 6½" in diameter. Example is ex-collections of Russell and Newwerk. Courtesy Charles West collection, Ohio.

PLATE 818: *Discoidal,* Mississippian period, from Boyd County, Kentucky. This example is made from a rare material, rose quartzite, and measures 1½" x 3" in diameter. Near-gemstone material adds to attractiveness and value. Courtesy Charles West collection, Ohio.

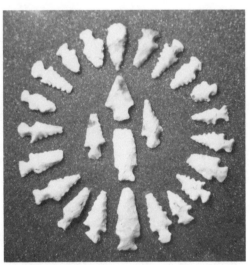

PLATE 821: *Sequoyah bird-points,* Mississippian and possibly Caddoan, with relatively large side notches and edge-serrations. The longest example here is 1⅜". This is a nice type display. Courtesy collection of L.A. Noblett; photograph by Victor A. Pierce, Missouri.

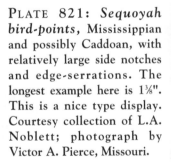

PLATE 819: *Discoidal,* Mississippian period, from Scott County, Missouri. This is a fine large artifact, made of variegated hardstone that is nicely polished. Size is 3" x 5" in diameter. A superior late prehistoric gamestone. Courtesy Charles West collection, Ohio.

PLATE 822: *Sequoyah bird-points,* Mississippian (possibly Caddoan) and all found in Maries County, Missouri. The center point is 1⅜" long. These are true late arrowheads, and well-made smaller examples as is typical of such point sizes. Courtesy collection of L.A. Noblett; photograph by Victor A. Pierce, Missouri.

PLATE 823: *Fort Ancient knife*, squared and shouldered base, made of grey Kentucky flint. It is from Brown County, Ohio, and was a personal find by the owner. Size is 1½" x 5½". This is one of the better large Fort Ancient knives, an overall superior artifact. Courtesy Donald E. Shuck collection, Ohio.

PLATE 826: *Midwestern chisels*, Mississippian period, all made of hardstone. Left, 4½", Ohio. Middle, 5¼", Kentucky. Right, 4¼", Kentucky. Courtesy Charles West collection, Ohio.

PLATE 824: *Triangular Fort Ancient knife*, Mississippian period, made from Ohio Brush Creek flint. It is from Brown County, Ohio, and came from the Eagle Creek area. This is a well-made blade, with size 1⅝" x 3½". Courtesy Donald E. Shuck collection, Ohio.

PLATE 827: *Chisel*, Mississippian tradition, made of a good grade of hardstone. It is well-shaped and highly polished, and an exceptional specimen. From Ohio County, Indiana, it is 1½" x 6½" long. Courtesy Charles West collection, Ohio.

PLATE 825: *Fort Ancient knives*, Mississippian period, and both from Brown County, Ohio. Left, shouldered blade made from Brush Creek flint, 1" x 2¾", personal find by owner. Right, bipointed blade, Carter County (KY) flint, 1" x 2⅞", personal find by owner. Courtesy Donald E. Shuck collection, Ohio.

PLATE 828: *Pottery vessel,* shell-tempered bowl, found in Henderson County, Kentucky. The freshwater mussel-shell spoon was associated with it. Size of bowl is 3¾" x 6¾". Ex-collection of Chalmer Lynch. Courtesy Marguerite L. Kernaghan collection, Colorado; photo by Marguerite & Stewart Kernaghan.

PLATE 830: *Mississippian plain jar,* double-lugged, a type which occurs in Early and Middle Mississippian Village Farmer localities. The exact origin of this vessel has been obscured for protective reasons, but is from St. Clair County, Illinois. Courtesy Gregory L. Perdun collection, Illinois.

PLATE 829: *Cahokia cord-marked vessel,* Mississippian period, very artistic form. It is from Madison County, Illinois, and is present in the Stirling, Moorehead, and Sand Prairie phases of the Village Farmer tradition. Courtesy Gregory L. Perdun collection, Illinois.

PLATE 831: *Tippetts bean pot,* or beaker, ca. AD 1000 - 1500. This may be the finest example found in Illinois, and is the only known bird effigy handle specimen to be recovered. This very fine vessel is from Brown County, Illinois. Courtesy Gregory L. Perdun collection, Illinois.

PLATE 832: *Discoidals*, Mississippian era, both from Sangamon County, Illinois. Each has a single cup on the wide faces. Left, polished hardstone, 2½" in diameter. Right, 3" in diameter, quartzite material. Courtesy Lee Fisher collection, Pennsylvania; Anthony Lang, photographer.

PLATE 833: *Head effigy pipe,* this form typical of the Fort Ancient peoples, Mississippian period. It is made of brown compact sandstone and measures 1½" x 2⅛". It was found in 1892 in Marion County, Ohio. Ex-collections of D. Beer and Stan Copeland for this fine piece. Courtesy Charles West collection, Ohio.

PLATE 834: *Vase-shaped pipe form,* made of golden tan quartzite. It measures 1¹³⁄₁₆" x 3⅛". This Mississippian piece is from Lake County, Ohio, and is well-shaped. Both the large bowl and smaller stem holes were begun, but not completed. Private collection, Ohio.

Chapter VI
Important Midwestern Collections

The typical Midwestern collector of prehistoric artifacts today has a few hundred to a few thousand artifacts. These are mostly average field-finds sprinkled with some above average specimens and topped with a very few superb pieces. Then there are beyond-average collectors who specialize in artifacts from their geographic regions and have amassed large collections of fine pieces. There are relatively few top collectors who have huge general collections plus an additional interest in one or two artifact classes and have the best of the best. Of course, there are many degrees of collecting achievement among the groups just-listed. It is enough to say that there are thousands of the former, only dozens of the latter.

All this is today, and dozens of Midwestern collectors could be named. The reason for such a concentration of collectors and artifacts is the almost endless variety and quality of high-grade prehistoric artifacts in the region. People in the Midwest have long been aware of the ancient past, and many have picked up bits and pieces of it. Some of this has been the result of purposeful searching, surface-hunting cultivated fields, that has taken place for the past two hundred years.

Of special interest to a book on Midwestern artifacts are the people there who once contributed in special ways or who put together huge collections. Some of these people were well-known and even nationally famous for the "relics" in their time. Today, it is hard to fully understand how big and important some of those collections were, even allowing for the fact that fewer people collected in a serious way 50 and 100 years ago, and prices were much lower back then even allowing for inflation.

Back then, prehistoric objects were considered more as curiosities ("curios") than artworks, at least by the general public. So the major collectors had a great deal less competition. But they also, in their searching out and love for the artifacts, were not only outstanding connoisseurs, but well ahead of their times. A good dictionary, by the way, defines connoisseurs as people with informed and astute discrimination, especially concerning the arts or matters of taste. These collectors had full measure of that rare and unwavering ability to see and appreciate and understand the beauty of certain classes of artifacts and they selected ancient things within those classes.

A note is in order regarding the difficulty of compiling even a brief historic record of great Midwestern collectors of prehistoric Amerind objects. To a certain extent, many of the important collectors of the past are practically unknown today because little was written about them. Or, any such articles packed with invaluable hard information (about the person and about the collection) tended to appear in local newspapers and so are generally unavailable for regional research. Most information, therefore, has come from specialized publications. It is known that a few old-time collectors preferred to be low-key, and only an occasional photograph or reference gives an idea of what they had really accomplished.

Some individuals were wealthy professionals or businessmen with the funds to acquire almost anything they desired, and they purchased by piece or group or entire collection. Others bought and traded as the opportunities arose, and gradually — often over many years — acquired stunning assemblages of top-level artifacts. Still others walked the fields every spring, rescuing what the plow had turned up and the rain had washed off. As these persons scoured the ancient village sites, their collections were assembled piece by piece.

What happened to all those great Midwestern collections, many hundred in all? Very few survive intact, because portions were sometimes donated to museums or bought by others to become part of even larger collections. Most, however, upon the death of the collector, were sold at auction. So even though most of the collections themselves do not exist as they were put together, as compact units, the artifacts now grace thousands of Midwestern collections. A relatively few were kept in the family through ongoing generations.

Due to factors already mentioned, only a small number of the great Midwestern collections are covered here. The sampling, however, will give some idea of who had what, and when. It also provides all Midwestern collectors (the writer included) with a dose of reality and humility in comparing what we have with what they had.

This brief and incomplete listing reminds everyone that the Midwestern region has been, and remains, a wonderful place to collect. On a population basis, the Midwest has a higher percentage of collectors than any other similar-size region in North America. This has been true since the mid-1800's and the observation is still valid today.

Albert L. Addis — Wolf Lake, Indiana   (d. 1951)

A collector for many years, Mr. Addis was friends with such notables as the author Warren K. Moorehead and Charles Heye (Heye Foundation and the Museum of the American Indian in New York City). Mr. Addis bought a large number of fine artifacts from farmers in his area, northeastern Indiana. Included were many top-grade glacial slate pieces, for which the region has long been noted. One large circular frame alone contained 61 superior examples of pendants, gorgets and Atl-atl weights of several varieties. His interest in collecting was so high that he called his farm (with name on the barn) "Arrowdale." A small museum was built on his farm property to display artifacts.

Mr. Addis also upgraded his collection at times. "FOR SALE / 1000 flint implements such as arrows, spears and knives, all good to fine, 15 pipes, 6 gorgets, 8 ceremonials, 10 celts, 10 fair to good roller pestles. All were found in Noble County, Indiana except the pipes. Pipes were found in vicinity of Portsmouth, Ohio, famous for its mound builder remains, and were in the Adams collection. This pipe collection was in the Ohio State Museum for many years. I am selling out duplicates to make room in museum which is too crowded. Will sell separately or as a whole."
Reference:
Advertisement, *The Archaeological Bulletin*, Vol. 5 No. 2, 1914.
Koup, Bill, and Kenny Simper, "Albert L. Addis," *Prehistoric Artifacts Of North America*, 1989, Vol. XXIII No. 2, pp 11-13.
Koup, Bill, and Kenny Simper, "The Albert Addis Photo Album Part II," *Prehistoric Artifacts Of North America*, 1989, Vol. XXIII No. 3, pp 12-15.

Clifford C. Anderson — Fort Ancient, Ohio   (d.1951)

Mr. Anderson did archeological work in the Eastern Midwest, and was associated for a time with Warren K. Moorehead. He excavated and studied prehistoric sites in Indiana, Kentucky and Ohio. Perhaps best known for his excavations at Ft. Ancient, Warren County, Ohio, Mr. Anderson helped publicize the spectacular Hopewell earthworks. His home was also near the great walls of this site. From about 1926-1945, the Andersons maintained a large public museum, built close to their home, in which were displayed many Indian artifacts. This collection was begun at Ft. Ancient in 1891, and the museum was located just outside the earthwork walls.
Reference:
McPherson, H.R., "Clifford C. Anderson—A Biographical Sketch," *Ohio Archaeologist*, January 1952, Vol. 2 No. 1, pp 29-31.

Thomas Beckwith — Southeastern Missouri   (d. 1913)

Born in the year 1840 in Mississippi County, southeastern Missouri, Mr. Beckwith had an early fascination with Indian things. There were 1100 cultivated acres on his father's much larger farm or plantation, including some mounds. The largest mound was 110 by 160 feet and 30 feet high. He began collecting artifacts at an early age, and eventually expanded farming operations that encompassed new land. The last 40 years of his life were spent in surface-hunting, collecting from eroded areas, and by controlled excavations. More than just a collector, Mr. Beckwith took care that his collection (from a limited geographic region, the Missouri low-lands) was orderly and fully documented. As an indication of the importance of the items to him, during his lifetime Mr. Beckwith never gave away or sold any artifacts.

The Thomas Beckwith Collection consisted of a large number of chert or flint hoes, and thousands of points and blades of all kinds. There were many fine specimens of axes and celts, but only one grooved example which in itself indicates the bulk of the material was from the Mississippian period, and late in prehistory. Other items included mortars and pestles, whetstones, pottery spools, cup-stones, paint cups and slabs, baked clay balls, many pipes, beads, earrings, labrets, and much more. This was the Beckwith general collection.

The Thomas Beckwith special collection consisted of pottery, and of vessels alone there were over 1100 specimens, these all whole or nearly so. The pottery pieces ranged from plain water bottles, to ornamented bottles, to effigy forms. The latter have animal or human designs or forms, and about 50 water bottles are the human form in various positions. Storage jars were represented, plus cooking pots either with suspension holes or ears. Many were effigy in form. In addition, there were numerous bowls and dishes, again many of them effigy types.

The Thomas Beckwith Collection was presented to the Southeast Missouri State University in June of 1913, shortly before Mr. Beckwith's death. In 1976, the Beckwith Collection of pottery was housed in the University Museum section of Memorial Hall, Southeast Missouri State University, where it can be seen today.
Reference:
Personal communication, 1 November 1990, Pat Reagan-Woodard, Museum & Gallery Director, University Museum, Southeast Missouri State University, Cape Girardeau, Missouri.

Dr. Rollin Bunch — Muncie, Indiana   (d. 1948)

Dr. Bunch had a very large collection, including effigy pottery, effigy pipes, Northwest Coast hardstone mauls, advanced Midwestern slate forms, and Intrusive Mound material. His axe collection was very large, and he once owned 113 fine birdstones. His collection was purchased by Dr. T. Hugh Young.

Reference:
Wachtel, Hubert C., *Who's Who In Indian Relics No. 1*, 1960, p 15.

Frank Burdett — Springfield, Ohio   (d. 1952)

Mr. Burdett's very large collection consisted of all Eastern Midwest fine artifact types. These included hardstone and slate bannerstones, expanded-base polished hardstone pestles and/or mauls, celts, birdstones, pipes of many kinds, axes, spades, hoes, cones or hemispheres, chisels, gorgets, pendants, chert and flint points and knives of most Midwestern types, and much else. His collection was sold to H.C. Wachtel.

Reference:
Wachtel, Hubert C., *Who's Who In Indian Relics No. 1*, 1960, pp 16-21.

Judge S.P. Dalton — Missouri   (d. 1965)

Judge Dalton was a member of the Greater St. Louis Archeological Society and Trustee of the Missouri Archeological Society. He was an experienced field-hunter, and in the central Missouri area he located and listed about 200 prehistoric sites. Judge Dalton collected thousands of artifacts which were carefully documented. A portion of his collection was donated to his alma mater, the University of Missouri, where he had received three degrees. The famous Dalton point cluster was named after this gentleman, who became Chief Justice of the Missouri Supreme Court.

Reference:
"Judge S.P. Dalton," *Central States Archeological Journal*, July 1965, Vol. 12 No. 3, p 108.
Perino, Gregory, *Selected Preforms, Points and Knives of the North American Indians*, Vol. I, 1985, p 97.

Warren Holland — Mt. Pleasant, Iowa   (d. 1988)

Mr. Holland was an avid surface-hunter for the years 1956-1976, and his activities centered in the Skunk River drainage area of Henry and Jefferson Counties, Iowa. He kept careful records of all finds. Mr. Holland is especially noted for the Holland Cache, a deposit of 14 large Late Paleo / Early Archaic blades found in Henry County, in 1966. The Holland points or blades have generally excurvate sides, were stemmed, and had varied basal treatments. Stem sides were parallel, expanded or contracted, and base-bottoms were straight, moderately concave or slightly concave. All points or blades were very well-chipped and quite thin. The Holland point or blade type was named in Warren Holland's honor.

Reference:
Perino, Gregory, *Guide to the Identification of Certain American Indian Projectile Points*, Special Bulletin No. 4, 1971, pp 56-57.
Vandyke, Gary, "Warren Holland," *Central States Archaeological Journal*, April 1989, Vol. 36 No. 2, p 104.

Byron W. Knoblock — Quincy, Illinois   (d. 1984)

Mr. Knoblock began collecting at a very young age, and eventually had one of the top artifact collections in the country. He was widely known throughout the collecting community, and was a founder of the Illinois State Archeological Society. In addition to his collecting activities, Mr. Knoblock was a commercial artist and did well-accepted work in oils. He is perhaps best known for a book he published in 1939, *Bannerstones Of The North American Indian*. This massive 600-page book has never been equalled in accurate and detailed coverage. Today the book is a sought-after collector item itself, and a must-have research volume for bannerstone collectors. Much of Mr. Knoblock's collection was donated to the Quincy Museum, and part went to the Illinois State Museum in Springfield.

Reference:
"Byron W. Knoblock," *Central States Archeological Journal*, January 1985, Vol. 32 No. 1, p 48.

Dr. Leon Kramer — Columbus, Ohio   (d. 1954)

Dr. Kramer, known as "The Flint King," specialized in fine Ohio flint artifacts. He "was known to be the possessor of some of the most outstanding and spectacular flint pieces in the world." In addition, Dr. Kramer had many other fine artifacts. The collection eventually was obtained by Dr. Young, Nashville, Tennessee.

Reference:
"In Memoriam," *Ohio Archaeologist*, April 1955, Vol. 5 No. 2, p 74.

Dr. Gordon Meuser — Columbus, Ohio   (d. 1971)

Dr. Meuser was famous for having the best collection, public or private, of high-grade Ohio prehistoric artifacts that had ever been put together. Many of the pieces were acquired when he made his rounds to patients in rural sections of the state. His specialties were slate and stone artifacts. While Dr. Meuser had celts and axes, some very fine, his collection consisted mainly of scarce to rare to unique pieces in each category. These included pipes, in platform, bowl, tubular and effigy forms, and bannerstones in a great variety of types. Some of these were crescents and knobbed lunates, picks, butterfly or winged forms, notched ovates, barrels and panels. In tubular banners alone there were short and long varieties, plus rounded, triangular and expanded-end.

Besides common gorgets, there were a number of rare Glacial Kame (Late Archaic) gorgets of the knobbed and spineback types, plus others. Dr. Meuser had many sandstone spools, bar amulets, and trophy axes, plus decorative and ornamental pieces of polished hardstone instead of the more usual slate materials. In addition to many discoidals and birdstones, Dr. Meuser had probably the largest individual collection of slate effigy or lizard stones. Ceremonial picks (Intrusive Mound), plummets and engraved pieces were present in quantity. The collection was so large it required seven auction sessions for dispersal.

Reference:

Converse, Robert N., *The Meuser Collection*, 1977.

Birdstones, all from the Late Archaic period. These specimens are mainly from Indiana and Ohio. This is a fine grouping that shows the varied forms for the type with different sizes. Material is glacial slate, usually the finely banded varieties. Courtesy Cameron W. Parks collection, photo taken in 1975. Lar Hothem photo.

Cameron Parks — Garrett, Indiana   (d. 1978)

A school-teacher, Mr. Parks devoted much of his life to collecting fine slate pieces from Indiana and the Midwest. He was known as "The Slate King of America," after having competed with Dr. Gordon Meuser of Ohio for the title. Since both had very extensive slate artifact collections, the agreement was that the survivor would be sole owner of the title. Dr. Meuser died in 1971, and Cameron Parks held the title for seven years. Mr. Parks had a wide range of prehistoric stone and flint objects,

some of very high quality. But his major interest was in glacial slate artifacts, especially birdstones. His slate artifacts included the usual pendants and gorgets, and he had entire old-fashioned glass-front display cabinets filled with such shelves. Rare slate pieces included most of the banner forms, such as ball, geniculate, pick, panel, barrel and tubular, plus bar amulets, and others. Birdstones, however, were his first love and at one time Mr. Parks had over 200 fine examples. These included elongated, flared-tail, Glacial Kame, animal-type, and additional types. He also had many fine hardstone birds, including the famous Parks Porphyry, a pop-eyed birdstone that could compete with the finest in the country. Mr. Parks would drive hundreds of miles for the chance to purchase or bid on birdstones. In a lifetime of surface-hunting, he found numerous slate pieces, including several damaged birdstones.

Reference:

Hothem, Lar, "A Visit With Cameron Parks," *Indian Artifact Magazine*, Jan-Mar 1987, Vol. 6 No. 1, pp 8-9, 53-54.

Edward W. Payne — Springfield, Illinois   (d. 1932)

Mr. Payne, a banker and businessman, had undoubtedly the largest and finest private Indian artifact collection in the Midwest, in North America, and in the world.

Truly, no one individual could have personally put together the collection of one-million-plus artifacts, and Mr. Payne had agents or buyers traveling the country, acquiring artifacts and entire collections. While part of the collection was kept in five huge underground steel vaults in Springfield, there was simply no room for storage or display of countless other pieces. Some boxes were never even unpacked between the time of purchase and Mr. Payne's death.

Also an author, Mr. Payne's book *The Immortal Stone Age* was published in 1938, after the gigantic collection had been dispersed. A listing of artifact classes in the Payne Collection would be lengthy, but some examples will indicate the extent of the collection. There were 13,000 stone axes, and 80,000 "arrowheads and spearheads." Among the major collections acquired were those of M.C. Long, Kansas City, MO, and Col. Bennett H. Young of Louisville, KY (author of *Prehistoric Men of Kentucky*), and C.E. Tribett of Darlington, IN. Eventually the enormous collection was offered to various government agencies, public museums and groups of collectors, but none could manage the finances. The bulk of the collection was put up for public auction in 1935.

Buyers came from all over the United States. Even in the Depression years — when a dollar would buy a multicourse dinner at a good restaurant — some of the artifact prices were high. A steatite pipe from Kentucky sold for $450, and two axes sold for $136 and $106, respectively. The largest known axe, almost 34 pounds, sold for $100. An effigy face pot brought $40, and three flint blades were $115. The unsold portions of the Payne collection were later displayed at a museum at the Dickson Mounds, Lewiston, Illinois. A large number of buyers attended the Payne auctions, and many important pieces were added to major collections. The Midwest will never again see the like of the fabulous Payne Collection.

Reference:
Photographs Of Interesting and Outstanding Specimens Of Indian Relics From The Edward W. Payne Stone Age Collection, First National Bank Of Springfield, 1937.

B.W. Stephens — Quincy, Illinois (d. 1970)

The huge collection of Mr. Stephens included a full range of fine Mississippian artifacts of the best quality, including the rare effigy pipes and hardstone spuds. Also included were large grooved axes, bannerstones of many kinds, notched hoes, long chipped blades, gorgets, pendants, a cache of 48 large turkeytail blades, a cache of 48 varied-size plummets, flint drills, Paleo points, notched-base blades, large and well-made celts, a mace and a scepter, large discoidals, shell beads, and much more. Mr. Stephens was one of the appraisers for the Edward Payne Collection and auction, and he helped organize the Illinois Archeological Society. In addition to his large collection (sold to Dr. T. Hugh Young) Mr. Stephens had a diverse and complete library.

Reference:
Mohrman, H.W., "In Memoriam — B.W. Stephens," *Central States Archeological Journal*, April 1971, Vol. 18 No. 2, p 93.
Parks and Thompson, *Who's Who In Indian Relics No. 3*, 1972, p 394.
Wachtel, Hubert C., *Who's Who In Indian Relics No. 1*, 1960, pp 89-100.

Claude U. Stone — Peoria, Illinois (d. 1957)

Mr. Stone was a multi-faceted man, being an attorney and at various times school principal and superintendent, Congressman, Postmaster of Peoria, and Editor and Publisher of *The Peoria Star*. It was as a collector of prehistoric artifacts, however, that his name is best known in Midwestern artifact circles. Mr. Stone had a very large collection, including for example over 100 birdstones and 1500 axes. He also had an outstanding collection of Temple Mound (Spiro, Oklahoma) material. Mr. Stone was a charter member of the Illinois Archeological Society, and held various offices there including president in 1947-1948. He also was influential in establish-

ing the Dickson Mounds as a State Park. Mr. Stone was, in the words of his son, one of those "great men with foresight and belief and curiosity."

Reference:
Personal communication, Claude U. Stone, Jr., 20 November 1990.
Wachtel, Hubert C., *Who's Who In Indian Relics No. 1*, 1960, p 109.

Hubert C. Wachtel — Dayton, Ohio (d. 1974)

Mr. Wachtel had an exceptionally large and comprehensive collection. It included many frames of chert and flint points and blades, axes, pottery, birdstones, bar amulets, winged and crescent bannerstones, gorgets, pendants, pestles and mauls, pipes in many sizes and styles, lizard effigies, boatstones, discoidals, and a great number of other artifacts. He had more than 130 large and fine St. Charles or Dovetail blades made of finest materials, plus many obsidian artifacts. The author of *Who's Who In Indian Relics No. 1* (1960) and *No. 2* (1968), Mr. Wachtel was widely known and respected. He eventually sold a number of pieces from his collection to friends, and his family kept the remainder. The Wachtel collection was noted for rare items and highest quality.

Reference:
Berner, John F., "Time Passes On . . .," *Artifacts*, Fall 1973, Vol. 3 No. 4, pp 3-7.
Wachtel, Hubert C., *Who's Who In Indian Relics No. 1*, 1960, pp 132-249.

Walter Wadlow — Dow, Illinois (d. 1965)

Mr. Wadlow was an amateur archeologist and collector in southwestern Illinois. He helped excavate at the Etley Site and Knight Site. At the last, he discovered the famous Knight Figurines, six Hopewell clay figures that showed the manner of dress in Middle Woodland times. Mr. Wadlow also discovered the Snyders Site, which indicated an association with Ohio Hopewell. Much of his work was written and published, so is available today. Mr. Wadlow is further distinguished by having an artifact type named for him, the Wadlow blade. This large square-base form was excavated by Mr. Wadlow at the Etley Site near Hardin, Illinois, where the cache of 75 was uncovered. They range from 5 to 12⅜ inches long.

Reference:
Browner, Tom, "Evolution Of The Illinois State Archeological Society," *Central States Archeological Journal*, 50th Anniversary Issue, October 1986, Vol. 33 No. 4, pp 198-199.
Perino, Gregory, *Selected Preforms, Points and Knives of the North American Indians*, Vol. I, 1985, p 389.

Joseph C. Walta — St. Louis, Missouri   (d. 1968)
Mr. Walta, an immigrant from Czechoslovakia, collected artifacts and had a preference for flint points and blades. Living near Cahokia Mound Group, he found about three thousand Cahokia points from 1930 to 1950. This may be a record for this point type for the region. Reference:
Fecht, William, "In Memoriam — Joseph C. Walta," *Central States Archeological Journal*, July 1969, Vol. 16 No. 3, p 141.

Warren K. Moorehead's monumental work, the two-volume set *The Stone Age In North America*, was published in 1910. As an indication of the importance of the Midwest — there were 48 contributors to the work — 16 were from this region. Midwestern Contributors were: Albert L. Addis, Indiana; E.E. Baird, Missouri; H.M. Braun, Illinois; H.F. Burkett, Ohio; F.M. Caldwell, Illinois; H.W. Franck, Illinois; F.P. Graves, Missouri; L.W. Hills, Indiana; W.A. Holmes, Illinois; G.Y. Hull, Missouri; W.C. Mills, Ohio; Missouri Historical Society; Ohio Archeological & Historical Society; Dr. C.L. Owen, Illinois; H.M. Whelpley, Missouri; Col. B.H. Young, Kentucky.

Chapter VII
Midwestern Prehistoric Facts

In the course of doing standard research for this book, a number of very interesting accounts were noted or facts gleaned from various sources. All relate in some way to this geographic region, and somehow involve the prehistoric time-frame. This information is well worth being summarized and reviewed in order to add an extra dimension to the study of ancient Midwestern material culture, the artifacts.

Postcard, the great Miamisburg Mound, Montgomery County, Ohio. This is the largest Adena (Early Woodland) mound in the Midwest. Its height (ca. 1925) was 68-70 feet, with a basal diameter of over 250 feet. Note the half a dozen people standing atop the mound for scale. Hothem collection.

Glaciation of the six Mid-western states covered in this book has relevance insofar as the glaciated areas came to have high-grade hardstones which served as raw material for certain artifact classes. These classes include (and are not restricted to) some bannerstones, some birdstones, some decorative pendants, some Atl-atl stones, ceremonial picks, plus many adzes, axes and celts. Midwestern states that had all or parts of continental glacial coverage were: The northwestern three-fourths of Ohio, Indiana, Illinois, Iowa, and northern Missouri. (Schuchert and Dunbar, *Textbook of Geology / Part II*, 4th Edition, 1945, pp 426-429.)

A rare cache of Late Archaic Ashtabula points or blades was found in Lorain County, Ohio, in the year 1918. There were at least ten in the cache, and all were large and very well-made. (*The Redskin — Prehistoric Art Classics*, Vol. XIV No. 3, 1979, pp 22-23, 38.)

One of the diagnostic artifacts associated with the Adena culture of the Early Woodland period is the grooved tablet. Most are made of fine-grained sandstone, a material which the Adena seemed to locate with ease and prefer for some artifacts. The Midwest has produced a few formal and classic decorated tablets with incised designs on one face and deep grooves on the other face. It is thought that the "design" side (often done in highly stylized raptorial birds) was coated with pigment and used as a body stamp. The other, grooved side may have been used to sharpen bone tattooing needles. Many other plainer Adena tablets have been found, some with red ochre or powdered hematite still caked in the grooves. (Hothem, various sources.)

Most prehistoric slate artifacts in the Midwest are made of glacial slate, much of it banded, and in colors of green, grey and black with contrasting colors in bands or streaks or swirls. Yellow slate may be the result of surface patination. Red slate is rare, and comprises no more than about 15% of all slate artifacts. The use of red slate is largely restricted to pendants and gorgets. (Hart, Steve, "Red Slate Ceremonials," *Prehistoric Art / Archaeology '81*, Vol. XVI No. 2, 1981, pp 44-47.)

Native silver, probably imported from the Lake Superior area or found alone or associated with copper in the glacial drift, has very sparingly been found in the Midwest. Silver was sometimes used to overlay Hopewell ear-spools with a thin veneer, but all silver objects or artifacts are extremely rare. At least two such occurrences have been noted. The Snake Den Mound B in Ohio (Adena Indian), excavated by Clarence Loveberry in 1897, produced the two hollowed halves of a concretion container. This held five native silver nuggets, with a total silver weight of 6.5 ounces. (Hothem, *Treasures Of The Mound Builders*, 1989, p 44.) Silver artifacts were found in Illinois, at the Liverpool Mounds Site Mound F-77, in Fulton County, opened by the Dickson brothers in 1926. This discovery within the Hopewell mound was a necklace of 120 silver beads. (Cole and Deuel, *Rediscovering Illinois*, Midway Reprint, 1975, pp 132-135.) This silver-bead necklace, by the way, was traded to the Smithsonian Institution for a pop-eyed porphyry bird-stone. (Townsend, *Birdstones Of The North American Indian*, 1959, p 76.)

The Hopewell Indians (Middle Woodland) of the Eastern Midwest are noted for the wide variety of materials used to make artifacts. This is especially true for the more ornate and cere-monial objects. Of inorganic mate-rials alone, they used slate, diorite, quartzite, granite, iron pyrite, flints, quartz crystal, chlorite (including goldstone), mica, chloritic schists, copper, hematite or iron ore, silver, obsidian, galena or lead ore, graphite and meteoric iron. (Mills, William C., "Explorations Of The Hopewell Group," *Certain Mounds And Village Sites In Ohio*, Vol. IV, 1926, p 295.)

Modoc Rock Shelter, Illinois, has given a good look at prehistory, including artifacts from stratified deposits that go back nearly to Paleolithic times. At the lower lev-els of the 27 feet of deposits, ca. 7900 BC, were found bone awls, choppers, scrapers, and side-notched blades or points. Even at this early age, a fairly wide range of tools was used. (Spencer and Jennings, *The Native Americans*, 1965, pp 47-49.)

A major concentration of rock art in the form of pet-roglyphs is located in Missouri, near the confluence of the Mississippi and Missouri Rivers. The designs are deeply pecked into limestone formations, and they include birds, humans, handprints, footprints and bird-tracks. (Grant, Campbell, *Rock Art Of The American Indian*, 1967, pp 137-139.)

Graham Cave, Missouri — now a Registered National Historic Landmark — lent its name to two dif-ferent point and blade types. The oldest is Paleo period, and is called Graham Cave Fluted. It is somewhat trian-gular, but has a wide and flared base and bold ears. The other type is Archaic, Graham Cave Notched, and has excurvate sides, shallow side notches, and a slightly incurvate baseline. (Chapman and Chapman, *Indians And Archaeology Of Missouri*, 1972, pp 30-37.)

Koster, the famous Illinois excavation, has produced a wealth of information about very early human habitation in the Midwest. Horizon 11, for example, was 32 to 35 feet below the present day ground surface, and was dated about 6400 BC, in the Early Archaic. To the surprise of many students of American prehistory, a complex lifeway already existed at that time, 8400 years ago. There were chipped points and blades in side-notched and bifurcated

Postcard, 1905. Portion of embankment (wall to left, interior ditch at center) of the extensive Newark Earthworks, Licking County, Ohio. This is the largest remaining Hopewellian (Middle Woodland) geometric system in the country. Hand-colored photo-graph, taken ca. 1905. Hothem collection.

types, stone adzes for woodworking, and slab mortars for seed-processing. Fish, clams and deer were utilized, dogs were kept, and people wove baskets and lived in houses. The village of Horizon 11 at Koster was about three-quar-ters of an acre in size. (Struever and Holton, *Koster — Americans in Search Of Their Prehistoric Past*, 1979.)

The Angel Mound Site, 435 acres located along the Ohio River in Vanderburgh and Warrick Counties, Indiana, was a large Middle Mississippian ceremonial complex. Excavated over many years, beginning in 1938, more than 1.8 million artifacts were found, of which over 99 percent were pottery sherds. The remainder were objects made of bone, clay, flint, native metal, shell and stone. Projectile points numbered 1407, most of which were the triangle form. Other artifacts included blades, perforators, scrapers and flake knives. Numerous chipped celts and ground celts were recovered, plus spades, pestles and mortars, and many other artifact classes. Of special interest were fluorspar pendants and beads. (Black, Glenn A., *Angel Site Vol. II*, Indiana Historical Society, 1967, pp 431-447.)

One of the finest Adena (Early Woodland) tubular pipes to come from the Midwest was found on Blennerhassett Island in the Ohio River. It was made of grey Ohio pipestone and was 8 inches long, very symmetrical. Highly polished, the rare object was recovered in 1889. (*The Redskin*, Genuine Indian Relic Society, Inc., Vol. II No. 3, July 1967, p 113.)

The Robbins is a Late Adena point or blade with a wide excurvate body, barbed or straight shoulders, and a straight-sided stem with a rounded or straight base-bottom. Fairly common in the Eastern Midwest, the type was named after the Robbins Mounds in Boone County, Kentucky. (Webb and Elliot, *The Robbins Mounds*, University of KY, Vol. V No. 5, 1942, pp 437-438.)

A very rare cache or subsurface deposit of prehistoric copper artifacts was found in Clinton County, Illinois, in 1969. The discovery consisted of five artifacts, with a bi-pointed pick at 8⅞ inches being the longest. Other items included three squared-end celts and a hollowed two-hole boatstone. In the author's opinion, these items would have been Hopewell (Middle Woodland) in origin. (*Central States Archeological Journal*, October 1970, Vol. 17 No. 4, p 170 fig 115.)

Northern Kentucky and southern Indiana have long been known as the major Midwestern areas for Shell Mound sites, with major components from Middle and Late Archaic times. In Kentucky, along with the famous Indian Knoll, the Carlson Annis Mound was an important site. Excavations, begun in 1939, revealed many flint, stone, bone, and shell and antler artifacts. As at Indian Knoll, stone Atl-atl weights were found with Atl-atl hooks and there were some 30 of these hooks at Carlson Annis. Of the stone weights, 22 were prismoidal, 49 were various types of flat bar weights, while one was a winged "butterfly" type. (Webb, *The Carlson Annis Mound*, University of KY, Vol. VII No. 4, 1950, pp 299, 304.)

Three important Early Archaic St. Charles or Dovetail points or blades have come from Ohio. Made of high-quality multi-colored Flintridge (VanPort) material

from Licking County, each is of exceptional size and beauty. The Hegler Spear is 7⁹⁄₁₆ inches long, and possibly came from near Washington Court House, Fayette County. The Fletcher Spear is 7⅜ inches long, and from near Pleasant Valley, Muskingum County. The Copeland Spear is 7³⁄₁₆ inches long, and came from Ross County. Dovetails of this size in perfect condition and in jewel material are exceptionally rare. (Townsend, Earl C. Jr., "Ohio Flint Ridge Dovetails," *The Redskin*, Genuine Indian Relic Society, Inc., Vol. I No. 1, July 1966, pp 6-9.)

Lost City was a large mound complex near Lewisburg, in Logan County, Kentucky. Funkhouser and Webb explored the site in 1929, when it was known as the Page Site. A total of 69 mounds were listed, and 18 were excavated. Under the auspices of E.F. Gibbs, the site was shown to the public as Lost City. A nearby bluff contained a village site, and a "serpent mound" about 900 feet in length. One very large "temple" mound was over 100 feet in diameter. (Gibbs, Erwin F., "Glover's Cave And Lost City Comparison," from Vietzen's *The Saga Of Glover's Cave*, 1956, pp 258-261.)

Without a doubt, the single most important overall food animal in the prehistoric Midwest was the deer. Excavations at most prehistoric sites show deer bones to be relatively common, suggesting that the meat was frequent fare. In addition, hides were used to make clothing, and antler and bone were used for artifacts of many kinds. Such artifacts include fish-hooks, projectile points, awls, perforators and punches, needles, and, less commonly, handles for knives, Atl-atls and scrapers. (Hothem, various sources.)

The 1893 World's Fair at Chicago featured, among other attractions, prehistoric North American artifacts from many states. It was a point of honor for each state to display the finest pieces, and the Midwest was well-represented. Artifacts and artworks included pipes from 2 to 8 pounds in weight, and from 4 x 5 to 6 x 7 inches, mainly effigy forms. Missouri examples were often kneeling figures. The Missouri Exhibit (with many items from the collection of W. J. Seever) had the best groups of flint, hematite and stone artifacts. This was the first time that very large numbers of the general public were able to see some of the best prehistoric artifacts. Again in reference to the Missouri Exhibit, ten thousand objects were shown, with flint artifacts alone ranging from ¼ inch to 18 inches in length. ("Prehistoric Sculptures of the Mississippi Valley At The Fair," *The Archaeologist*, Vol. I No. II, 1893, forepage advertisement, pp 208-212.)

Many Midwestern prehistoric tools and weapons

were made of hematite, natural iron ore that exists in many grades of color and hardness. Ancient quarries for mining hematite are found in the Iron Mountain region of Missouri. This particular ore was dark, hard, and accepted a high polish. (Sellers, Paul V., "Hematite Artifacts," *Central States Archeological Journal*, July 1967, Vol. 14 No. 3, pp 114-117.)

One of the most unusual artifacts to be found in the Midwest is probably completely unknown to the average collector — and in fact is an artifact that cannot (or should not) even be collected because it is somewhat a landscape feature. Many cliff areas of the Midwest have rock-shelters, also called roof-shelters, and a number of the shelters have the so-called "hominy holes." Technically, these are called "bed-rock mortars." They are narrow, deep holes sunk into solid rock, and were no doubt used to pulverize nuts and seeds, perhaps even beans and maize. Likely, long hardwood pestles were used with the holes. The artifacts above-mentioned were sometimes used when the hominy-holes were worn too deep for ease of use. Rather than begin a new hole, the original hole was refurbished by inserting a cone-shaped piece of stone that in effect made the hole less deep. These hominy-hole plugs are extremely rare. (Webb and Funkhouser, *Ancient Life In Kentucky*, 1928, p 144.)

The peoples who constructed Midwestern mounds, especially the Middle Woodland Hopewell, often made elaborate and highly specialized artifacts. No doubt some were for decoration or ceremony or ritual, for they are sometimes far too large for any utilitarian uses. Among such discoveries was a great cache of blades or knives or spearpoints which came from Ohio's Hopewell Mound Group in 1891. One gigantic obsidian notched/stemmed blade was about 9½ inches wide and over 17 inches long. The Seip Mound Group in Ohio provided an elongated celt of copper, weighing 27 pounds. The Hopewell Group also produced a celtiform copper axe which weighed 38 pounds. (Shetrone, *The Mound Builders*, 1931, pp 148-149.)

The Green River region of Kentucky is noted for a unique type of Atl-atl balance weight. These were made of river mussel shell in triangular forms, drilled with a large hole in the center, and lined in a series on the Atl-atl shaft. From seven to fifteen units made a single (composite) weight set. (Kellar, *The Atlatl In North America*, Vol. III No. 3, 1955, p 317.)

A brief survey of Ohio's copper (from the glacial drift and from the Great Lakes region) artifacts is worthy of note. The artifacts are listed here as to type, as well as to numbers known to have been collected by the year 1877.

Axes (celts) and adzes, 33; chisels and gouges, 9; spearpoints, lance-heads or daggers, 6; knives and cutting tools, 1; perforators (awls, borers, drills, etc.), 8; tubular beads, 650; plates (head, breast, ear) 9; pendants, 1; bracelets, 30; buttons, studs, bosses, more than 4; miscellaneous, 33. ("Ancient Copper Implements In Ohio," *Ohio Centennial Report*, Ohio State Board, 1877, pp 107-112.)

The Adena of Early Woodland times were the first Eastern Midwest people to make widespread use of pottery or fired clay utensils. They made at least 14 different kinds of ceramics, as follows: Adena Plain, Johnson Plain, Limestone-tempered Check-stamp, Montgomery Incised, Sand-tempered Plain, Sand-tempered Check-stamp, Grit-tempered 5-line Diamond, Levissa Cord-marked, Paintsville Simple Stamped, Fayette Thick, Woodland Plain/Adena Variety, Woodland Cord-marked, Grit-tempered Check-stamp, and, Grit-tempered Fabric-marked. (Webb and Snow, *The Adena People*, 1945, pp 102-103.)

A very unusual and important cache of Mississippian sheet-copper effigy plates was found near Malden, Dunklin County, Missouri, around 1908 or just prior to that year. The cache was plowed up by a Ray Groomes, and came from a depth of 16 to 18 inches and below. There were eight copper effigies, which had been buried with flat faces touching and at about a 45-degree angle. Some of the plates were slightly plow-damaged and there was some corrosion, but otherwise the artwork was intact. The figures depicted were of stylized raptorial birds (6), a chief-warrior human (1), and a double-headed raptorial bird (1). Fowke, Gerard, *Antiquities Of Central And Southeastern Missouri*, 1910, p 98, plates 15-19.)

The Simonsen Site, in Cherokee County, Iowa, is an important Early Archaic bison-kill area. There, the remains of about 25 extinct animals (*Bison occidentalis*) were found eroding from a bank along the Little Sioux River. The bone layer was under 15 feet of natural soil deposits, indicating considerable age. Excavations determined that the bison had been killed by human hunters, as charcoal and artifacts were associated with the remains. There were six fragmentary side-notched points or blades, plus chipped knives and scrapers. A radio-carbon date on hearth charcoal indicated an age of 6470 BC +/- 520 years. (McKusick, *Men Of Ancient Iowa*, 1964, pp 59-64, 223.)

A cache of ten fine Turkeytail points or knives was found in Iroquois County, Illinois. They were made of blue-grey chert, and the lengths were from 4¾ to 7 inches. (*The Redskin*, Genuine Indian Relic Society, Inc, Vol. III No. 4, October 1968, pp 134-135.)

The George West Pipe was owned by its namesake in the early 1900's. (Mr. West was the author of the noted two-volume work, *Tobacco Pipes And Smoking Customs Of The American Indians*, published in 1934.) Found in Floyd County, Indiana, the pipe is one of the Middle-Late Woodland Great Pipes. It is ca. AD 500-600, and represents a bird with folded wings and tucked legs and talons. Made of grey-brown Tennessee steatite, the pipe is 8 inches long. There is a large, raised bowl in the middle of the upper back. Overall, the pipe is extremely well-designed and crafted. One of the top Great Pipes from the Midwest, the George West pipe resided in many famous collections before joining the Hart Collection. (Hart, Gordon, *Hart's Prehistoric Pipe Rack*, 1978, pp 91-93.)

J.R. Nissley was a major collector and dealer who lived at Ada, Ohio, in the late 1800's. He traveled to the World's Fair in 1893, and an account of his trip gives clues to how collecting was done a century ago, and his notes provide facts on regional artifact differences. "We set out from Ohio on the fifth of last June with wagon, collecting on the way to this locality (Carlyle, Illinois), obtaining, however, nothing that would interest an old or experienced collector. Hence disappointment was our share very often. The writer was much interested in the great variety of material and local oddity of types as he slowly wended his way westward. He was also favored with excellent facilities to observe peculiarities in other localities; and also to meet on the way types and materials originating in Ohio which gradually grew less as the distance from that state was increased. It is hard to tell where is situated the line that divides Ohio objects from those that were brought from the west and south-west. This, the writer supposes, can be determined by a number of overland trips eastward or westward through Indiana." (Nissley, J.R., "Relics On The Kaskaskia River," *The Archaeologist*, Vol. I No. II, 1893, p 217.)

Most collectors are aware that fish-hooks are quite old, and that no flint fish-hook has ever been found in the Midwest — or anywhere else in the country, for that matter — that was without a doubt old and authentic. This refers to the traditional bent hook type. Gorge-hooks, designed to be swallowed, are short and usually straight, and were secured by line at the center. These were occasionally made of flint, often from what appears to be a section of drill-shaft, perhaps salvaged in this fashion. Others were made of wood, bone or antler. Most bent fish-hooks were made in the Midwest by cutting a section of hollow bone at an angle. A piece with an elongated cross-section, if cut correctly, produced two hooks. Fish-hooks were also made from deer and elk teeth. (Hothem, various sources.)

In the early 1900's, the purpose of Midwestern earthen mounds was the subject of much speculation. Some, but not all, mounds were used for burial purposes, and several types were simply elevated cemeteries. Other suggested reasons for the presence and purpose of mounds included observation platforms, sacrificial sites, signaling mounds (smoke by day, fire by night), low mounds as the result of collapsed earth-roofed houses, for defense (at strategic locations), heaps of camp refuse, and for ceremonial purposes. (Webb and Funkhouser, *Ancient Life In Kentucky*, 1928, pp 71-101.)

There are numerous hilltop "fortifications" in southern Indiana, southern Ohio, and northern Kentucky that defy ready explanations. These earthworks are generally quite large in acreage enclosed, and even small villages were in the interior of some. The walls, of varying heights and thicknesses, were generally made of earth and some stone, though walls mainly of stone are found where this construction material was readily available. Most of the "forts" in the region named were put up late in the Hopewell or Middle Woodland period; early writers explained in great (and imaginary) detail how they protected the industrious inhabitants. The only problem is, there is very little evidence of ferocious battles or villages being burned to the ground or the walls purposely demolished. So the real purpose for the hilltop earthworks is yet to be determined. They may have in fact been a form of prehistoric insurance, rarely needed but there anyway, just in case. (Hothem, various sources.)

A series of mounds along the Illinois River in Illinois denotes the presence of a people known variously as the Illinois culture or Bluff culture. Their characteristic artifacts, such as at Dickson Mounds, included pottery vessels of many sizes, mussel-shell spoons, marine-shell pendants, bone needles, L-shaped pipes, flint points, stone celts, and bone ornaments. (Shetrone, *The Mound Builders*, 1931, pp 324-329.)

In 1968, an unusual Atl-atl hook-end was found in Christian County, Kentucky. Made of polished antler or bone, it had a typical length of 5 inches and the usual small, raised hook to engage the lance-base. It was atypical, however, in having tally marks on the upper face, a slotted or inset base, and a hole at right angles to the slot for pin attachment. Most such Atl-atl end-hooks have simple socketed bases. (*Central States Archeological Journal*, January 1969, Vol. 16 No. 1, pp 22 fig 15.)

One of the most interesting materials used for artifacts in the Midwest was cannel coal, a jet-black lightweight material composed originally of plant spores and compressed into solid form over countless millions of years. Cannel coal was easily carved by prehistoric artisians and the substance accepted a high polish. It was especially favored by Indians of the Woodland and Mississippian periods in the Midwest. They carved many decorative and ornamental objects from it, including gorgets, pendants, many kinds of beads, plus imitation animal teeth and talons of birds of prey. Among other places, cannel coal was found near flint formations at Ohio's famed Flintridge quarries. (Hothem, various sources.)

One point type that is found throughout the Midwest, though sparingly, is the Early Paleo Clovis point. This specialized lance or spear point has a concave base and shallow flutes on one or both lower faces, driven in from base toward tip. The Clovis is the basic type, and there are many varieties in the Midwest. Sub-types or related points found in all or part of the Midwest include the Ross County, Redstone, and Holcombe. (Justice, Noel, *Stone Age Spear And Arrow Points Of The Midcontinental And Eastern United States*, 1987, pp 17-24.)

The Red Ochre phase, a mysterious Midwestern prehistoric people that apparently were not large in numbers, left behind distinctive and diagnostic artifacts. One of their best-known traits was to bury caches of long bipointed blades with shallow side-notches near one end, the Turkeytail. These are usually made of Indian hornstone or Kentucky material. Early Woodland in time, this people almost invariably sprinkled liberal amounts of red ochre or powdered hematite over the deposits. Other artifacts from Red Ochre peoples include wide, flat hardstone "gorgets" (probably Atl-atl emblems) and elongated bar amulets, possibly Atl-atl handles. Their main living area was in the Eastern Midwest, but Turkeytail caches turn up elsewhere. A very interesting sideline is that the Red Ochre people may have put up a walled earthwork in Peoria County, Illinois, near Elmore. This consisted of three mounds and a multi-sided linear wall with a bluff-line forming a concave finishing side. Early excavations produced bits of galena or lead ore, leaf-shaped blades, copper awls or needles, two white chert or flint blades 4 and 4½ inches long, respectively, and copper beads and tubes. Red ochre was found with many of the artifacts. The main mound was 19 by 62 feet, and only 18 inches high. Dates for Red Ochre are within the 700 BC - AD 1 period. If the site is indeed Red Ochre, it may be unique for Illinois. (Maginel, Dr. C.J., and John P. Wilson, "A Red Ocher Earthwork Enclosure in Illinois?" *Central States Archeological Journal*, January 1970, Vol. 1, pp 4-16.)

The Heavy Duty is a point or blade type that is much-admired by collectors in the Eastern Midwest. It is Archaic in time, and unresharpened specimens are medium-large in size. Made of quality flints, the type has a wide, strong stem which may be somewhat bi-lobed in some examples. The body is thick and there is often a median ridge. Flaking is well-done, and many of the flake-scars are long and ribbon-like. (Edler, Robert, "The Heavy Duty Point," *The Redskin*, Vol. V No. 1, January 1970, pp 16-17.)

Some of the most valued and unusual materials ever used for Archaic bannerstones of advanced design and nearly ultimate forms were the rose quartzites, once called "blooded quartz." It was used often for hourglass and bottle banner forms. The material is most common (or least scarce) in the Western Midwest, although a solitary example can turn up almost anywhere in the Midwest. The material is exceptionally hard, beautifully variegated or shaped with one or more colors, and takes (after much work) a beautiful polish which it holds well. According to one source (Hamilton, et al, *A Guide To Minerals, Rocks and Fossils*, 1974, pp 128-129) the color is rose-red to pink, and it "is usually found massive rather than as crystals." This explains why prehistoric peoples were able to find large-enough masses for their bannerstones. Another source (Fritzen, *The Rock-Hunter's Field Manual*, 1959, p 190) mentions that the deeper colors "may fade to a very light pink after long exposure to the weather." A related material is ferruginous quartz, in dark red to yellow. There has been much discussion as to where this beautiful material originated, before it or the artifacts made from it entered early trade routes. Moorehead (*Stone Ornaments Of The North American Indians*, 1917, p 40) states that rose quartzite comes from Arkansas.

A cache of plummets was found prior to 1964 in Calhoun County, Illinois. All examples were made of hematite or natural iron ore, and all were drilled for attachment or suspension. The fourth largest of the group was long and slender, and measured 5⅛ inches long. (*Central States Archeological Journal*, July 1964, Vol. II No. 3, p 99 fig 65.)

Looking at the Midwest by way of an early map showing mounds and walls, the location of such massive geographic artifacts is of interest. In general, and with exceptions, such works are located within the drainage systems of major rivers. As examples, the following rivers (among others) in these Midwestern states once had numerous earthworks: Scioto, Ohio; Cumberland, Kentucky; Wabash, Indiana; Illinois, Illinois; Des Moines, Iowa, and Missouri, Missouri. Such locations suggest that to the mound-building peoples, rivers were important for transportation and trade and communication purposes. (Shetrone, *The Mound Builders*, 1931, pp 28-29 fig 8.)

In the Midwest, only a relatively few prehistoric woven fabrics have been preserved. Such preservation is usually whole in one case, and partial in the other. In the former, various fabrics have been found in dry rock-shelters, where the overhangs protected the interior and the fabrics from moisture and prevented the growth of destructive bacteria. Additionally, dry dust helped protect and preserve such fabrics. In the latter case, partial samples have come from mounds, mainly of the Middle Woodland period, where the fabrics have been in contact with copper artifacts such as decorative plates or large celts. Copper salts helped preserve fabrics that were in direct contact with the copper. (Hothem, various sources.)

One of the largest pipes found in the Midwest was an obtuse angle elbow example, thought to be ca. AD 1150. The bowl was 8 inches long and with the wide, flat base/stem was 17 inches in overall length. This fantastic pipe came from a mound in Marion County, Kentucky. (Moorehead, Warren K., *The Stone Age In North America*, 1910, Vol. 22, p 43 fig 444.)

Creased-top celts are a rare form of ungrooved axe, and they seem to be found mainly along a short segment of the Mississippi Valley from Keokuk, Iowa, to Hannibal, Missouri. Most of these celt forms are the squared-poll type, and as the name suggests, the poll top is lightly and thinly grooved or incised or creased. This crease is at right angles to the edge dimension, or across the short part of the poll. The crease is usually nearer one corner of the poll, not in the center. The most plausible theory for such creases is that they may have somehow served as a hafting aid when the celt was mounted in a sturdy hardwood handle. (Sellers, Paul V., "The Creased Top Celts," *Central States Archeological Journal*, January 1968, Vol. 15 No. 1, pp 4-6.)

Two of the largest celts ever made in North America came from Kentucky, and are probably Mississippian in origin. One was a long, narrow form, 17½ inches long, and with greatest width of 3½ inches. Another had a slightly triangular form, and was 18 inches long and 7¾ inches wide at the excurvate bit. (Moorehead, Warren K., *The Stone Age In North America*, 1910, Vol. I, p 266.)

In 1981, a cache of 84 Hopewell (Middle Woodland) blanks was found in St. Charles, Missouri. Probably preforms for North-type blades or points, the cache was buried about 4 feet down and was uncovered during land-scape work. Artifact materials were either white Missouri chert or a glossy pinkish or pink and white. The artifacts ranged from 3¼ to 4¾ inches long. (Kinker, Joe, "Recent Cache Find," *Central States Archeological Journal*, April 1982, Vol. 29 No. 2, pp 88-99.)

An interesting cache was found in St. Clair County, Illinois, in 1897. It was important because it was not the typical cache of single-type artifacts of similar size and material. Included were a flint spade 15¾ inches long, four flared-bit hoes, three flint chisels, a "turtle-back" (preform?) blade, a 6-inch knife, a cupped stone and a celt. (The artifacts suggest the cache dated from Mississippian times.) (Throop, Addison J., *Mound Builders Of Illinois*, 1928, p 17.)

In 1978, a cache of large Wadlow blades was found, probably in the St. Louis area of Missouri. There were ten blades in the cache, the longest of which was 8⁵⁄₁₆ inches. All blades appeared to be made of a mottled and speckled chert. (Turin, John, "Wadlow Cache Blades," *Central States Archeological Journal*, January 1980, Vol. 27 No. 1, pp 30-31.)

Cup-stones or the so-called nut-stones are found throughout the Midwest, usually on Archaic village sites. These common but mysterious artifacts have also been called lap-stones or flat mortars, also spindle-rod foot-rests. They are quite simple, just a depression in softer rock like sandstone, the indentations an inch or less in depth, and the size of a quarter to a silver dollar across. Some cups, at bottom center, show a faint or bold conical pit depression, as if the depth had been enhanced with a chert or flint drill. Hundreds of thousands of these artifacts exist, and the stones may have from one to dozens of the strange depressions, often on both faces or even the edges of slabs. Despite their high find-frequency – the writer once picked up seven on one site in an hour – and their relatively unsophisticated design, no one knows for sure what they were used for. It is possible they are related to food preparation, but it is possible they are not. There have been many theories and explanations for cup-stones advanced, but all have drawbacks and seemingly equal-value counter-theories. Whoever comes up with some proof as to actual use will have done the study of Midwestern prehistory a great favor. (Hothem, various sources.)

Two of the largest grooved axes found in the Midwest have come from Kentucky. One, made of dark-colored hardstone, was 8 by 13½ inches. From Warren County, it weighed 30 pounds. The largest axe, from Christian County, was 8½ by 15 inches and weighed 32 pounds. Both axes were full-grooved. (Young, Col.

Bennett H., *The Prehistoric Men Of Kentucky*, The Filson Club, 1910, pp 93, 125-126.)

In 1977, a cache of about 30 large blades was found in southern Indiana. Most were ovate with one pointed end, very well-made, and of Harrison County flint or Indiana hornstone. Colors were beige to blue-grey, sometimes with the several colors in one artifact. These were Woodland in origin, and the largest blade was 4⅛ by 9⅛ inches. (Lawson, Eric J., "The Williams Cache," *Central States Archeological Journal*, April 1978, Vol. 25 No. 2, pp 78-80.)

Wyandotte Cave, in Crawford County, Indiana, was one source for a variety of the famous Harrison flint or Indiana hornstone. The material is blue-grey, and one quarry site was located about one mile from the cave entrance. One cave room at that distance had the floor covered with 5 to 6 feet of flint nodules and flakes. (Lilly, Eli, *Prehistoric Antiquities Of Indiana*, Indiana Historical Society, 1937, p 106.)

One of the more fascinating aspects of the Middle Woodland Hopewell people is their embankments or "sacred ways." Truly, as earlier writers have referred to them, the Hopewells were the Romans of the Midwest (and North America) in terms of engineering with earth. In addition to fortified hilltops and valley earthworks in geometric patterns (squares, octagons, circles) they constructed innumerable mounds large and small. But perhaps the most mysterious of their works is the matter of the missing walls, or lines not present today. A good example is, or was, located at Portsmouth, Ohio, in Scioto County. A large group of earthworks was on the Ohio side of the Ohio River, while two additional and apparently associated groups were on the Kentucky side. The whole stretched along the river for about 8 miles. The first widely publicized reporting of this site was by Squier and Davis, in *Ancient Monuments of the Mississippi Valley*, Smithsonian Vol. I, 1847, pp 77-78, plate XXVII. Parallel walls or embankments often connected Hopewellian ceremonial centers, and they had various names: graded ways, sacred ways, covered ways, avenues. The parallel embankments of the Portsmouth group for the walls discussed here were about 4 feet high, 20 feet thick at the base, and were as much as 150 feet across or between the walls. This in itself is very interesting, but the walls on the Portsmouth side went to the Ohio River and re-emerged from the Ohio River on the Kentucky side. A mighty river was not allowed to interfere with whatever the walls meant in prehistoric times. People may have crossed the water by swimming, raft, dugout, bark boats, or even a floating walkway might have been used, impossible as it might seem. (Hothem, various sources.)

In 1916, a cache of beautifully worked blades was found in Tazewell County, Illinois. There were about 40 in the original cache, some broken. Of 31 examples studied, 12 were unnotched and 19 were corner-notched with deep and narrow notches. The unnotched specimens were slightly more squared in the basal region that were the notched examples. The artifact material was a light-colored chert from the Crescent Quarries which are located near St. Louis. The artifact forms suggest Hopewell (Middle Woodland) manufacture. (Weedman, William L., "The Mackinaw Cache Revisited," *Central States Archeological Journal*, April 1985, Vol. 32 No. 2, pp 60-62.)

Central Kentucky is noted for rock shelters, mainly in the layers of Waverly sandstone. Softer portions weathered away and left protective, solid-rock overhangs; some of these shelters are 50 to 60 feet deep. Many artifacts were found in such protected areas years ago, and interesting features of some were dwelling remains with rock walls. (Young, Col. Bennett H., *The Prehistoric Men Of Kentucky*, The Filson Club, 1910, pp 30-31.)

True Folsom points of Late Paleo times have been found well beyond their normal Western U.S. distribution ranges, and have turned up in the Midwest. These thin, fully-fluted points have been found in Illinois, and may well be present as very rare finds in other Midwestern states. (Perino, Gregory, "Early Projectile Points Found," *Central States Archeological Journal*, July 1967, Vol. 14 No. 3, pp 103-106.)

For those who look hard and long for a fine grooved axe, there is yet hope. Several years ago, a man was surface hunting a small ridgeline near a stream in Iowa. Before the morning was out, he had picked up seven grooved axes, all in good to perfect condition. One axe was full-grooved and six were three-quarter grooved. (Hothem, personal communication.)

An interesting and rare pendant form is found in Illinois, and perhaps elsewhere in the Midwest. It is an elongated animal effigy with four stubby legs indicated, and a long tail. They are outline forms, as if seen from the side. Forequarters terminate in a tapered head. These were first chipped from chert or flint, then ground and polished to remove flaking scars. About mid-back a small raised and rounded knob was left to serve as an attachment point, apparently for a thong or cord. These rare effigy pendants, 3 to 6 inches long, are probably ca. AD 500, in the Late Woodland period. Very few collectors, even within the geographic area, have examples. (Hothem, various sources.)

Fluorspar or fluorite is a mineral found in many light colors: blue, brown, green, violet or yellow. Barite or "heavy spar" is a colorless crystalline mineral. Both minerals were used in late prehistoric times in the Midwest to make small and attractive decorations or ceremonial objects. These included pendants and effigy heads. A figurine of barite from southern Illinois was 2 by 4½ inches, and 1½ inches thick. (*Central States Archeological Journal*, July 1970, Vol. 17 No. 3, p 111, fig 73.)

Plummets are found throughout the Midwest in more than half a dozen different forms or named types, such as Elm Point, Snyders, Gilcrease and Godar. Many are made of hematite, natural iron ore, while others exist in high grades of hardstone. Recent thought is that plummets — named for similarity to a carpenter's plumb-bob — were used as throwing weights, since they are sometimes found as sets of from three to five specimens. These would have been secured to lines, cords or nets, perhaps to entangle or enmesh waterfowl. In support of this theory, plummets are often found near ponds, marshes and lakes. They are Late Archaic and Early Woodland in time. A few rare specimens were made of jasper and even rock crystal. Most are somewhat teardrop-shaped, may have a suspension hole or groove at the smaller end, and are from 1 to 4 inches long. (Hothem, various sources.)

In 1976, a fine cache of Late Paleo/Early Archaic points or blades was found in Illinois by E.R. Smith. The artifacts were surface-found and were made of high-grade mottled chert in tans to white colors. Lengths were 5¼ to 6 inches, and only one example was broken, near the tip. The type is probably a Dalton variant. Early artifacts such as these are rarely found in groups or caches. (Thompson, Ben, "Illinois Cache Found," *Central States Archeological Journal*, October 1976, Vol. 23 No. 4, p 157, fig 108.)

One of the great mysteries to those interested in Midwestern artifacts is what the Late Archaic birdstones were really used for. There have been numerous theories over the years, some fanciful, some practical. Recent thought is that the elongated flat-bottomed forms with holes drilled at each end are somehow associated with the Atl-atl or lance-thrower. These suggest that birdstones might have been weights or counter-balances or handles or hand-grip guides or positioners. However, no firm evidence has ever been found to support any of these theories — or any other theory for that matter. (Hothem, various sources.)

The largest Fort Ancient (Mississippian period) site in Indiana is reported to be near the mouth of Laughery Creek, in Ohio County. It consists of two nearby sites, these separated by about 500 feet. One site was 250 by 1030 feet, while the other was 300 by 1720 feet. In addition, six mounds were once associated with the site. (Lilly, Eli, *Prehistoric Antiquities Of Indiana*, Indiana Historical Society, 1937, p 68.)

Four of the greatest caches of prehistoric artifacts ever found have come from the Midwest. The artifacts were large, roughly ovoid quarry blanks or preforms, possibly stored as raw material for manufacturing points and blades, possibly placed as some sort of ceremonial offering. The first was found in Schuyler County, Illinois, many years ago. It consisted of 3500 specimens, all found about five feet underground, with no mound over them. The second came from the base of a 30-foot mound in Brown County, Illinois, and the 6000-plus examples were made of black hornstone. The third cache came from Mound Number 2 of the Hopewell Group, Ross County, Ohio. The disc-like flints were placed in small groups or pockets surrounded with sand. They were in two layers and covered an area of 22 x 26 feet. There were 8185 specimens. The fourth cache came from the Crib Mound, in southern Indiana. Grey flint blanks were found in a large deposit, and eventually more than 12,000 were recovered. (Fowke, Gerard, *Archeological History Of Ohio*, 1901, pp 628-632; Meek, Maurice, "Another Crib Mound Bannerstone," *Central States Archeological Journal*, October 1969, Vol. 16 No. 4, p 163.)

One type of pipe found throughout the Midwest is the effigy platform pipe, once known as the Curved-base Monitor pipe. These were made in the Middle Woodland (Hopewell) period. Such specimens were either made by the Hopewell Indians or their original designs spawned and inspired similar designs by others. Trade may also have been involved. Many of the pipes had small depictions of animals, birds or other creatures. These were always extremely well-executed and true to life. The effigies either faced the smoker (along the drill-hole in the platform/stem end) or the side. Several hundred of these effigy pipes were found in Mound 8, Mound City Group, Ohio. (Lilly, Eli, *Prehistoric Antiquities of Indiana*, Indiana Historical Society, 1937, pp 198-199.)

Two caches of elongated ovate knives or blades were found in Kentucky, the first prior to June, 1965, the second in April, 1966. The artifacts in both caches were made of Dover flint. The first cache consisted of 37 blades 4 to 7 inches long, and came from Calloway County. The second cache consisted of 44 blades 3¾ to 6½ inches long, from Hickman County. (*Central States Archeological Journal*, April 1966, Vol. 13 No. 2, pp 52-55.)

One of the largest and most symmetrical Adena cache blades ever found came from LaGrange County, Indiana. It was made of Flintridge multi-colored chalcedony and measured precisely 4 by 8 inches. Blades this size and in perfect condition are only rarely found. (*The Redskin*, Genuine Indian Relic Society, Inc., Vol. XI No. 2, 1976, p 53.)

Knife River flint is a high-grade translucent material in various shades of amber, often with white "clouds" or inclusions of various sizes. While the material is from Montana, points and blades made from it are found very thinly scattered across the Midwest, often in the form of large Early Paleo fluted artifacts. A very large St. Louis type (oversized Clovis, used probably as a knife) Paleo artifact was found years ago in St. Louis County, Missouri. Another Clovis of Knife River flint, measuring 1¼ x 4¼ inches, was found in Marion County, Iowa. It is not known whether Paleo hunters traveled great distances carrying such individual points or whether the material and/or artifacts were traded into the area where found, or both. (Perino, Gregory, "Early Projectile Points Found," *Central States Archeological Journal*, July 1967, Vol. 14 No. 3, pp 102 fig 60, 103-105; Perino, Gregory, "St. Louis," *Selected Preforms, Points and Knives Of The North American Indians*, Vol. I, 1985, p 334; Swim, Jerry, "An Unusual Iowa Find," *Central States Archeological Journal*, October 1983, Vol. 30 No. 4, p 184 fig 1.)

In general — but with exceptions and discounting inter-regional artifact styles — there is a difference between chipped flint and chert artifacts in eastern and western portions of the Midwest. Points and blades in the western part are somewhat larger than those in the eastern part, especially in the Paleo to Woodland time-frames. To the author's knowledge, no one has yet developed a convincing explanation as to why this is so. Western examples tend to be made more frequently of chert, while eastern examples tend to be made more frequently of flint — since these were the regional raw materials available. Other than this obvious and well-known difference, the size matter has yet to be settled. (Hothem, various sources.)

Potatoes and prehistory in the Midwest might seem to have nothing to do with each other, but occasionally they in fact do. The author, around 1954, was picking potatoes by hand in a commercial field on the floodplain of the Tuscarawas River in Coshocton County, Ohio. One of the results of a hard day's work was a fine Hopewell tapered-poll celt, nearly 9 inches long. Cameron Parks, noted birdstone collector, related to the author in 1978 that one of his prize pop-eyed hardstone

birds was unearthed by a mechanical potato-digger in Indiana, and was found undamaged after passing over the cleaning rods. And in Lexington, Kentucky, a lady noticed something unusual in the 10-pound bag of potatoes she had purchased. It was a fine pink and white quartzite discoidal (Mississippian period), about 3 inches in diameter. (Thompson, Ben, "The Potato-Bag Discoidal," *Central States Archeological Journal*, April 1971, Vol. 18 No. 2, pp 76-77.)

The Feurt Site, near Portsmouth, Scioto County, Ohio, was a Mississippian-period village and ceremonial area. Many interesting artifacts were recovered during excavations from 1896 through 1916, including a variety of pipes. A large number of these were made of Ohio pipestone, which outcrops extensively nearby. Colors for the Feurt pipes ranged from light reddish-grey to a dark red resembling Catlinite or Minnesota pipestone. Other Ohio pipestone colors were near-white to brown and yellow. Feurt produced plain, ornamented, and effigy pipe forms. Plain forms were mainly of the bowl, elbow and vase varieties. Decorated pipes included incised lines around the bowls. Effigy forms included human heads with the features facing away from the stem-hole. Bird-heads were also popular with the Feurt people. There was a wide range of pipe forms, and no one special type seems to have predominated. (Mills, William C., "The Feurt Mounds And Village Site," *Certain Mounds And Village Sites In Ohio*, Vol. III, 1922, pp 6, 88-102.)

About 25 years ago, a narrow, thick flint point was found in Hopkinsville, Kentucky. The point was not that unusual, but it was nearly unique because it was still secured to a bone shaft. The bone handle or shaft had a single barb-like protrusion on one side, and a pointed and spiraled projection at the base that may have screwed into a wooden shaft. The remains of pitch or natural glue used as an adhesive could be seen between the flint point and the bone holder. Such examples showing how prehistoric tool parts were fitted are very scarce, and invaluable artifacts. (Nance, G.A., "Unusual Artifact From Kentucky," *Central States Archeological Journal*, October 1964, Vol. 11 No. 4, p 144.)

One of the most interesting books ever done on a Midwestern state was *Archeological Atlas Of Ohio*, written by William C. Mills and published in 1914. In it, the prehistoric remains of the state — including earthworks (mounds and enclosures), village sites, petroglyphs, flint quarries and rock-shelters — were located on a per-county basis. Each of Ohio's 88 counties was mapped and the prehistoric features drawn in red symbols. While it is easy to criticize this work today because many features were incorrectly positioned on maps and very many features were not included, the pioneering effort is still a basic, much-referred-to source. The oversize book, 13¾ by 17 inches, was printed in a limited edition of 500 hardbound copies, and is itself a top collector book in the Eastern Midwest. Depending on condition, copies in 1991 sell in the $500-$750 range. (Hothem; reference Mills, William C., *Archeological Atlas Of Ohio*, Ohio State Archeological and Historical Society, Columbus, 1914.)

The Crib Mound, located in Spencer County, along the Ohio River in southern Indiana, was one of the great Midwestern sites. Named for the corn-crib on it, this was a large shell mound with occupation levels that extended from Middle Archaic through Woodland times. Probably comparable to the famous Indian Knoll Site in Kentucky in many ways, but multi-component; some similar items were found. These included a large number of very fine bannerstones. While numerous articles have been written on this very important site, a book should one day be done so all the facts can be pulled together and no information lost. (Hothem, various sources.)

The good old days:
"The Humphrey Stone Age Collection
Consisting of about 3000 specimens and collected principally in the states of Indiana and Illinois, is for the first time offered for sale. It was started 32 years ago, enabling us to acquire a great number of the very finest specimens. It is exceptionally strong in fine flints and ceremonials, and for general quality is excelled but by few, if any. As a large and comprehensive showing for any college, museum or private collector, it will be hard to improve. It will be sold as a whole only. We have always refused to part with any individual specimens to its detriment. Price $1200. We have catalogued it. If interested, will send you a copy. The price is very reasonable when quality is considered. We will be glad to go into particulars or show the collection to intending buyers. H.S. Humphrey, 29 Union Trust Bldg., Indianapolis, Ind." (Advertisement, *The Archeological Bulletin*, Vol. V No. 1, 1914, inside back cover.)

The major method for dating Midwestern organic (once-living) matter from archeological sites has long been the C-14 technique. Carbon-14 testing measures the decay rate of that substance and compares it with Carbon-12, which serves as a stable scale because it does not decay. C-14 is valid for measurements up to about 50,000 years. A newer method is particle acceleration, which requires only a small fraction of material compared with C-14. This method may prove to be valid for objects up to 100,000 years of age. (While ages in excess

of 11,500 before present are not yet known for the Midwest, there are yet thousands of sites and millions of potential samples.) (Gardner, Nielsen, et al, *Mysteries Of The Ancient Americas*, 1986, p 75.)

Some students (the author included) have long suspected that chipped chert and flint points were, for the most part, used either exclusively as knives or more as knives than as projectile points. Except for small, late prehistoric true arrowheads, the majority of chipped artifacts with tips and cutting edges seem designed more for cutting than piercing purposes. Extensive resharpening of many examples suggests this is true in a very high percentage of cases. This of course brings up the question as to what objects or materials in fact were used to tip the lances thrown by the launcher, the Atl-atl. At least part of the answer may have been found at the Read Shell Midden Site in Butler County, Kentucky. Excavated in 1937-39, the usual chert and flint artifacts typical of Archaic times were found, but also "projectile points" made of other materials. There were 30 of these made of splintered bone, and at least 43 made of cut antler. (Webb, *The Read Shell Midden*, Vol. VII No. 5, 1950, pp 382, 386, 388.)

Two Adams Counties in the Midwest are directly associated with the so-called serpent mounds, or linear earthworks in the form of snakes. Both are believed to have been constructed sometime in the Woodland period. One is in Adams County, Ohio, and is in the shape of a semi-extended snake with open mouth, as if to swallow an egg-shaped oval earthwork. It is about 1335 feet long. Another is in Adams County, Illinois, on a long bluff above the Mississippi River. The contours of this effigy were reported to be at least 1500 feet. (Randall, E.O., *The Serpent Mound*, 1907, pp 10, 53-54.)

An interesting book, *Indian Relics And Their Values*, was written by Allen Brown and published in 1942. Very many Midwestern artifacts were illustrated. It is informative to look back almost half a century and study price-ranges for artifacts at that time. The purpose of the book, as stated in a single sentence, is as valid today as when the book was published: "It is designed to be of practical and helpful use in appraising and marketing the artifacts that a country boy would find, as well as a coach and mentor to those who are taking up the hobby." Examples from the book are: Blades 7 to 8 inches long, $25-50; Dovetails 3 to 6 inches long, $1-8.50; Cumberland point 4¾ inches long, $27.50; Notched ovate slate bannerstone 6 inches wide, $100; Saddle-face green quartzite bannerstone 3½ inches long, $125-175; Pop-eyed spotted porphyry birdstones, $50-200; Duck effigy "Great Pipe" 10 inches long, $150-250; (Brown, Allen, *Indian Relics And Their Values*, Lightner Publishing, 1942.)

Boatstones — so-called because some scooped-out versions roughly resemble watercraft such as dugout canoes — are one of the rarest artifacts of the Midwest. Very highly developed forms, both in glacial slate and hardstone, may have thin walls and large longitudinal basal cavities. Only a few bits of evidence exist to suggest what they were used for. Ohio's Tremper Mound, Hopewell (Middle Woodland), provided some interesting facts. Two effigy boatstones, one resembling a swimming beaver and the other a beetle, were recovered. Copper boatstones were also found, and perhaps are the key to the mystery. These boatstones, most with two holes equidistant from the ends, had once contained quartzite pebbles. This suggests that boatstones, at least the ones with pebbles, were not only a form of Atl-atl stone or weight, but additionally served as ceremonial or ritual rattles or noise makers. (Mills, William C., "Explorations Of The Tremper Mound," *Certain Mounds and Village Sites In Ohio*, Vol. II, 1917, pp 206-210.)

Artifacts made of calcite — the crystalline form of natural calcium carbonate, which helps make up substances like chalk, limestone and marble — are rare in the Midwest. At least two artifacts made of this material have been found, and both were large-size effigies or representations of oak-nuts or acorns. One was found in Edmonson County, Kentucky, in 1903. Another was found more recently in Vanderburgh County, Indiana, and was slightly more than 2 inches across the base. This specimen was of translucent white calcite. Both specimens depict the acorn with the basal hull still attached. (A guess is that these may be effigy cones or hemisphere forms, which would place them in the Woodland timeframe.) (*Central States Archeological Journal*, October 1971, Vol. 18 No. 4, p 183 fig 135; Hansen, Randall R., "Another Calcite Acorn," *Central States Archeological Journal*, January 1974, Vol. 21 No. 1, pp 24-25.)

Midwestern prehistoric artifacts were known by different (and often fanciful) names in early days. There has been a certain evolution of terminology, and some examples are given here with today's word(s) or term(s) given first.

Birdstones; effigy stones, brooding effigies.
Hardstone bannerstones; net-gauges, Mound-Builder maces.
Slate bannerstones; badges or wands of distinction, insignia, emblems.
Adena pipes; stone tubes, whistles, flutes, calls, telescopes.
Gorgets; weaving shuttles, pierced tablets, thread-sizers, rope-makers, perforated plates, ensigns, coat of mail.
Grooved mauls; net-sinkers, war-club heads.
Spuds; bark-peelers, skinners.
Celts; skinners, fleshers.
Shell gorgets; head-plates, breast-plates.
Hardstone earspools; spindle whorls, sockets, balances.

(Hothem, various sources.)

Some years past a cache of Turkeytail blades, 17 in all, was found in Louisville, Kentucky. The material was chert or flint "of light bluish cast." The average size of the artifacts was 2¼" by 5½". The blades were beautifully chipped, and slate gorgets and awls and needles of bone were also found with the cache. (Young, Col. Bennett H., *The Prehistoric Men of Kentucky*, The Filson Club, 1910, pp 158, 166, 193.)

One of the finest effigy pipes ever found was picked up in Posey County, Indiana. Made of black steatite and highly polished, the figure represents a crouched panther or cougar (mountain lion), once fairly common in the Midwest. The pipe bowl was on the back, the head was raised, and the tail curled up along one side. The right front foot, missing at the time of discovery, was found 15 years later and the pipe was again complete. The panther pipe has resided in a number of well-known collections. The size is 2³⁄₁₀" high and 6⅜" long. (Knoblock, Byron W., "Superb Sculptured Art of the Eastern United States," reprint of 1951 *Illinois State Archeological Society Journal* article, *Central States Archeological Journal*, January 1972, Vol. 19 No. 1, pp 26-27.)

As of the year 1959, over 4000 whole or broken birdstones had been found, many in the Eastern Midwest. Likely thousands are yet unfound. (Townsend, *Birdstones Of The North American Indian*, 1959, p 117.)

There were two important sources of hard or tool grade hematite in the Midwest. One is in eastern Missouri, near the town of Lessley. The other is in westcentral Illinois, near the town of Hardin. (Seeman, Mark, *The Hopewell Interaction Sphere*, Vol. V No. 2, 1979, p 294.)

Throughout the Midwest from the late 1800's into the 1930's and 1940's, the word "collection" was not often used to denote a purposeful gathering together of prehistoric artifacts. Instead, the word "cabinet" was used, due to a common method of displaying fine pieces. So in that time period, it was a person's cabinet instead of a person's collection. The artifacts themselves were often termed "relics" or "curios" or "Indian stones."

Value Guide

PLATE 1: *Clovis fluted point* $600-700
PLATE 2: *Clovis point* ....museum quality
PLATE 3: *Agate Basin point*........................$100-115
PLATE 4: *Clovis fluted point* $600-725
PLATE 5: *Paleo points*
      left & right, each........................$150
      center, large Clovis $900
PLATE 6: *Ross County type Clovis point* $750-1100
PLATE 7: *Clovis Fluted point* $700-1000
PLATE 8: *Clovis point* $300-375
PLATE 9: *Lanceolate* $450-700
PLATE 10: *Fluted Clovis* $275-300
PLATE 11: *Lanceolate* $150-175
PLATE 12: *Agate Basin lanceolate* $350-500
PLATE 13: *Agate Basin point*........................$500-750
PLATE 14: *Agate Basin point*........................$100
PLATE 15: *Agate Basin point*........................$45
PLATE 16: *Clovis point* $150
PLATE 17: *Dalton point*........................$350-400
PLATE 18: *Late Paleo stemmed lanceolates*
      Left........................$800-900
      Right $350-500
PLATE 19: *Late Paleo points or blades* $100-250
PLATE 20: *Folsom point*........................$300
PLATE 21: *Late Paleo blades or points* $1,200-1,800
PLATE 22: *Agate Basin point*........................$300
PLATE 23: *Ross County fluted point*........................$450
PLATE 24: *Knife*........................$110
PLATE 25: *Clovis point* $200
PLATE 26: *Tang knife* ....value unknown
PLATE 27: *Lanceolate point or blade*........................$95
PLATE 28: *Scottsbluff* $550
PLATE 29: *Lanceolate point*........................$175
PLATE 30: *Cumberland fluted point* $900
PLATE 31: *Paleo knife* $85
PLATE 32: *Paleo points or blades*............the two, $300
PLATE 33: *Paleo points and blades* $50-350
PLATE 34: *Late Paleo points and blades* ..each, $35-175
PLATE 35: *Lanceolate points* ....each, $40-65
PLATE 36: *Late Paleo lanceolates* ....each, $150-450
PLATE 37: *Knife*........................museum quality
PLATE 38: *Clovis point* $200
PLATE 39: *Paleo points or blades* ....each, $25-100
PLATE 40: *Agate Basin points*........................each, $175
PLATE 41: *Clovis points*
      left........................$350
      center........................$675
      right........................$500
PLATE 42: *Fluted Paleo points*
      left........................$150
      right........................$235
PLATE 43: *Ross County fluted point*........................$1000
PLATE 44: *Clovis point* ....study piece

PLATE 45: *Agate Basin* $395
PLATE 46: *Agate Basin point*........................$100
PLATE 47: *Clovis points*
      left........................$175-250
      right........................$275-350
PLATE 48: *Large blade or point*........................$450
PLATE 49: *Agate Basin* $275
PLATE 50: *Agate Basin* $525
PLATE 51: *Lanceolate point* $175
PLATE 52: *Clovis point* $175-250
PLATE 53: *Clovis point* $275
PLATE 54: *Paleo point* $250-300
PLATE 55: *Clovis point* $125-150
PLATE 56: *Agate basin* $550
PLATE 57: *Lanceolate points or blades*
      left........................$70-90
      middle and right $40-50
PLATE 58: *Stemmed lanceolate*........................$100-150
PLATE 59: *Agate Basin point*........................$250-325
PLATE 60: *Agate Basin point*........................$825
PLATE 61: *Agate Basin* $275
PLATE 62: *Agate Basin point*........................$375-425
PLATE 63: *Sloan Dalton* $300-375
PLATE 64: *Agate Basin point*........................$225-275
PLATE 65: *Agate Basin point*........................$75-125
PLATE 66: *Knife blade* $300-400
PLATE 67: *Agate Basin point* $1,000-plus
PLATE 68: *Agate Basin point*........................$400-500
PLATE 69: *Paleo point*........................$200-250
PLATE 70: *Paleo points and artifacts* ...each $100-1,000
PLATE 71: *Lizard effigy* $700-900
PLATE 72: *Archaic axes*
      top left $200
      bottom center........................$250-500
      top right $150
PLATE 73: *Hematite bell pestles*
      left........................$250
      right........................$100
PLATE 74: *Archaic axes*
      left........................$250-300
      right........................$150-250
PLATE 75: *¾ groove axe* $200-225
PLATE 76: *Archaic points or blades* ....each $5-30
PLATE 77: *¾ groove axe* $800
PLATE 78: *Gilcrease grooved plummet* $225-300
PLATE 79: *Bowl-type pipe* $100
PLATE 80: *Antler flakers* $25-50
PLATE 81: *Graham Cave variant* $700-850
PLATE 82: *¾ groove axes* $350-750
PLATE 83: *¾ groove axe* $1,000-plus
PLATE 84: *Early Archaic blade* $350-400
PLATE 85: *Thebes blade* $325-375
PLATE 86: *¾ groove axe* $1,000

PLATE 87: ¾ *groove axe* $1,600
PLATE 88: *Bannerstone* ....museum quality
PLATE 89: *Flared-bit axes*
    left & right, each.............................$950
PLATE 90: *Bannerstone*.........................$450-700
PLATE 91: *Hardin points or blades*
    left $250
    right $400
PLATE 92: *Birdstone* $700-750
PLATE 93: ¾ *groove axe* $1,200-plus
PLATE 94: ¾ *groove axe* $150-200
PLATE 95: *Plummets* ....each, $100-300
PLATE 96: *Riverton points* ....each, $5-20
PLATE 97: *Plummets* $100-300
PLATE 98: ¾ *groove axe* $45-70
PLATE 99: *Pendant* $45-60
PLATE 100: *Loafstone* $85-110
PLATE 101: *Etley or Mehlville point or blade* ..$150-175
PLATE 102: *Kings corner-notch point or blade* $50-75
PLATE 103: *Bannerstone* $375-525
PLATE 104: *Pendant* $50-70
PLATE 105: *Tapered-tube pipe*......................$800
PLATE 106: *Archaic corner-notch points or blades*
    left $60
    center..$35
    right $55
PLATE 107: *Blades or knives*
    left $85
    right $185
PLATE 108: *Pick bannerstone*....................$250
PLATE 109: *Iowa Straight-side ¾ groove axe* ..$2500-plus
PLATE 110: *Atl-atl weight*....................$160-210
PLATE 111: *Hafted shaft-scrapers*
    left $40
    right $55
PLATE 112: *Archaic deep-notch blade* $250
PLATE 113: *Archaic knives* ....each, $10-25
PLATE 114: *Archaic blades*
    left $30
    right $45
PLATE 115: *Heavy-duty blade*.....................$100
PLATE 116: *Hardin points or blades*
    left $175
    right $160
PLATE 117: *St. Charles or Dovetail blade* $750
PLATE 118: *Drills*........................the two, $60
PLATE 119: *Plummet* $125
PLATE 120: *Plummet* $210
PLATE 121: *Thebes cluster points or blades*
    ....group, $200-300
PLATE 122: *Bell-type pestle*....................$95-125
PLATE 123: *Halfted end-scraper* $30
PLATE 124: *Sedalia* $195
PLATE 125: ¾ *groove axe* ....museum quality
PLATE 126: *Winged bannerstone* $325
PLATE 127: *Archaic blades*
    Ohio-notch Thebes $200-275
    Thebes $300-400

    Notched-base $250-300
    Ashtabula $200-250
PLATE 128: *Midwestern chipped artifacts*
    ....group, $125-175
PLATE 129: *Archaic knife* $45
PLATE 130: *Sedalia point* $125
PLATE 131: *Archaic knife* $45
PLATE 132: ¾ *groove axe* $90
PLATE 133: *Slant-grooved ¾ axe* $500
PLATE 134: *Large knife blade*....................$225
PLATE 135: ¾ *grooved axe* $500
PLATE 136: *Slant-grooved ¾ axe* $375
PLATE 137: *Knife blade*...........................$225
PLATE 138: *Bone needles* ....each, $10-25
PLATE 139: *Hematite plummet* ....museum grade
PLATE 140: *Bannerstone*...........................$650
PLATE 141: ¾ *groove axe* $135
PLATE 142: *Early Archaic points and blades*
    ....each, $65-300
PLATE 143: *Dalton points or blades* ....each, $75-300
PLATE 144: *Sloan Dalton* $475
PLATE 145: ¾ *groove axe* $90-115
PLATE 146: *Hardin*...............................$75-90
PLATE 147: *Corner-notched point or blade* $275-325
PLATE 148: *St. Charles or Dovetail blade* $500
PLATE 149: ¾ *groove axe* $100-125
PLATE 150: *Dalton point or blade*....................$75
PLATE 151: ¾ *groove axe* $300
PLATE 152: *Sedalia point or blade* $165
PLATE 153: *Illinois River type axe* ....museum quality
PLATE 154: *Stone mortar* $150-200
PLATE 155: *Dalton point or blade* $350
PLATE 156: *Archaic blades*
    left $300-400
    right..$250-325
PLATE 157: *Graham Cave blade* $75
PLATE 158: *Missouri points or blades* ...each, $200-300
PLATE 159: *Illinois points or blades*
    left..$350-500
    center, left.....................................$175-250
    center, right $150-200
    right..$350-450
PLATE 160: *Large stone hammers or mauls*
    ....each, $85-110
PLATE 161: *Lost Lake* $375-425
PLATE 162: *Adzes*
    left $180
    right..$150-175
PLATE 163: *St. Charles or Dovetail blades* $500-650
PLATE 164: *Archaic blades*
    left $100
    right..$125
PLATE 165: *Winged bannerstone* $375
PLATE 166: ¾ *groove axe* $150-200
PLATE 167: ¾ *groove axe* $275-325
PLATE 168: *Saddle-face bannerstone* $800-1000
PLATE 169: *Saddle-face bannerstone* $800-1000
PLATE 170: ¾ *groove axe* $250-325

PLATE 171: *Gouge* $400-650
PLATE 172: *¾ groove axe* ....museum quality
PLATE 173: *Half-groove axe* $1,500-2,500
PLATE 174: *¾ groove axe* ....museum quality
PLATE 175: *¾ groove axe* ....museum quality
PLATE 176: *Full-groove axe*.........................$350-450
PLATE 177: *¾ groove axe* ....museum quality
PLATE 178: *¾ groove axe* $750-900
PLATE 179: *¾ groove axe* $500-600
PLATE 180: *Full-groove axe*.........................$350-450
PLATE 181: *¾ groove axe* ....museum quality
PLATE 182: *¾ groove axe* ....museum quality
PLATE 183: *Half-groove axe*................museum quality
PLATE 184: *¾ groove axe* $500-675
PLATE 185: *Miami Valley axe* $550-700
PLATE 186: *¾ groove axe* $400-550
PLATE 187: *Hump-backed adz*......................$500-725
PLATE 188: *Hump-backed adz*......................$450-700
PLATE 189: *Full groove ¾ axe* $700-925
PLATE 190: *¾ groove axe* ....museum quality
PLATE 191: *Hardin barbed points or blades*
....each, $85-350
PLATE 192: *Half-groove axe* $700-850
PLATE 193: *¾ groove axe* ....museum quality
PLATE 194: *Wadlow blade*...........................$175-250
PLATE 195: *Etley point or blade* $350-450
PLATE 196: *Sedalia points or blades*........each, $50-300
PLATE 197: *Etley points or blades*..........each, $50-275
PLATE 198: *Mehlville point or blade*.............$175-200
PLATE 199: *Hardin point or blade* $195-265
PLATE 200: *Graham Cave point or blade* $450-525
PLATE 201: *Sedalia point or blade* $225-275
PLATE 202: *Stanfield knife* $150-200
PLATE 203: *Pebble pendant* $60
PLATE 204: *Thebes point or blade* $365-415
PLATE 205: *Smith point or blade* $425-525
PLATE 206: *Double crescent bannerstone* $900
PLATE 207: *Fox Valley points or blades*.....each, $15-50
PLATE 208: *Dalton point or blade*.................$450-575
PLATE 209: *Double-notched ovate bannerstone*
....$975
PLATE 210: *Fox Valley points or blades*.....each, $10-35
PLATE 211: *¾ groove axe* $155
PLATE 212: *¾ groove axe* $100
PLATE 213: *Pick bannerstone*..................................$800
PLATE 214: *Full groove or ¾ axe* $175
PLATE 215: *Full groove or ¾ axe* $75
PLATE 216: *Osceola point or blade* $65
PLATE 217: *Table Rock or Bottleneck blade*............$45
PLATE 218: *Drills and perforators* ....each, $4-15
PLATE 219: *Stanfield knife* $130
PLATE 220: *Godar point or blade* $40
PLATE 221: *Thebes* $225
PLATE 222: *Thebes* $175
PLATE 223: *¾ groove axe* $800
PLATE 224: *Thebes* $175
PLATE 225: *Thebes* $100
PLATE 226: *¾ groove axe* $950
PLATE 227: *¾ groove axe* $2,000
PLATE 228: *¾ groove axe* $100
PLATE 229: *¾ groove axe* $225
PLATE 230: *¾ groove axe* $800-1,200
PLATE 231: *¾ groove axe* $1,200-1,700
PLATE 232: *¾ groove axe* $600-800
PLATE 233: *¾ groove axe* $3,000-plus
PLATE 234: *Slant-groove ¾ axe* $275
PLATE 235: *Thebes point or blade* $325
PLATE 236: *Pestle or monolithic maul*..........$175-225
PLATE 237: *Pestle or double-ended maul*......$250-300
PLATE 238: *Pestle or monolithic maul*..........$200-225
PLATE 239: *Pestle or monolithic maul*..........$250-325
PLATE 240: *Double-groove axe* $450-575
PLATE 241: *Godar point or blade* $35
PLATE 242: *St. Charles or Dovetail blade* ...$800-1,100
PLATE 243: *St. Charles or Dovetail blade* $400-600
PLATE 244: *Indented-base Dovetail*..............$550-650
PLATE 245: *Plummet*.....................................$250-350
PLATE 246: *Plummet group*.................each, $200-275
PLATE 247: *Plummets*
left...$200
right...$175
PLATE 248: *Plummet*.....................................$275-350
PLATE 249: *Plummet*.....................................$225-350
PLATE 250: *Plummet* $150
PLATE 251: *Pendant* $175
PLATE 252: *Pentagonal point or blade* $35
PLATE 253: *Full-grooved or ¾ axe* $125
PLATE 254: *Glacial Kame Indian gorget* $575
PLATE 255: *Archaic ¾ grooved adz* $165
PLATE 256: *Archaic points or blades*
left...$110
middle...$140
right...$150
PLATE 257: *Archaic points or blades*
left...$25
middle...$90
right...$30
PLATE 258: *Fluted ball bannerstone*.......................$400
PLATE 259: *Slate pendant* $175
PLATE 260: *St. Charles or Dovetail blades*
left...$350
right...$450
PLATE 261: *Archaic blades or knives*
left...$65
middle...$125
right...$135
PLATE 262: *Merom (Riverton cluster) points*
....each, $3-10
PLATE 263: *Loafstone* $125-150
PLATE 264: *¾ groove axe* $650-750
PLATE 265: *Full-grooved maul*..............................$135
PLATE 266: *¾ groove axe* $295
PLATE 267: *Nebo Hill point*..................................$150
PLATE 268: *Archaic axes*
left...$90
right...$125

PLATE 269: *Pestles*

 left $145

 right $145

PLATE 270: *Mortar and pestle set* ....set, $295

PLATE 271: *Thebes point or blade* $150

PLATE 272: *Dalton point or blade* $125

PLATE 273: *¾ groove axes* ....each, $125-300

PLATE 274: *Archaic slate artifacts*

 top $325

 bottom $185

PLATE 275: *Early Archaic bifurcated blades*

 left $25

 upper center $20

 lower center $25

 right $30

PLATE 276: *Surface-found collection* ....each, $5-65

PLATE 277: *St. Charles or Dovetail blade* $450

PLATE 278: *¾ and ¼ grooved axes* ....each, $75-600

PLATE 279: *Surface-found collection* ....each, $3-25

PLATE 280: *Points or blades* ....each, $25-60

PLATE 281: *Sedalia point* $195

PLATE 282: *¾ groove axe* $225

PLATE 283: *Archaic points and blades* ....each, $40-225

PLATE 284: *Bifurcate points or blades* ....each, $5-35

PLATE 285: *Archaic blades* ....group, $900-1400

PLATE 286: *Archaic concave-base* $50

PLATE 287: *Palmer corner-notch* $45

PLATE 288: *Archaic points or blades*

 left $20

 middle $30

 right $35

PLATE 289: *Bifurcate points or blades*

 left $30

 middle $30

 right $30

PLATE 290: *Short-tube bannerstone* $150

PLATE 291: *Winged "butterfly" bannerstone* ..$800-950

PLATE 292: *Bannerstones*

 left $250

 right $350

PLATE 293: *Barrel-shaped bannerstone* $165

PLATE 294: *Winged bannerstone* $165

PLATE 295: *Drill grouping*

 left $65

 center $95

 right $65

PLATE 296: *Corner-notched blade* $30

PLATE 297: *Side-notched blade* $75

PLATE 298: *Godar point or blade* $30

PLATE 299: *Archaic knife* $175

PLATE 300: *Smith points or blades* ....each, $55-90

PLATE 301: *Bifurcated-base blades* ....each, $25-30

PLATE 302: *Humped-back gorget* $350

PLATE 303: *Tube bannerstone* $325

PLATE 304: *Dalton variant* $185

PLATE 305: *Earbob Ferry* $30

PLATE 306: *Dalton point* $90

PLATE 307: *Dalton* $285

PLATE 308: *Bifurcate* $30

PLATE 309: *Stilwell point or blade* $75

PLATE 310: *Dalton* $375

PLATE 311: *Dalton* $90

PLATE 312: *Hidden Valley point or blade* $65

PLATE 313: *Mehlville point or blade* $225

PLATE 314: *Dalton variant* $50

PLATE 315: *Graham Cave point or blade* $65

PLATE 316: *Notched/stemmed blade* $65

PLATE 317: *Thebes Cache-type blade* $140

PLATE 318: *Holland point or blade* $450

PLATE 319: *Drill or heavily resharpened knife* $50

PLATE 320: *Sedalia* $90

PLATE 321: *Knife* $70

PLATE 322: *Drill or perforator* $50

PLATE 323: *Late lanceolate* $65

PLATE 324: *Dalton points or blades*

 top $70

 bottom $70

PLATE 325: *Plummet* $275-375

PLATE 326: *Plummet* $200-250

PLATE 327: *Plummet* $325-450

PLATE 328: *Plummet* $250-375

PLATE 329: *Bannerstone* $3,000-4,000

PLATE 330: *Plummet* $185-265

PLATE 331: *Plummet grouping* ....each, $195

PLATE 332: *¾ groove axe* $400-500

PLATE 333: *Tube bannerstones*

 top $300-400

 bottom $400-470

PLATE 334: *Notched ovate bannerstone* ...$4,000-5,000

PLATE 335: *¾ groove axe* $275-375

PLATE 336: *Quartzite popeyed birdstone*

 ....museum quality

PLATE 337: *Hump-backed adz or gouge*

 ....museum quality

PLATE 338: *Plummet* $1,200-1,500

PLATE 339: *¾ groove axe* $175-250

PLATES 340 & 341: *Crescent or lunate bannerstone*

 ....$1,000-1,350

PLATE 342: *¾ groove axe* $800

PLATE 343: *Elongated birdstones* ....unlisted

PLATE 344: *Harpoon heads* ....each, $75-110

PLATE 345: *Birdstone* $1,800-3,000

PLATE 346: *Frog effigy* ....value unknown

PLATE 347: *Winged bannerstone* $350

PLATE 348: *Winged bannerstone* $500-800

PLATE 349: *Birdstone* $1,200-2,000

PLATE 350: *Butterfly-type bannerstone* $600-750

PLATE 351: *Rounded bar weight* $225-275

PLATE 352: *¾ groove axe* $425

PLATE 353: *Winged bannerstone* $1,500-1,900

PLATE 354: *Saddle-face prismoidal bannerstone*

 ....$850-1,100

PLATE 355: *Single-ridge prismoidal bannerstone*

 ....$900-1,200

PLATE 356: *Slant-grooved ¾ axe* $425

PLATE 357: *¼ groove axe* $150

PLATE 358: *¾ grooved axe* $450
PLATE 359: *Archaic corner-notch*..........................$425
PLATE 360: *¾ groove axe* $125
PLATE 361: *Half-grooved Keokuk type axe* $700
PLATE 362: *Thebes point or blade* $95
PLATE 363: *"Hardove"* $60-70
PLATE 364: *Stilwell point or blade*..................$95-115
PLATE 365: *Thebes point or blade* $125
PLATE 366: *Hardin point or blade* $50-65
PLATE 367: *Winged bannerstone variant* $375
PLATE 368: *Pentagonal point or blade* $20
PLATE 369: *Archaic unhafted blade* $70-80
PLATE 370: *Archaic unhafted blade* $50-60
PLATE 371: *E-notch Thebes*.........................$195-245
PLATE 372: *Pentagonal*................................$135-160
PLATE 373: *Dovetail blades*
left...$35-45
right...$50-60
PLATE 374: *¾ groove axe* $150-175
PLATE 375: *Archaic points*......................each, $25-35
PLATE 376: *¾ groove axe* $135-160
PLATE 377: *¾ groove axe* $165-250
PLATE 378: *Archaic artifacts*
top right $150
bottom left $245
PLATE 379: *¾ groove axe* $95-115
PLATE 380: *Drills* ....each, $20-30
PLATE 381: *Tama points or blades*...........each, $10-15
single specimen, bottom right.............$15-20
PLATE 382: *Side-notched point or blade*............$50-60
PLATE 383: *St. Charles or Dovetail blade* $525
PLATE 384: *Table Rock points or blades*
left...$4-7
right...$15-25
PLATE 385: *Pestle or monolithic maul*..........$150-200
PLATE 386: *Ashtabula point or blade* $150-125
PLATE 387: *Hardin points or blades*
left...$35-45
middle...$95-115
right...$35-45
PLATE 388: *Sedalia*.....................................$150-200
PLATE 389: *Archaic side-notched points or blades*
left...$40-50
right...$35-45
PLATE 390: *Archaic points or blades*
left...$15-20
middle...$30-40
right...$15-20
PLATE 391: *Nebo Hill point* $135-185
PLATE 392: *Archaic points or blades*
left...$60-70
right...$55-65
PLATE 393: *Dalton points or blades*
left...$65-75
center $115-125
right...$80-95
PLATE 394: *Thebes blade*...............................$60-70
PLATE 395: *Archaic points or blades*
left...$35-40
right...$25-30
PLATE 396: *Archaic Corner-notched blades*
left...$70-80
right...$90-100
PLATE 397: *Thebes blade*...............................$75-85
PLATE 398: *Knife blade* $90-105
PLATES 399 & 400: *Borroughs point*............$150-175
PLATE 401: *Stanfield blade* $100-120
PLATE 402: *Sedalia point or blade* $50-60
PLATE 403: *Godar point or blade*.......................$60-70
PLATE 404: *Thebes blades*
left...$75-95
right...$85-110
PLATE 405: *Short-stemmed Hardin-barbed*........$70-90
PLATE 406: *Archaic artifacts*
left...$300-400
right...$300-400
PLATE 407: *Loafstone*
left...$200-300
right...$200-300
PLATE 408: *Missouri knife collection*........each, $25-60
PLATE 409: *Etley blades*........................each, $50-125
PLATE 410: *Half-groove axe* $700-850
PLATE 411: *Half-groove axe*.................museum quality
PLATE 412: *Midwestern axes*...............listed elsewhere
PLATE 413: *¾ groove axe* $225-275
PLATE 414: *Half-groove axe* $1,500-3,000
PLATE 415: *Half-groove axe*.................museum quality
PLATE 416: *Half-groove axe*.................museum quality
PLATE 417: *Winged bannerstone* $900-1,100
PLATE 418: *Plummets*......................each, $800-1,000
PLATE 419: *Plummets*
left...$400-600
center $400-600
right...$200-250
PLATE 420: *Expanded-center bottle bannerstone*
....$750-950
PLATE 421: *Grooved-end plummet*..........$1,250-1,500
PLATE 422: *Chlorite pick bannerstone*.....$1,200-1,850
PLATE 423: *Elongated ball bannerstone*...$1,500-2,200
PLATE 424: *Loafstone* $165-215
PLATE 425: *Chlorite pendant* $250-300
PLATE 426: *Humped gorget*..........................$400-550
PLATE 427: *Elongated ball bannerstone*......$800-1,100
PLATE 428: *Elongated ball bannerstone*...$1,500-2,200
PLATE 429: *Chlorite pick bannerstone*.....$3,500-4,100
PLATE 430: *Rounded bar Atl-atl weight* $225-275
PLATE 431: *Chlorite pick bannerstone*.....$1,100-1,500
PLATE 432: *Tubular fluted bannerstone* $900-1,250
PLATE 433: *Ellipsoidal bar Atl-atl weight*
....$1,000-1,400
PLATE 434: *Bannerstone*.........................$1,200-2,000
PLATE 435: *Pick bannerstone* $1,400-1,900
PLATE 436: *Pebble pendant* $300-425
PLATE 437: *St. Charles or Dovetail blade*
....$425
PLATE 438: *Pendant*....................................$200-250

PLATE 439: *¾ groove axe* $1,200-1,500
PLATE 440: *Bannerstone* .... museum quality
PLATE 441: *Archaic knives* .... museum quality
PLATE 442: *Iowa axes* .... each, $65-450
PLATE 443: *¾ groove axe* .... museum quality
PLATE 444: *St. Charles or Dovetail blade* $425
PLATE 445: *Saddle-faced bannerstone*...museum quality
PLATE 446: *Square-back ¾ groove axe*...museum quality
PLATE 447: *Full groove or 4/4 axe* $135
PLATE 448: *¾ groove axe* .... museum quality
PLATE 449: *Half-groove or Keokuk axe* $365
PLATE 450: *Full groove or 4/4 axe* .... museum quality
PLATE 451: *St. Charles or Dovetail blade* $600-725
PLATE 452: *Pine Tree point or blade* $90
PLATE 453: *Keokuk axe* $350
PLATE 454: *¾ groove axe* $500-625
PLATE 455: *St. Charles or Dovetail blade* $575
PLATE 456: *Fractured-base Dovetail* $125-165
PLATE 457: *Half-groove Keokuk axe* $695
PLATE 458: *Bow-tie type bannerstone*...museum quality
PLATE 459: *Miniature Keokuk axe* .... museum quality
PLATE 460: *Birdstone* $1,500-2,000
PLATE 461: *Half-groove axe* .... museum quality
PLATE 462: *Half-groove axe* $700-1,000
PLATE 463: *Bone awls* .... each, $45-90
PLATE 464: *¾ groove axe* $500-plus
PLATE 465: *St. Charles or Dovetail* $325-450
PLATE 466: *¾ groove axe* .... museum quality
PLATE 467: *Bone gorget* .... museum quality
PLATE 468: *Iowa Keokuk axes* .... each, $125-625
PLATE 469: *Hardin point or blade* $550
PLATE 470: *Archaic prehistoric artworks*
.... museum quality
PLATE 471: *Birdstone effigy forms*
top left $7500
top right $10,000
center right $8,500
lower left $12,000
lower center $12,500
lower right $15,000
PLATE 472: *Saddle-faced bannerstone preform*
.... museum quality
PLATE 473: *Thebes point or blade* $425
PLATE 474: *St. Charles or Dovetail blades*
.... each, $600-3,000
PLATE 475: *¾ groove axe* .... museum quality
PLATE 476: *St. Charles or Dovetail blades*
.... each, $85-400
PLATE 477: *St. Charles or Dovetail blades*
.... each, $75-900
PLATE 478: *4/4 groove axe* .... unlisted
PLATE 479: *St. Charles or Dovetail blades*
.... each, $150-550
PLATE 480: *Keokuk axes*
left $2,000
right .... value undetermined
PLATE 481: *St. Charles or Dovetail blades*
.... each, $100-495
PLATE 482: *Early Archaic blades* .... each, $45-400
PLATE 483: *St. Charles or Dovetail blades*
.... each, $275-700
PLATE 484: *St. Charles or Dovetail blades*
.... each, $100-425
Missouri blade $675
PLATE 485: *Goddard axe collection* ....range, $75-4,000
PLATE 486: *Archaic knives and a lanceolate*
left $175-250
center $200-300
right $250-350
PLATE 487: *¾ groove axe* $600-700
PLATE 488: *Full groove or 4/4 axe* $295
PLATE 489: *4/4 groove axe* $325-500
PLATE 490: *¾ groove axe* $600-700
PLATE 491: *Half-groove axe* $275
PLATE 492: *¾ groove axe* $600-800
PLATE 493: *¾ groove axe* $300-425
PLATE 494: *¾ groove axe* $500-600
PLATE 495: *Basal notch type Dovetail* $200
PLATE 496: *¾ groove axe* $800-900
PLATE 497: *St. Charles or Dovetail blade* $225-325
PLATE 498: *Large blade* $200-250
PLATE 499: *Large blade* $125-175
PLATE 500: *Thebes blade* $50-75
PLATE 501: *Godar point or blade* $120-150
PLATE 502: *Archaic side-notch* $300-400
PLATE 503: *Hardin point or blade* $175-200
PLATE 504: *Thebes blade* $125-175
PLATE 505: *Thebes blade* $100-150
PLATE 506: *Thebes blade* $75-125
PLATE 507: *Corner-notch blade* $50-80
PLATE 508: *Hardin barbed point or blade* $175-225
PLATE 509: *Thebes blade* $150-200
PLATE 510: *Side-notch point or blade* $175-225
PLATE 511: *Side-notch point or blade* $140-190
PLATE 512: *Thebes blade* $140-190
PLATE 513: *Sedalia point or blade* $140-190
PLATE 514: *Sedalia point or blade* $75-115
PLATE 515: *Large blade* $225
PLATE 516: *St. Charles or Dovetail points or blades*
.... each, $500-1,000
PLATE 517: *Thebes blade* $400
PLATE 518: *Table Rock or Bottleneck point or blade*
.... $25-50
PLATE 519: *Grooved adz* $325-375
PLATE 520: *Half-groove Keokuk axe* $450-575
PLATE 521: *Etley point or blade* $275-350
PLATE 522: *Wadlow blade* $160-210
PLATE 523: *Mantanzas point or blade* $40-75
PLATE 524: *Hopewell point or blade* $100-150
PLATE 525: *Waubesa point or blade* $150-175
PLATE 526: *Pendant* $175-200
PLATE 527: *North and Snyders blades* ....each, $75-400
PLATE 528: *Snyders blades* .... each, $125-450
PLATE 529: *Tubular pipe* $900-1,500
PLATE 530: *Hopewell double-notched blade*
.... museum quality

PLATE 531: *Decorative artifacts* ....museum quality
PLATE 532: *Adena blade*..............................$150-200
PLATE 533: *Adena slate artifacts*....site and study value
PLATE 534: *Black Creek blade* ....museum quality
PLATE 535: *Celts*
       left..$250-350
       right...$175-195
PLATE 536: *Pendants*
       left...$125
       right...$275
PLATE 537: *Quadriconcave gorget* $500-600
PLATE 538: *Hardstone adz* $125-175
PLATE 539: *Celt*...............................museum quality
PLATE 540: *Bell-shaped pendant* $750
PLATE 541: *Full groove axe* ....museum quality
PLATE 542: *Celt* $450-550
PLATE 543: *Adena leaf-shaped blade* ....museum quality
PLATE 544: *Jersey Bluff pipe*.............................$100
PLATE 545: *Hopewell platform pipe* $225
PLATE 546: *Pottery pipes* ....each, $90
PLATE 547: *Jersey Bluff discoidal* $900
PLATE 548: *Corner-notch*..............................$200-240
PLATE 549: *Celt* $195-270
PLATE 550: *Waubesa point or blade*......................$150
PLATE 551: *Creased-poll celt*..........................$225-275
PLATE 552: *Quadriconcave gorget* $90-140
PLATE 553: *Steuben points*......................each, $8-20
PLATE 554: *Squared-stem Adena points or blades*
       left...$30-35
       middle..$40-50
       right...$30-35
PLATE 555: *Stemmed Adena points or blades*
       ....each, $15-40
PLATE 556: *Celt* $75-105
PLATE 557: *Celt* $75-105
PLATE 558: *Celts*
       left...$45-60
       right...$45-60
PLATE 559: *Spud-like celt* $175-250
PLATE 560: *Adz*..$75-100
PLATE 561: *Dickson point or blade* $75-125
PLATE 562: *Dickson point or blade* $125-175
PLATE 563: *Dickson point or blade* $125-200
PLATE 564: *Hopewell celt* ....$ 200-275
PLATE 565: *Peisker Diamond blades* ....museum quality
PLATE 566: *Copper celt*.......................museum quality
PLATE 567: *Ceremonial pick* ....museum quality
PLATE 568: *Celt*.................................museum quality
PLATE 569: *Square-sided celt* $275-375
PLATE 570: *Creased-poll celts* ....museum quality
PLATE 571: *Square-sided celt* ....museum quality
PLATE 572: *Knife blade*.....................................$350
PLATE 573: *Adena pendants*
       left..$325-400
       right...$200-275
PLATE 574: *Hopewell celt* $325-375
PLATE 575: *Pipe*...$700-900
PLATE 576: *Adena slate artifacts*

       left...$400-475
       center....................shown elsewhere in book
       right..$350-425
PLATE 577: *Bar-type gorget* $750-1,000
PLATE 578: *Adena gorget* ....as-is, $100-125
PLATE 579: *Boatstone or keeled gorget* $700-850
PLATE 580: *Adena expanded-center gorget* $325
PLATE 581: *Bar amulet*................................$450-550
PLATE 582: *Edged tool* $75-105
PLATE 583: *Celt* $70-100
PLATE 584: *Boatstone* $400-475
PLATE 585: *Pipe* $650-900
PLATE 586: *Boatstone* $275-400
PLATE 587: *Rectangular celt*........................$175-225
PLATE 588: *Ceremonial pick* ....museum quality
PLATE 589: *Ceremonial pick* ....museum quality
PLATE 590: *Celt* $160-210
PLATE 591: *Tapered-poll celt*.......................$150-200
PLATE 592: *Gorget*.......................................$400-500
PLATE 593: *Hardstone gorget* $500-600
PLATE 594: *Cones*...............................each, $75-165
PLATE 595: *Hematite cones*..................each, $75-165
PLATE 596: *Cone* $400-500
PLATE 597: *Elongated ball bannerstone*........$650-900
PLATE 598: *Boatstone* $400-550
PLATE 599: *Cone* $150-250
PLATE 600: *Pentagonal pendant* $350-400
PLATE 601: *Four-hole gorget* $300-425
PLATE 602: *Knobbed pendant* $150-200
PLATE 603: *Celt or adz blade* $250-335
PLATE 604: *Semi-keeled gorget* $450-600
PLATE 605: *Convex gorget*............................$300-350
PLATE 606: *Cone* $300-400
PLATE 607: *Turkeytail point or blade*.................$5,500
PLATE 608: *Rectangular gorget* $350-550
PLATE 609: *Dickson point or blade* $45-65
PLATE 610: *Knife blade* $50-75
PLATE 611: *Missouri points or blades* ....each, $15-30
PLATE 612: *Rice side-notch* $45-65
PLATE 613: *Turkeytail blade* $250-300
PLATE 614: *Missouri points or blades* ....each, $20-55
PLATE 615: *Hopewell celts*
       top $75
       bottom $350
PLATE 616: *Boatstone* $400-450
PLATE 617: *Cones*
       left...$200-300
       right...$150-250
PLATE 618: *Bar amulet*................................$500-750
PLATE 619: *Two-hole gorget* $400-500
PLATE 620: *Adz*.......................................$700-1,000
PLATE 621: *Anchor-type pendant* $300-340
PLATE 622: *Trapezoidal pendant* $275
PLATE 623: *Celt grouping*....................each, $30-85
PLATE 624: *Pendant* $165
PLATE 625: *Celt* $40-50
PLATE 626: *Jersey Bluff pipe* $1,800
PLATE 627: *Jersey Bluff pottery*.......................$800

PLATE 628: *Flared celt or spud-like axe* $350
PLATE 629: *Pottery human effigy* $200
PLATE 630: *Celt*...$260
PLATE 631: *Waubesa point or blade*....................$240
PLATE 632: *Adena points or blades*

       left $175

       middle $115

       right $135
PLATE 633: *Anchor pendant* $185
PLATE 634: *Hopewell point or blade* $350
PLATE 635: *Cone*...$85-100
PLATE 636: *Pendant*................................$325-425
PLATE 637: *Woodland rectangular poll adz* $40
PLATE 638: *Adena point or blade* $550
PLATE 639: *Adena rectangular celt* $85
PLATE 640: *Adena tapered poll adz* $125
PLATE 641: *Adena adz* $75
PLATE 642: *Woodland rectangular poll adz* $45
PLATE 643: *Woodland rectangular poll adz* $70
PLATE 644: *Adena tapered poll adz* $75
PLATE 645: *Glacial slate artifacts*...................unlisted
PLATE 646: *Adena tubular pipe* $550-900
PLATE 647: *Adena rounded-poll adzes*

       left $45

       right $45
PLATE 648: *Hopewell point or blade* $400-550
PLATE 649: *Hopewell point or blade* $400-525
PLATE 650: *Celt* $180-210
PLATE 651: *Turkeytail point or blade* $175-250
PLATE 652: *Adena point or blade* $550-850
PLATE 653: *Adena point or blade* $500-700
PLATE 654: *Adena adz* $65-95
PLATE 655: *Celt* $450-550
PLATE 656: *Snyders point or blade* $400-450
PLATE 657: *Dickson point or blade*................$75-150
PLATE 658: *Bar amulet*.....................................$750
PLATE 659: *Celts*

       left $45

       center..$50

       right $40
PLATE 660: *Celt*...$115
PLATE 661: *Celt*...$160
PLATE 662: *Ceremonial celt* $800-1,400
PLATE 663: *Adz* $400-650
PLATE 664: *Hopewell platform pipe* $900
PLATE 665: *Jersey Bluff handled pipe* $600
PLATE 666: *Adena adz*.............................$500-650
PLATE 667: *Celt* $195-225
PLATE 668: *Hopewell squared-poll celt* $350-450
PLATE 669: *Celt* $375-475
PLATE 670: *Celt* $450-750
PLATE 671: *Celt* $400-750
PLATE 672: *Hopewell celt* $600-850
PLATE 673: *Adz* $550-800
PLATE 674: *Celt* $250-325
PLATE 675: *Snyders point or blade*.....................$120
PLATE 676: *Three-hole shell gorget* $150-175
PLATE 677: *Celt* $200-375

PLATE 678: *Necklace*................................$400-550
PLATE 679: *Snyders point or blade*.......................$85
PLATE 680: *Dickson broad-blade* $265
PLATE 681: *Quadriconcave gorget* $220
PLATE 682: *Snyders point or blade*.......................$75
PLATE 683: *Snyders point or blade*......................$270
PLATE 684: *Woodland pendants*

       left $250

       right $275
PLATE 685: *Celt*...$275
PLATE 686: *Woodland-period blades* ....each, $45-85
PLATE 687: *Rice shallow side-notched points or blades*

       ....each, $45-95
PLATE 688: *Dickson points or blades* ....each, $35-75
PLATE 689: *Woodland-era blades*...........each, $65-125
PLATE 690: *Hopewell points or blades*

       left $20

       center..$40

       right $30
PLATE 691: *Woodland-era blades*

       left $35

       middle $85

       right $35
PLATE 692: *Hopewell points or blades*

       top left $25

       top right $20

       bottom left $20

       bottom center $15

       bottom right $20
PLATE 693: *Hopewell blades*

       left $55

       middle $70

       right $45
PLATE 694: *Woodland-era blades*

       left $20

       right $40
PLATE 695: *Woodland artifacts*

       top $400

       bottom $225
PLATE 696: *Adena blades*

       left $90

       center..$300

       right $75
PLATE 697: *Late Woodland blades*

       left $50

       right $65
PLATE 698: *Celt*...$265
PLATE 699: *Celts* ....each, $15-65
PLATE 700: *Hematite cone* $75
PLATE 701: *Snyders points or blades*.........each, $25-40
PLATE 702: *Fulton Turkeytail* $190
PLATE 703: *Adena tubular pipe*............................$190
PLATE 704: *Woodland pendant*............................$265
PLATE 705: *Adena blocked-end pipe* $375
PLATE 706: *Elbow pipe*............................$300-plus
PLATE 707: *Hopewell platform pipe* $950
PLATE 708: *Celt* $250-325
PLATE 709: *Copper rings and tubes* ......museum quality

PLATE 710: *Ceremonial celt* ....museum quality
PLATE 711: *Apple Creek points or blades*
      left $75
      right $55
PLATE 712: *Late Woodland points*
      ....individual values, $15-95
PLATE 713: *Shield-shaped pendant* ....museum quality
PLATE 714: *Large classic Adena blades*
      left $8,500
      left center $7,500
      center right $6,500
      right $6,000
PLATE 715: *Hopewell platform pipes*
      top left $6,000
      top right $8,000
      center right $15,000
      lower left $8,000
      lower right $10,000
PLATE 716: *Bust-type birdstone* $3,000-4,000
PLATE 717: *Hopewell blade* $750
PLATE 718: *Celt* $275-375
PLATE 719: *Mississippian pottery* ....pair, $5,000
PLATE 720: *Mississippian pottery* $375
PLATE 721: *Wood duck effigy pot* $195
PLATE 722: *Pottery vessel* $125-175
PLATE 723: *Pottery vessel* $110-140
PLATE 724: *Pottery vessel* $110-140
PLATE 725: *Pottery vessel* $110-140
PLATE 726: *Pottery vessel* $110-140
PLATE 727: *Effigy pot* $500-600
PLATE 728: *Effigy pot* ....museum quality
PLATE 729: *Flint hoe or adz* $165-180
PLATE 730: *Pottery vessel* $275-350
PLATE 731: *Effigy pendant* ....museum quality
PLATE 732: *Salt River discoidal* $375
PLATE 733: *Mississippian artifacts* ....museum quality
PLATE 734: *Effigy pipe* $600
PLATE 735: *Oval spade* $225-325
PLATE 736: *Pottery vessel* $200-225
PLATE 737: *Compound pottery bottle* $300-400
PLATE 738: *Double-bitted hoe* $195-250
PLATE 739: *Salt River type discoidal* $375-425
PLATE 740: *Spud or spatulate* $1,500-2,000
PLATE 741: *Flared-bit celt or spud* ....museum quality
PLATE 742: *Ohio pipes* ....each, $400
PLATE 743: *Engraved pipe* $350-450
PLATE 744: *Perforated-center discoidals*
      left $500
      right $500-750
PLATE 745: *Mystery artifact* ....value unknown
PLATE 746: *Pottery vessel* $225-275
PLATE 747: *Pottery vessel* $175-225
PLATE 748: *Bi-pointed knife* $170-220
PLATE 749: *Bi-pointed blade* $175
PLATE 750: *Celt* $325-375
PLATE 751: *Spade* $95-145
PLATE 752: *Discoidals* ....each, $45-95
PLATE 753: *Spade* $125-165

PLATE 754: *Mississippian-era artifacts*
      top $900-1,400
      bottom $300-375
PLATE 755: *Pottery vessel* ....museum quality
PLATE 756: *Human effigy* ....value unknown
PLATE 757: *Discoidal* $125
PLATE 758: *Pottery effigy* $50-75
PLATE 759: *Effigy pipe* $800
PLATE 760: *Fort Ancient pipe* $500
PLATE 761: *Elbow pipe* $350
PLATE 762: *Effigy pipe* $450
PLATE 763: *Effigy pipe* $800
PLATE 764: *Disc-bowl pipe* $595
PLATE 765: *Cahokia type discoidal* $195
PLATE 766: *Celt* $195
PLATE 767: *Triangular point or blade* $50
PLATE 768: *Bi-pointed blade* $325-400
PLATE 769: *Mississippian bi-points*
      left $70
      right $35
PLATE 770: *Cahokia points* ....each, $25-100
PLATE 771: *Schugtown point* $15
PLATE 772: *Cahokia points* ....each, $10-100
PLATE 773: *Cahokia Sharktooth* $60
PLATE 774: *Hooded human effigy water bottle*
      ....$500-750
PLATE 775: *Pottery bowl* $125-175
PLATE 776: *Pottery bowl* $125-175
PLATE 777: *Pottery bowl* $125-175
PLATE 778: *Columella bead* $35
PLATE 779: *Spud* $900-1,200
PLATE 780: *Celt* $250-325
PLATE 781: *Modified elbow pipe* $400
PLATE 782: *Vase-type pipe* $300
PLATE 783: *Vase-type pipe* $375
PLATE 784: *Elbow pipe* $475
PLATE 785: *Disc pipes*
      top $650
      bottom $400
PLATE 786: *Disc pipes* ....each, $450
PLATE 787: *Disc pipes*
      top $425
      bottom $345
PLATE 788: *Mississippian agricultural implements*
      left $100-150
      center 150-175
      right $200-225
PLATE 789: *Madison points* ....each, $1-6
PLATE 790: *Midwestern drills* ....each, $12-25
PLATE 791: *Double-bitted celt* $175-250
PLATE 792: *Hairpin* $125-175
PLATE 793: *Pendant, bead or disc* $125-165
PLATE 794: *Human effigy mask* ....museum quality
PLATE 795: *Engraved pendant* $135
PLATE 796: *Ft. Ancient knife* $400
PLATE 797: *Chipped spade* $125
PLATE 798: *Chipped celt* $45
PLATE 799: *Chipped hoes* ....each, $30-50

PLATE 800: *Pottery vessel* $175
PLATE 801: *Mississippian chalice* $650
PLATE 802: *Spoon River vessel* $225
PLATE 803: *Mississippian pipe forms* ...each, $65-1,600
PLATE 804: *Effigy pipe* $1,600
PLATE 805: *Bear effigy bowl* $200
PLATE 806: *Wood-duck effigy bowl* $325
PLATE 807: *Plainware* $135
PLATE 808: *Plainware* $185
PLATE 809: *Mississippian artifacts* ....museum quality
PLATE 810: *Pottery* $350
PLATE 811: *Tippets bean pot* $750
PLATE 812: *Discoidal* $500-725
PLATE 813: *Discoidal* $450-650
PLATE 814: *Discoidal* $275-400
PLATE 815: *Discoidal* $375-575
PLATE 816: *Discoidal* $375-575
PLATE 817: *Scooped discoidals* ....each, $300-425
PLATE 818: *Discoidal* $500-700
PLATE 819: *Discoidal* $500-750

PLATE 820: *Discoidal* $450-650
PLATE 821: *Sequoyah bird-points* ....each, $3-15
PLATE 822: *Sequoyah bird-points* ....each, $8-25
PLATE 823: *Fort Ancient knife* $175-250
PLATE 824: *Triangular Fort Ancient knife* $90-120
PLATE 825: *Fort Ancient knives*
            left $45-55
            right $40-50
PLATE 826: *Midwestern chisels* ....each, $115-225
PLATE 827: *Chisel* $250-325
PLATE 828: *Pottery vessel* $225-300
PLATE 829: *Cahokia cord-marked vessel* $295
PLATE 830: *Mississippian plain jar* $450
PLATE 831: *Tippetts bean pot* $1,400
PLATE 832: *Discoidals*
            left $200
            right $120
PLATE 833: *Head effigy pipe* $325
PLATE 834: *Vase-shaped pipe form* $165-215

BOOKS ON COLLECTIBLES

This is only a partial listing of the books on antiques that are available from Collector Books. All books are well illustrated and contain current values. Most of the following books are available from your local bookseller, antique dealer, or public library. If you are unable to locate certain titles in your area, you may order by mail from COLLECTOR BOOKS, P.O. Box 3009, Paducah, KY 42002-3009. Customers with Visa or MasterCard may phone in orders from 7:00–4:00 CST, Monday–Friday, Toll Free 1-800-626-5420. Add $2.00 for postage for the first book ordered and $0.30 for each additional book. Include item number, title, and price when ordering. Allow 14 to 21 days for delivery.

DOLLS, FIGURES & TEDDY BEARS

2382	**Advertising Dolls**, Identification & Values, Robison & Sellers	$9.95
2079	**Barbie** Doll Fashions, Volume I, Eames	$24.95
3957	**Barbie** Exclusives, Rana	$18.95
3310	**Black Dolls**, 1820–1991, Perkins	$17.95
3873	**Black Dolls**, Book II, Perkins	$17.95
3810	**Chatty Cathy** Dolls, Lewis	$15.95
2021	Collector's **Male Action Figures**, Manos	$14.95
1529	Collector's Encyclopedia of **Barbie** Dolls, DeWein	$19.95
3727	Collector's Guide to **Ideal Dolls**, Izen	$18.95
3728	Collector's Guide to Miniature **Teddy Bears**, Powell	$17.95
4506	**Dolls in Uniform**, Bourgeois	$18.95
3967	Collector's Guide to **Trolls**, Peterson	$19.95
1067	**Madame Alexander** Dolls, Smith	$19.95
3971	**Madame Alexander** Dolls Price Guide #20, Smith	$9.95
2185	**Modern Collector's** Dolls I, Smith	$17.95
2186	**Modern Collector's** Dolls II, Smith	$17.95
2187	**Modern Collector's** Dolls III, Smith	$17.95
2188	**Modern Collector's** Dolls IV, Smith	$17.95
2189	**Modern Collector's** Dolls V, Smith	$17.95
3733	**Modern Collector's** Dolls, Sixth Series, Smith	$24.95
3991	**Modern Collector's** Dolls, Seventh Series, Smith	$24.95
3472	**Modern Collector's** Dolls Update, Smith	$9.95
3972	Patricia Smith's **Doll Values**, Antique to Modern, 11th Edition	$12.95
3826	Story of **Barbie**, Westenhouser	$19.95
1513	**Teddy Bears & Steiff** Animals, Mandel	$9.95
1817	**Teddy Bears & Steiff** Animals, 2nd Series, Mandel	$19.95
2084	**Teddy Bears, Annalee's & Steiff** Animals, 3rd Series, Mandel	$19.95
1808	Wonder of **Barbie**, Manos	$9.95
1430	World of **Barbie** Dolls, Manos	$9.95

TOYS, MARBLES & CHRISTMAS COLLECTIBLES

3427	**Advertising Character** Collectibles, Dotz	$17.95
2333	Antique & Collector's **Marbles**, 3rd Ed., Grist	$9.95
3827	Antique & Collector's **Toys**, 1870–1950, Longest	$24.95
3956	Baby Boomer **Games**, Identification & Value Guide, Polizzi	$24.95
1514	Character **Toys** & Collectibles, Longest	$19.95
1750	Character **Toys** & Collector's, 2nd Series, Longest	$19.95
3717	**Christmas** Collectibles, 2nd Edition, Whitmyer	$24.95
1752	**Christmas** Ornaments, Lights & Decorations, Johnson	$19.95
3874	Collectible Coca-Cola Toy **Trucks**, deCourtivron	$24.95
2338	Collector's Encyclopedia of **Disneyana**, Longest, Stern	$24.95
2151	Collector's Guide to **Tootsietoys**, Richter	$16.95
3436	Grist's Big Book of **Marbles**	$19.95
3970	Grist's Machine-Made & Contemporary **Marbles**, 2nd Ed.	$9.95
3732	**Matchbox®** Toys, 1948 to 1993, Johnson	$18.95
3823	**Mego** Toys, An Illustrated Value Guide, Chrouch	15.95
1540	**Modern Toys** 1930–1980, Baker	$19.95
3888	**Motorcycle** Toys, Antique & Contemporary, Gentry/Downs	$18.95
3891	Schroeder's Collectible **Toys**, Antique to Modern Price Guide	$17.95
1886	Stern's Guide to **Disney** Collectibles	$14.95
2139	Stern's Guide to **Disney** Collectibles, 2nd Series	$14.95
3975	Stern's Guide to **Disney** Collectibles, 3rd Series	$18.95
2028	**Toys**, Antique & Collectible, Longest	$14.95
3975	**Zany Characters** of the Ad World, Lamphier	$16.95

JEWELRY, HATPINS, WATCHES & PURSES

1712	Antique & Collector's **Thimbles** & Accessories, Mathis	$19.95
1748	Antique **Purses**, Revised Second Ed., Holiner	$19.95
1278	Art Nouveau & Art Deco **Jewelry**, Baker	$9.95
3875	Collecting Antique **Stickpins**, Kerins	$16.95
3722	Collector's Ency. of **Compacts, Carryalls & Face Powder Boxes**, Mueller	$24.95
3992	Complete Price Guide to **Watches**, #15, Shugart	$21.95
1716	Fifty Years of Collector's **Fashion Jewelry**, 1925-1975, Baker	$19.95
1424	**Hatpins** & Hatpin Holders, Baker	$9.95
1181	100 Years of Collectible **Jewelry**, Baker	$9.95
2348	20th Century Fashionable Plastic **Jewelry**, Baker	$19.95
3830	Vintage **Vanity Bags & Purses**, Gerson	$24.95

FURNITURE

1457	American **Oak** Furniture, McNerney	$9.95
3716	American **Oak** Furniture, Book II, McNerney	$12.95
1118	Antique **Oak** Furniture, Hill	$7.95
2132	Collector's Encyclopedia of **American** Furniture, Vol. I, Swedberg	$24.95
2271	Collector's Encyclopedia of **American** Furniture, Vol. II, Swedberg	$24.95

3720	Collector's Encyclopedia of **American** Furniture, Vol. III, Swedberg	$24.95
1437	Collector's Guide to **Country** Furniture, Raycraft	$9.95
3878	Collector's Guide to **Oak** Furniture, George	$12.95
1755	Furniture of the **Depression Era**, Swedberg	$19.95
3906	**Heywood-Wakefield** Modern Furniture, Rouland	$18.95
1965	**Pine** Furniture, Our American Heritage, McNerney	$14.95
1885	**Victorian** Furniture, Our American Heritage, McNerney	$9.95
3829	**Victorian** Furniture, Our American Heritage, Book II, McNerney	$9.95
3869	**Victorian** Furniture books, 2 volume set, McNerney	$19.90

INDIANS, GUNS, KNIVES, TOOLS, PRIMITIVES

1868	Antique **Tools**, Our American Heritage, McNerney	$9.95
2015	Archaic **Indian** Points & Knives, Edler	$14.95
1426	**Arrowheads** & Projectile Points, Hothem	$7.95
1668	**Flint Blades** & Projectile Points of the North American Indian, Tully	$24.95
2279	**Indian** Artifacts of the Midwest, Hothem	$14.95
3885	**Indian** Artifacts of the Midwest, Book II, Hothem	$16.95
1964	**Indian** Axes & Related Stone Artifacts, Hothem	$14.95
2023	**Keen Kutter** Collectibles, Heuring	$14.95
3887	Modern **Guns**, Identification & Values, 10th Ed., Quertermous	$12.95
2164	**Primitives**, Our American Heritage, McNerney	$9.95
1759	**Primitives**, Our American Heritage, Series II, McNerney	$14.95
3325	Standard **Knife** Collector's Guide, 2nd Ed., Ritchie & Stewart	$12.95

PAPER COLLECTIBLES & BOOKS

1441	Collector's Guide to **Post Cards**, Wood	$9.95
2081	Guide to Collecting **Cookbooks**, Allen	$14.95
3969	Huxford's **Old Book** Value Guide, 7th Ed.	$19.95
3821	Huxford's **Paperback** Value Guide	$19.95
2080	Price Guide to **Cookbooks** & Recipe Leaflets, Dickinson	$9.95
2346	**Sheet Music** Reference & Price Guide, Pafik & Guiheen	$18.95

OTHER COLLECTIBLES

2280	Advertising **Playing Cards**, Grist	$16.95
2269	Antique **Brass & Copper** Collectibles, Gaston	$16.95
1880	Antique **Iron**, McNerney	$9.95
3872	Antique **Tins**, Dodge	$24.95
1714	**Black** Collectibles, Gibbs	$19.95
1128	**Bottle** Pricing Guide, 3rd Ed., Cleveland	$7.95
3959	**Cereal Box** Bonanza, The 1950's, Bruce	$19.95
3718	Collector's **Aluminum**, Grist	$16.95
3445	Collectible **Cats**, An Identification & Value Guide, Fyke	$18.95
1634	Collector's Ency. of Figural & Novelty **Salt & Pepper Shakers**, Davern	$19.95
2020	Collector's Ency. of Figural & Novelty **Salt & Pepper Shakers**, Vol. II, Davern	$19.95
2018	Collector's Encyclopedia of **Granite Ware**, Greguire	$24.95
3430	Collector's Encyclopedia of **Granite Ware**, Book II, Greguire	$24.95
3879	Collector's Guide to Antique **Radios**, 3rd Ed., Bunis	$18.95
1916	Collector's Guide to **Art Deco**, Gaston	$14.95
3880	Collector's Guide to **Cigarette Lighters**, Flanagan	$17.95
1537	Collector's Guide to **Country Baskets**, Raycraft	$9.95
3966	Collector's Guide to **Inkwells**, Identification & Values, Badders	$18.95
3881	Collector's Guide to **Novelty Radios**, Bunis/Breed	$18.95
3729	Collector's Guide to **Snow Domes**, Guarnaccia	$18.95
3730	Collector's Guide to **Transistor Radios**, Bunis	$15.95
2276	**Decoys**, Kangas	$24.95
1629	**Doorstops**, Identification & Values, Bertoia	$9.95
3968	**Fishing Lure** Collectibles, Murphy/Edmisten	$24.95
3817	**Flea Market Trader**, 9th Ed., Huxford	$12.95
3819	**General Store Collectibles**, Wilson	$24.95
2215	Goldstein's **Coca-Cola** Collectibles	$16.95
3884	Huxford's Collector's **Advertising**, 2nd Ed.	$24.95
2216	**Kitchen Antiques**, 1790–1940, McNerney	$14.95
1782	**1,000 Fruit Jars**, 5th Edition, Schroeder	$5.95
3321	Ornamental & Figural **Nutcrackers**, Rittenhouse	$16.95
2026	**Railroad** Collectibles, 4th Ed., Baker	$14.95
1632	**Salt & Pepper Shakers**, Guarnaccia	$9.95
1888	**Salt & Pepper Shakers** II, Identification & Value Guide, Book II, Guarnaccia	$14.95
2220	**Salt & Pepper Shakers** III, Guarnaccia	$14.95
3443	**Salt & Pepper Shakers** IV, Guarnaccia	$18.95
2096	**Silverplated Flatware**, Revised 4th Edition, Hagan	$14.95
1922	Standard **Old Bottle** Price Guide, Sellari	$14.95
3892	**Toy & Miniature Sewing Machines**, Thomas	$18.95
3828	Value Guide to **Advertising Memorabilia**, Summers	$18.95
3977	Value Guide to **Gas Station** Memorabilia	$24.95
3444	**Wanted to Buy**, 5th Edition	$9.95

Schroeder's
ANTIQUES
Price Guide

. . . is the #1 best-selling antiques & collectibles value guide on the market today, and here's why . . .

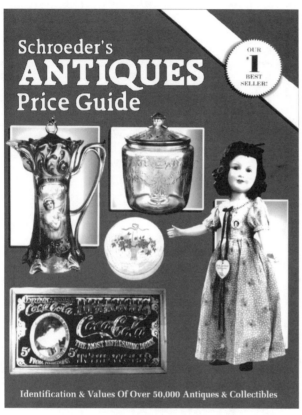

8½ x 11, 608 Pages, $14.95

- *More than 300 advisors, well-known dealers, and top-notch collectors work together with our editors to bring you accurate information regarding pricing and identification.*

- *More than 45,000 items in almost 500 categories are listed along with hundreds of sharp original photos that illustrate not only the rare and unusual, but the common, popular collectibles as well.*

- *Each large close-up shot shows important details clearly. Every subject is represented with histories and background information, a feature not found in any of our competitors' publications.*

- *Our editors keep abreast of newly developing trends, often adding several new categories a year as the need arises.*

If it merits the interest of today's collector, you'll find it in *Schroeder's*. And you can feel confident that the information we publish is up to date and accurate. Our advisors thoroughly check each category to spot inconsistencies, listings that may not be entirely reflective of market dealings, and lines too vague to be of merit. Only the best of the lot remains for publication.

Without doubt, you'll find
SCHROEDER'S ANTIQUES PRICE GUIDE
the only one to buy for
reliable information and values.

COLLECTOR BOOKS
A Division of Schroeder Publishing Co., Inc.